CENSORSHIP, INC.

CENSORSHIP, INC.

The Corporate Threat to Free Speech in the United States

Lawrence Soley

Monthly Review Press

New York

Library of Congress Cataloging-in-Publication Data
Soley, Lawrence C.
Censorship, Inc. : The Corporate Threat to Free Speech in the United States
    / by Lawrence Soley.
        p. cm.
Includes bibliographical references and index.
ISBN 1-58367-067-X (hardcover) – ISBN 1-58367-066-1 (pbk.)
1. Free speech–United States. 2. Corporate image–United States. 3. Corporations
–Corrupt practices–United States. 4. Censorship–United States. I. Title.

JC591 .S65 2002
323.44'3'0973–dc21   2002007530

Monthly Review Press
122 West 27th Street
New York, NY 10001

www.monthlyreview.org

Designed and typeset by Terry J. Allen, New York, NY

Manufactured in Canada
10 9 8 7 6 5 4 3 2 1

CONTENTS

PREFACE

Many legal histories of the First Amendment begin with discussions of colonial-era violations of speech and press; describe the debates that raged when the Constitution was being written; and review laws and court decisions that infringed on free speech and press during the first two hundred years of the Republic.[1] The most sweeping of the speech-infringing laws include the Alien and Sedition Acts of 1798; state-imposed speech restrictions of the pre–Civil War period; "Palmer Raid–era" laws such as the Espionage Act of 1917 and state criminal sedition laws; and World War II and postwar "Red Scare" laws such as the federal Smith Act of 1940 and the McCarran Act of 1950. These legal histories invariably also discuss significant court decisions such as Gitlow v. New York, De Jonge v. Oregon, and United States v. Eichman,[2] which have slowly expanded free speech in the United States by applying the First Amendment to states rather than just the federal government, distinguishing between advocacy and action, and recognizing that some acts, such as flag burning, constitute forms of protected, symbolic speech.

Although most legal histories provide laudable discussions of speech-infringing laws and judicial review, they invariably emphasize the roles that governments have played in adopting speech-stifling laws, while simultaneously de-emphasizing or neglecting the roles that businesses, trade associations, and other private-sector groups have played in their adoption. For example, *Freedom of Speech in the United States* describes the restriction of the pre–Civil War Virginia Act of 1836, which prohibited "speaking or writing that the owners of slaves have no property in the same" or advocating "the abolition of slavery," but fails to mention that the law was adopted by slave owners, who feared that abolitionists were jeopardizing their control over slaves.[3]

Free Speech in the United States devotes a chapter to the criminal syndicalist laws and prosecutions during the post–First World War (or Palmer Raid) era, but fails to mention the role that businesses, farm owners, and trade associations played in the passage of these laws. These business groups, fearing that the Industrial Workers of the World (I.W.W.) would organize and ideologically influence their employees, lobbied vigorously for the adoption of criminal syndicalist laws.[4]

Similarly, businesses were involved in many attempts by local governments to suppress speech. Many of the pre–First World War ordinances banning speech on downtown street corners were adopted at the urging of businesses, which maintained that political speeches on public streets interfered with their rights to engage in commerce. For example, the lawyer for the Merchants' Association of San Diego urged the city council to adopt an ordinance against public speaking, claiming the rights of shop owners, whose businesses were being blocked by crowds listening to I.W.W. speakers, outweighed the rights of orators.[5] The city council adopted the ordinance, precipitating a free speech fight led by the I.W.W. and Free Speech League.

Some of the most famous cases of book banning were orchestrated by business associations and nongovernmental groups. In 1939, the Associated Farmers of Kern County, incensed by *The Grapes of Wrath*'s exposé of agribusiness's treatment of migrant farm workers, launched a campaign against the John Steinbeck novel. The campaign sought to ban the novel from public libraries, limit its distribution, and keep Twentieth Century Fox from adopting the novel into a motion picture. The Associated Farmers succeeded in getting the book banned from the Kern County libraries and schools, sought similar bans in other agricultural counties of California, and applied pressure on the movie studio. Its campaign collapsed after the Oil Workers Union, Brotherhood of Engineers, American Civil Liberties Union, and other groups denounced and exposed the Associated Farmers' ham-fisted censorship.[6] Other books have been banned at the urging of the National Anti-Communist League of America (a.k.a. The Textbook Study League, Inc.), the American Legion, the National Association for the Advancement of Colored People, and other groups. Although book bannings are frequently approved by government bodies such as school boards or boards of supervisors, the pressure to ban books usually originates with private, nongovernmental groups.

If private entities are willing to pressure government bodies into adopting speech-restricting laws or instigating censorial actions such as book bannings, it should come as no surprise that these entities will also restrict speech among members and employees, in civil relationships such as contracts, and over property. Ironically, when government capitulates to private groups and commits speech-stifling acts, the acts are described as "censorship." When private entities commit the same acts, they are described as exercises in "property rights," "editorial control," or simply "business policies."

Although not usually called censorship, speech-stifling acts by private parties occur more frequently than similar acts by governments. Private restrictions on speech are enforced daily, are deeply rooted, and go unnoticed. For example, mall owners in most states prohibit free speech within their shopping centers and parking areas and enforce these bans on an ongoing basis. If similar prohibitions of free speech were adopted and enforced by a government body, the enforcement would be immediately publicized, branded as censorship, challenged in court, and doubtlessly overturned.

This distinction between private and government action developed during a vastly different economic past. Until the early to mid-nineteenth century, businesses were small and powerless when compared to government. The typical business of the eighteenth and early nineteenth century was owned by an individual or a small group, who managed the firm.[7] For that reason, citizens had more to fear from government than business.

But times have changed. Modern-day multinational corporations have greater resources and power than local or state governments—and even more power and resources than the governments of all but the largest nation states.

Another reason why private acts are not defined as censorship is the ideology of anti-Communism, which has pervaded American consciousness since the birth of the Soviet Union.[8] Anti-Communism, an ideology promoted by corporate chieftains such as defense contractors Lynde and Harry Bradley, textile magnate Alfred Kohlberg, and publishers such as Henry Luce and DeWitt Wallace, identifies unfettered capitalism with freedom and government regulation with repression.[9] Free enterprise represents the essence of freedom from this ideological perspective, and therefore actions of the private sector cannot be called "censorship." Censorship is what Communist governments practice; it is not practiced by capitalists. This ideological definition of censorship, a bulwark of the anti-Bolshevik era, continues to affect public and legal definitions of censorship even in the post-Soviet era.

A third reason why private acts that restrict speech are not defined as censorship arises from conventional thinking, particularly among lawyers and legal scholars, who use traditional legal categories, such as "torts" and "contracts," to characterize private actions that may have censorial elements to them. Speech-restrictive clauses in employment contracts are simply viewed as legitimate parts of business contracts that protect trade secrets, even if the clauses objectively curtail employees' speech. These conventional approaches to legal thinking might help lawyers identify specific trees, but they keep lawyers from understanding the ecology of the forest.

For example, the legal concept of "state action" is often viewed as an established judicial doctrine asserting that the Constitution protects individuals against encroachment by governments, not private entities, when it is actually a wild card used by courts to justify ideologically based decisions. The "state action" concept has been used by courts to protect and limit property rights, often in trade-offs with free speech and civil rights. When conservative courts have sought to protect property rights, they narrowly define state action, claiming that government must have "significantly involved itself" before state action exists. Using this definition of state action, a court dominated by Nixon appointees found no state action when a government granted a liquor license to a private club practicing racial discrimination.[10] By contrast, a more liberal court earlier concluded that mere court enforcement of a racially discriminatory private contract constituted state action.[11]

Similarly, conventional thinking has kept lawyers from recognizing that Strategic Lawsuits Against Public Participation (or SLAPP suits) constitute a group of legal actions that collectively restrict speech. As George W. Pring and Penelope Canaan wrote in their seminal work, *SLAPPs: Getting Sued for Speaking Out*:

> When we began studying [Slapp suits], there was virtually no recognition—by the legal profession, courts, academia, government or the public—of their similarity or linkages. The tendency was (and often still is) to view them as unrelated and to apply conventional legal labels: a "libel" case, a "business interference" case, a "conspiracy" case. Looking deeper, we found what they have had in common: every case was triggered by defendants' attempts to influence government action—the exact activity covered by the Petition Clause of the First Amendment.[12]

Only by shedding conventional thinking was it possible to discern this new category of legal action—SLAPP suits—that has censorship as its primary purpose.

A major purpose of this book is to challenge conventional thinking about the nature of censorship: Conventional definitions are challenged, new definitions are proffered, and commonly accepted interpretations of laws and court decisions are questioned. The purpose of this book is to stimulate a debate about what constitutes censorship in the "land of the free."

The book would never have been completed without the assistance of Marquette University, which provided me with a sabbatical leave to develop the outline, proposal, and preliminary chapters. The author is also indebted to the late Herb Schiller, whose ideas stimulated this book.

1

Private Censorship, Corporate Power

The tobacco companies have repeatedly squawked about their First Amendment right to advertise cigarettes. In 1998, as Congress considered a bill that would ban outdoor and sports advertising reaching adolescents and children, the tobacco companies denounced the proposed legislation for trampling on their free speech rights. "We intend to assert our First Amendment, due process, and other constitutional rights to overturn [this legislation] in courts," threatened tobacco industry attorney J. Phil Carlton, as the companies withdrew from negotiations on the bill until it offered them more protection from liability suits. The tobacco company representatives asserted that they would not surrender their First Amendment rights to promote cigarettes unless Congress capped the industry's annual liability claims.[1] In other words, the tobacco companies were willing to give up their cherished First Amendment rights for the right price.

In an effort to derail a proposed federal ban on cigarette advertising a decade earlier, the Philip Morris Corporation sponsored an essay-writing contest about the First Amendment rights of cigarette advertising. The contest was a continuation of an earlier Philip Morris promotional campaign, inaugurated during the American Bicentennial, heralding the Bill of Rights and the freedoms it enshrines.

Advertisements for the contest appeared in large circulation magazines and newspapers, including *The New Yorker* and the *New York Times*, asking entrants to write about why a ban on cigarette advertising infringed on free speech. The purpose of the heavily advertised contest was to suggest that the proposed ban threatened the average citizen's First Amendment rights.[2]

The campaign represented the height of corporate hypocrisy, suggesting that billion-dollar, multinational conglomerates such as Philip Morris are just "average citizens" being pushed around by big government. Philip Morris is not, after all, an average citizen; it is a multibillion-dollar, multinational conglomerate, whose annual sales exceed the gross domestic product of Iraq, Chile, and many other nations, and whose Kraft Food and Miller Brewing divisions produce more food and drink annually than most countries consume.[3]

The contest also erroneously implied that commercial advertising has the same First Amendment protection as political and social speech, which is untrue. While commercial speech enjoys First Amendment protection, that protection is less than that afforded political and social speech.

Ironically, at the same time they were clamoring about free speech rights, the tobacco companies were using their profits and power to suppress information about the health hazards of cigarette smoking. This corporate-sponsored censorship had been ongoing for decades.

When the tobacco companies sponsored television programs in the 1940s and 1950s, they prohibited shows from mentioning the health risks of cigarette smoking, using words that might suggest smoking was unhealthy or inadvertently refer to marketplace competitors. For example, Jack Benny refused to mention a cancer treatment center on his show, admitting that "I am sponsored by a cigarette maker, [and] we are not permitted at any time to mention the word cancer."[4] In the 1950s, R. J. Reynolds, the sponsor of NBC's *Camel News Caravan*, even banned the filming of news events where "No Smoking" signs were observable and prohibited dramatic shows from naming characters "Lucky," the brand name of its chief competitor.[5]

When magazines ran articles about the hazards of smoking, the tobacco companies quickly withdrew their advertising to financially punish the magazines. *Mother Jones, Reader's Digest,* and other magazines had their tobacco advertising accounts cancelled after publishing articles about the health hazards of smoking.[6] Having learned that the tobacco companies will not allow magazines in which they advertise to publish stories about the hazards of smoking, magazines carrying cigarette advertising have studiously avoided the subject.[7]

> Even advertising agencies have felt the wrath of the tobacco conglomerates. When Saatchi and Saatchi developed an advertisement for Northwest Airlines promoting the airline's nonsmoking flights, R. J. Reynolds had its parent company, R. J. R. Nabisco, pull its advertising business from the agency. Because Saatchi did not handle any of the tobacco company's cigarette advertising, R. J. R. Nabisco pulled its accounts for biscuits and sweets, part of its Nabisco division.[8]

The problems of tobacco company censorship are far graver than suggested by these neanderthal attempts to directly pressure the media. Magazines that carry cigarette advertising frequently act as tobacco company toadies, refusing to carry antismoking advertisements. Of 36 magazines carrying such advertisements, 22 refused outright to run ads for antismoking clinics, an investigation of magazine advertising practices found. In rejecting antismoking advertisements, *Cosmopolitan* explained that it would not "jeopardize $5 or $10 million worth of business" from the tobacco companies. An executive with *Psychology Today*, a self-help magazine that claims to be devoted to readers' well-being, said the magazine would not accept the antismoking ads because "we have a lot of money that comes in from tobacco companies, and frankly, we don't want to offend our tobacco advertisers."[9]

Not content with merely stopping magazines from publishing antismoking articles, the tobacco companies have recently moved into the publishing business, producing their own magazines with tobacco-friendly content. Brown & Williamson produces *Simple Living* and *Flair* with Hearst Publications and *Real Edge* with EMAP Peterson Publishing. The three are written by employees of Hearst and EMAP Peterson so they appear to be bona fide consumer magazines. However, the contents are carefully controlled by Brown & Williamson, which determines what can be written about, forbids references to cancer or other tobacco-induced diseases, and even prohibits mentions of cigarette smoking in stories.

Smoking is promoted through advertising and other visuals, rather than hard-sell stories.[10] Philip Morris and R. J. Reynolds produce similar magazines. Philip Morris produces *Unlimited* with Hachette Filipacchi Publishing and R. J. Reynolds produces *CML* with Time, Inc.

Tobacco companies employ many other methods to suppress information about the hazards of smoking, one of which is to have tobacco company employees sign confidentiality agreements that prohibit them from speaking about the company and its products during and after their employment. When Dr. Victor DeNoble, a scientist working for Philip Morris, discovered that nicotine was not just addictive, but altered smokers' brain chemistry, he was fired. To ensure DeNoble's silence, Philip Morris reminded him that a secrecy clause in his employment contract prohibited him from speaking publicly about his research, warning him that if he violated his contract, Philip Morris would sue.[11]

The same fate befell Jeffrey Wigand, a Brown & Williamson employee, who became aware of the company's research demonstrating the addictive nature of nicotine and its manipulation of cigarette nicotine levels. When Brown & Williamson discharged Wigand, he was warned to remain silent about the company and repeatedly threatened with legal action if he violated the secrecy clause in his employment contract. Eventually, Wigand told his story to *60 Minutes*.

Brown & Williamson then threatened to sue CBS if *60 Minutes* broadcast Wigand's interview, claiming that *60 Minutes* had intentionally interfered with a civil contract by encouraging Wigand to violate his confidentiality agreement with the company.[12] The threat of legal action came as CBS's owners were negotiating the sale of the network. Fearing that the lawsuit would lower CBS's value, CBS suppressed the interview, an act of self-censorship criticized by many newspapers. For example, the *New York Times* called the suppression "a chilling message to journalists investigating industry practices everywhere."[13] The *Wall Street Journal* also scooped CBS, publishing a story based on interviews with Wigand. After being denounced and scooped, CBS allowed *60 Minutes* to air the Wigand interview, hoping to salvage its by then tarnished reputation as a muckraker.

A movie, *The Insider*, was subsequently made about the Wigand-*60 Minutes* debacle. Although *The Insider* was based on widely known events, Brown & Williamson threatened to sue the film's distributor for libel, alleging that scenes suggesting that the tobacco company physically threatened Wigand were untrue.[14] Significantly, the tobacco company didn't challenge the main premise of the movie, which was that Brown & Williamson sought to silence former employees and even reporters who sought to expose its potentially criminal practices.

Several years earlier, Brown & Williamson publicly discussed suing cartoonist Gary Trudeau for defamation after his *Doonesbury* comic strip showed Thomas Sandefur, the company's CEO, being indicted for perjury because of his testimony before Congress. Sandefur testified that nicotine wasn't addictive, even though company documents show that he was well aware of nicotine's addictive power.[15]

Such tactics have not been unique to Brown & Williamson. R. J. Reynolds threatened to sue Dr. Paul M. Fischer, who published research showing that children were well acquainted with Joe Camel, the cartoon character used to promote Camel cigarettes. As a result of the threats, Fischer gave up studying tobacco advertising.[16]

Philip Morris and Reynolds filed libel suits against ABC after the network's *Day One* program featured a segment alleging that the tobacco companies "spiked" the nicotine in cigarettes. During those suits, the tobacco companies sought and obtained a court order limiting the number of ABC executives who were allowed to see subpoenaed tobacco company documents. Each Philip Morris document delivered to ABC carried legal warnings stamped on it that "this document and its content shall not be used, shown, or distributed as provided in the court's order."[17]

An out-of-court settlement was reached on the eve of ABC's sale to Disney Corporation, in which ABC agreed to publicly apologize for the segment and pay the tobacco companies' legal costs. The carefully worded apology stated that ABC could not prove that the companies "spiked" or increased nicotine levels, even though ABC had evidence clearly showing they manipulated and controlled the levels. Critics charged that

ABC settled the suit to allow the sale of the network to proceed without impediments.

The settlement prohibited ABC and Philip Morris executives from commenting on the case and required the sealing of the briefs filed by Philip Morris and ABC.[18] *USA Today* nevertheless obtained a copy of the secret ABC brief, discovering that accompanying Philip Morris documents showed that the tobacco company did indeed add nicotine to cigarettes. The newspaper concluded that the "evidence appears at odds with both the tobacco company's public statements and the network's apology," suggesting that ABC might have settled in order to make the network's sale easier.[19]

Lawsuits such as these, which are filed to stifle criticism rather than remedy injustice, are called Strategic Lawsuits Against Public Participation, or SLAPPs. These suits tie up critics in court for years, forcing them to incur massive legal expenses. Burdened by such suits, critics often gag themselves. Shortly after Philip Morris filed its $10 billion libel suit against ABC over the spiking segment on *Day One*, the network cancelled a one-hour documentary on *Turning Point* about tobacco companies, suggesting that SLAPPs are an effective form of censorship.[20]

When sued or being sued, the tobacco companies also seek and obtain protective orders to suppress information about tobacco industry practices. As Marc Z. Edell, an attorney who sued the tobacco companies, explained, the companies "have protective orders [gag orders] entered in every case, you can't share information among plaintiff's lawyers, and they try to paper you to death and outspend you, which they are quite capable of doing."[21] These tactics have been used repeatedly in civil and class action suits filed against the tobacco companies, making it very hard for injured parties to finance their suits against the tobacco companies because each suit begins at square one.

The tactics used by the tobacco companies to suppress information— advertising pressures, secrecy agreements, defamation suits, and protective orders— are not unique to the tobacco industry. A survey of television news reporters and editors found that more than two-thirds of television stations had been threatened by advertisers, who tried to intimidate the stations with threats to withdraw advertising because of the content of news stories. Forty-four percent of the televison journalists reported that advertisers had "actually withdrawn advertising because of the content of a news report."[22]

Corporations even withdraw funding to punish nonprofit institutions and community groups, just as they withdraw advertising to punish media. For example, Nike Chairman Philip Knight cancelled a promised $30 million contribution to the University of Oregon for renovating the athletic stadium when the university joined the Workers' Rights Consortium, which had criticized the use of foreign sweatshops by U.S. manufacturers.[23] Holland America Cruise Line cut off contributions to several charitable groups in Juneau, Alaska, after Juneau voters approved a tax on cruise ship passengers who arrive annually in that city. When the cruise line withdrew support for the arts council, Civil Air Patrol, and other nonprofit organizations, it said it was reassessing its relationship with the city as a result of the vote.[24]

General Growth Properties, Inc., which operates 130 malls nationwide, banned Salvation Army bell ringers from its Wisconsin properties during the 1999 holiday season. The corporation wasn't punishing the Salvation Army because of anything it did or said. Rather, as Bernie Freibaum, the chief financial officer of General Growth, explained, the company's motivation for acting like Scrooge was that "if you let one group in, then all of a sudden you have to let the rest in and the next thing you know you're in court arguing the First Amendment."[25] In Wisconsin, like most other states, mall owners can prohibit all free expression on their property. General Growth feared that the presence of the Salvation Army might set a precedent for other nonprofit groups, which might then demand to distribute handbills or engage in other forms of free expression.

Corporations also commonly seek protective orders sealing evidence or impose confidentiality agreements in the settlement of civil cases, as Philip Morris did in its lawsuit against ABC. "This practice has exploded in the last 20 years," reports Arthur Bryant of the nonprofit Trial Lawyers for Public Justice. "Corporations have realized how they can be successful, and it's cheaper to hide the truth from the public."[26] Secret settlements are often reached by the manufacturers of pharmaceuticals, medical devices, and hazardous products such as lead paint, but are also used by retailers such as Home Depot, Inc., and Wal-Mart, which successfully keep secret information about injuries sustained by shoppers in their stores, who are struck by merchandise falling from shelves or tripped by goods lying the floor.

Bridgestone, Inc., the manufacturer of the dangerous ATX tires that came on Ford sports utility vehicles and delaminated in hot weather, quietly settled many cases arising from crashes and injuries caused by the tires over an eight-year period. The settlements usually included secrecy agreements, barring parties in the suits from discussing the case. The court files and evidence were also sealed, keeping information about the dangers posed by the tires from reaching the public.[27]

Secrecy clauses such as those used by Philip Morris and Brown & Williamson to silence Victor DeNoble and Jeffrey Wigand are not just used by the tobacco companies or in employment contracts. They have increasingly been inserted into a variety of other contracts, including university-corporate research contracts, which often contain clauses restricting when researchers can publish their findings. For example, a study published in the *New England Journal of Medicine* reported that a majority of companies entering into biomedical research agreements with universities require that the findings be "kept confidential to protect [their] proprietary value beyond the time required to file a patent."[28]

According to the National Cancer Institute's Steven Rothenberg, these restrictions on publishing impede scientific research because uninhibited "discussion among scientists, even about preliminary results of ongoing experiments . . . can play an important part in advancing research."[29]

Some university-corporate contracts restrict more than when research findings can be published. They contain paragraphs giving the corporate sponsor the right to determine whether the results can ever be released. A British pharmaceutical corporation, the Boots Company, gave $250,000 to the University of California San Francisco for research comparing its hypothyroid drug, Synthroid, with lower-cost alternatives. Instead of demonstrating Synthroid's superiority, as Boots had hoped, the study found the drugs were bioequivalents. Professor Betty Dong, who conducted the study, submitted her findings to the *Journal of the American Medical Association*, which, after subjecting the study to rigorous blind review, agreed to publish it. The information could have saved consumers $356 million if they had switched to cheaper alternatives, but would have undermined Synthroid's domination of the $600 million synthetic hormone market.

When Boots found out about the scheduled article, it stopped publication, citing provisions in the research contract that results "were not to be published or otherwise released without [Boots'] written consent." After Boots blocked publication of the article, it announced that Dong's research was badly flawed, and that Sythroid was actually superior to alternatives. Dong was unable to counter the claim because she could not release the study.[30]

Some research contracts have even had speech restrictions imbedded in them. In 1996, the University of Wisconsin signed a multimillion-dollar contract with Reebok, granting the running shoe manufacturer exclusive rights to make and market athletic apparel bearing the Wisconsin logo. In addition to paying coaches for promotional appearances and giving financial support for the university's athletic program, the contract included this speech-restricting clause: "The university will not issue any official statement that disparages Reebok . . . [and] will promptly take all reasonable steps to address any remark by any university employee, including a coach, that disparages Reebok."

Although university administrators publicly disclosed many other provisions of the contract, they kept the speech-restriction clause secret until the last moment. When news of it did become public, dozens of professors signed a letter of opposition. Embarrassed by the flak and the exposure of their willingness to sell out free speech, university administrators retreated, asking Reebok to cancel the speech-prohibition paragraph. Facing a public relations disaster, Reebok quickly agreed.[31]

Because such tactics are widely used to restrict speech, businesses and corporations now pose a greater threat to free speech than does government.

Government Censorship

Despite claims by Waco wackos, paranoid militiamen, and hard-right Republicans, the U.S. government is not the chief censor in the United States. In fact, government infringements on speech in the U.S. are far fewer today than in the past. Citizens are no longer prosecuted or jailed for their political advocacy, as they were during much of the twentieth century. Most of the repressive legislation passed during the World War I and World War II eras, such as the criminal syndicalist laws and Smith Act, have been declared unconsitutional.

One reason for the change is that the federal courts have become far more protective of speech during the past two decades. The protections have come about because courts now distinguish between mere advocacy and incitement, view acts such as flag burning as symbolic speech, and carefully scrutinize state and local laws that might infringe on the First Amendment.

When local, state, and federal governments have tried to restrict speech and assembly, organizations such as the American Civil Liberties Union and National Lawyers Guild have challenged their actions in court and have frequently won. Many of these aborted government attempts at censorship have been widely publicized. For example, New York City mayor Rudolph W. Giuliani's refusals in 1998 and 1999 to issue permits for the "Million Youth" marches in Harlem made headlines across the United States. In both cases, courts ordered the city to issue the permits because the city had acted unconstitutionally, arbitrarily, and with a "lack of standards."[32]

In September 1998, the same month that the first "Million Youth" march took place in the streets of Harlem, protesters in New Hampshire were in court on trespassing charges for passing out leaflets in the Mall of New Hampshire after being asked to stop. The protesters, known as the "Footlocker Eight," were arrested for simply distributing leaflets critical of conditions in foreign sweatshops producing running shoes and other products. The eight were convicted and sentenced to thirty days in jail, suspended, and $117 fines.[33] The "Million Youth" and "Footlocker Eight" court cases are sharp contrasts between the constitutional rights that citizens have in public versus private places.

Another widely publicized example of a local government's failed attempt to limit speech occurred in the upscale St. Louis suburb of Ladue, which adopted an ordinance in 1991 that banned homeowners from posting all but "For Sale" signs on their property, claiming that signs were a visual blight that contributed to the deterioration of property values. During the 1991 "Gulf War," the city ordered resident Margaret Gilleo to remove an 8½-by-11 inch sign in her window that read: "For Peace in the Gulf." Federal courts struck down this ordinance because it violated citizens' free speech rights.[34]

Although the courts have ruled that city ordinances banning political signs are unconstitutional, courts have upheld similar bans when imposed by private companies. In *Murphy v. Timber Trace Association* and *Linn Valley Lakes Property Owners Association v. Brockway,* bans on signs imposed by housing associations were declared legal.[35] Housing associations are corporations created to govern planned developments such as condominiums. In these cases, the actions taken by private housing corporations were not viewed as state action and therefore did not violate the First Amendment. As the court observed in *Linn Valley Lakes Property Owners Association,* "there is nothing constitutionally impermissible per se in a private agreement restricting signs in a residential neighborhood, and enforcement thereof does not constitute improper state action."[36]

On the state level, Missouri officials denied the Ku Klux Klan's request to participate in the state Adopt-A-Highway program, where organizations post signs about their efforts to pick up trash, pull weeds, and plant flowers along their stretch of adopted highway. As with the Million Youth March, a federal judge ordered Missouri to allow the hate group to participate in the program. As a result, the Klan was assigned a one-mile stretch of Interstate 55 to clean up and was given a sign recognizing its participation. (Shortly after the sign was put up, it was taken by irate citizens or souvenir collectors.[37])

Federal attempts to attempts to infringe free expression have been no more successful than state and local attempts. In a 5–4 decision, the

Supreme Court struck down a federal anti–flag burning law in 1990, ruling that flag burning was a constitutionally protected form of political expression.[38] (Because of the Supreme Court decision, conservative senators and representatives have pushed for a constitutional amendment to ban flag burning, which so far has gone nowhere.)

Under most circumstances, citizens are free to speak in public places such as parks, streets, sidewalks, and other public forums, subject to reasonable "time, place, and manner" constraints.[39] If a local, state, or federal government body interferes with this right, citizens can take the government to court, and will frequently prevail there.

When governments have passed speech-stifling legislation, it has often been at the urging of private sector institutions, which have a vested interest in the legislation and have clout with legislators. For example, the old California Criminal Syndicalism Act, under which 504 persons were arrested and 264 persons prosecuted during the post–World War I "Palmer Raid" era, was adopted at the urging of agribusiness, which sought to stop the Industrial Workers of the World union from organizing migrant farmworkers in California's Central Valley.[40] Other California business associations also lobbied for the criminal syndicalism law, as did business associations in Idaho, Indiana, and other states. "In every state which enacted a criminal syndicalism law, with the exception of Wyoming," there is evidence that "business and industrial interests and groups had some connection with the[ir] enactment," concluded Professor Eldridge Foster Dowell in a 1939 study of the laws.[41]

More recent example example of speech-suppressing legislation passed on the state level at the urging of business are food disparagement laws, which have been enacted in thirteen states. Food disparagement laws extend libel to generic product categories such as beef, opening critics to lawsuits that would otherwise be thrown out of court. These state disparagement laws allow corporations to sue critics of their products in civil courts, even when critics are speaking in other states. The specter of food disparagement suits has had a stifling effect on publishers, broadcasters, and even health advocates.

On the federal level, Monsanto used its lobbying clout to keep information about genetically altered foods from the public. Monsanto, the leading patent holder and producer of genetically altered food products, often referred to as "Frankenfoods," convinced Congress and the Food and Drug Administration (FDA) that genetically altering plants and animals was not vastly different from older methods of plant breeding and animal husbandry and that consumers should not be informed that products they were consuming were genetically altered.[42] As a result, the FDA ruled that food labels need not mention the presence of genetically altered contents, depriving consumers of important health information.

Companies have also lobbied vigorously for their "right" to act as censors. In Florida, a bill was introduced by Democratic state representative Mimi McAndrews that would have made it more difficult for companies to file SLAPP suits. The bill would have required plaintiffs to prove the merits of the case to a judge before the suit could proceed, thereby eliminating suits filed for the purpose of intimidating or harassing citizens for exercising their free speech rights. Representatives of environment groups, consumer groups, and trial lawyers testified in favor of the bill, but it was killed in committee after business lobbyists spoke against it. Business lobbyists also spoke against a similar bill that was introduced and eventually passed in Massachusetts.[43]

There are numerous instances where companies have withheld information, in addition to taking censorial action to prevent vital information about the company and its products from becoming public. Several large pharmaceutical companies, including Warner-Lambert and American Home Products (now known as Wyeth), have settled lawsuits which asserted that they withheld information about their products from the public. The information affected public health. For example, Warner-Lambert withheld information about problems with four of its drugs, including one widely used to treat epilepsy. American Home Products withheld information that fen-phen, a diet drug combination, caused dangerous heart valve problems. Lead pigment manufacturers and their trade association were apparently knowledgeable about the dangers of lead paint long before the information was disseminated to the public.[44]

Corporations also lobby intently against laws and regulations that would require them to make even small amounts of information public. For example, the Securities and Exchange Commission (SEC) in 1999 proposed a regulation prohibiting publicly traded corporations from divulging information that can affect stock prices, except through public disclosure. The proposed regulation stated that if information were inadvertently disclosed to one investor, the information needed to be publicly released. The purpose of the regulation was to prevent companies from giving preferred investors information while withholding the same information from others. "The all-too-common practice of selectively disseminating material (company) information is a disservice to investors and undermines the fundamental principle of fairness," said SEC chairman Arthur Levitt about the disclosures that the regulation was trying to curb. "In a time when instantaneous and free-flowing information is the norm, these sorts of whispers are an insult to the principles of free and open disclosure."

Rather than embracing the regulation, Wall Street immediately opposed it, claiming the proposal was unnecessary. "I would question the assumption that there is a widespread practice that gives rise to the stain," one securities lawyer said. Other Wall Street firms lobbied against the regulation or lobbied to water down the disclosure requirements.[45]

In contrast to corporations, which are legally private entities even if publicly traded, governments are required to make vast amounts of information available to the public. Federal agencies and most state and city governments operate under freedom of information and open-meetings laws, which allow citizens to examine government operations.[46] Without access to such information about government operations, free speech would mean little. As James Madison said, " A popular government without popular information or the means of acquiring it, is but a Prologue to a Farce or a Tragedy, or perhaps both."[47]

The U.S. Freedom of Information Act (FOIA) requires government agencies to disclose information, but it contains an exemption for information collected from businesses. The exemption states that trade secrets and commercial or financial data are "privileged or confidential" and government agencies are not required to make that information public. The purpose of this exemption is to keep competing businesses from using the Freedom of Information Act to obtain sales inventories, customer lists, or scientific and manufacturing developments that can be used for commercial advantage.[48] Despite the intent of this exemption, businesses have repeatedly invoked it to keep even publicly important information about their operations secret.

In one of the major challenges to the FOIA, called a "reverse FOIA case," Chrysler Corporation attempted to keep secret a report on affirmative action compliance that it was required to file as a federal contractor. The report described the composition of Chrysler's work force and its attempts to comply with affirmative action programs. After Chrysler was informed that the U.S. Department of Defense's Logistics Agency was planning to release the information in response to a FOIA request, the corporation sought an injunction in federal court to prohibit the release. The District Court sided with Chrysler, but the case was appealed and reached the Supreme Court in 1978. The Supreme Court ruled that companies that submit data to government agencies have an interest in confidentiality under the FOIA "only to the extent that this interest is endorsed by the agency collecting the information."[49] The ruling was a setback for Chrysler and other corporations' attempts to block important information from being made public by the federal government.

Unlike federal and state government agencies, corporations need not divulge any information, except where ordered to by government. Even then, corporations try to keep the information from becoming public, as the Chrysler case shows. Sometimes, relatively innocuous disclosure requirements, such as the SEC's requirement that publicly traded corporations make public their earnings reports, are often undermined by companies, which bury important information in footnotes or which publicly release confusing and misleading information immediately prior to the public disclosure.[50]

Privately held corporations need not even release this information. Given their ability to withhold information—even information that affects public health—corporations are far more effective in choking off public debate and discussion than government.

The Growth of Corporate Power

As railroads in the United States developed and grew in the last half of the nineteenth century, American industry was transformed. The railroad companies became the first large interstate corporations, but they also built the infrastructure that allowed other corporations to become large national operations. The size of U.S. companies is reflected in the number of miles of railway track laid. Between 1840–1850 7,000 miles of track were opened; between 1850–1860, 24,000 miles were opened; between 1860–1870, another 24,000; and between 1870–1880, 51,000 miles of track were laid and opened.[51]

During these decades of railway expansion, businesses intrinsically tied to the railway industry, such as telegraph, steel, and oil, evolved into large corporations. Other corporations became national once the railways allowed goods to be easily distributed nationally.

During the same era that corporations grew from local to national enterprises, labor unions developed. The Knights of Labor, which was forced to organize underground beginning in 1869, emerged publicly in 1881. In 1886, thirteen unions merged to form the American Federation of Labor. These unions protected workers from exploitative companies, which used numerous tactics to keep wages down and unions out. The tactics included dismissal, blacklists, lockouts, brutality, and yellow dog contracts, which employees signed, promising never to join a union.

When unions gained enough power to influence legislation, such as state laws passed during the 1890s that prohibited blacklisting, companies used a variety of methods to circumvent the laws or to challenge them in court. An important method for countering legislation protecting workers came in 1886 when the Supreme Court ruled in *Santa Clara County v.*

Southern Pacific Railroad that corporations were legally "persons" and entitled to protection under the equal protection clause of the Fourteenth Amendment to the Constitution.[52] The Fourteenth Amendment, written to redress the legal inequality between whites and blacks in former slave states, prohibits states from "depriv[ing] any person of life, liberty, or property without due process." Rather than protecting blacks, the Fourteenth Amendment after 1886 was primarily used to challenge child labor, health, and safety laws imposed by states, and to protect corporations from any state actions that limited corporate activities. "Of the Fourteenth Amendment cases brought before the Supreme Court between 1890 and 1910, nineteen dealt with the Negro, 288 dealt with corporations," reports historian Howard Zinn.[53]

Using the Fourteenth Amendment as the basis for their claims, corporations filed suits claiming that state laws creating the eight-hour day, prohibiting employers from discharging pro-union employees, and banning yellow dog contracts were unconstitutional abridgements of employers' rights. The employers frequently won. In 1895, the Supreme Court struck down an Illinois law establishing the eight-hour day, ruling that the law "substitutes the judgement of the legislature for the judgement of the employer and employee in a matter which they are competent to agree with each other. But the police power of the state can only be permitted to limit or abridge such a fundamental right as the right to make contracts, when the exercise of such power is necessary to promote the health, comfort, welfare, or safety of society to the public; and it is questionable whether it can be exercised to prevent injury to the individual engaged in a particular calling."[54] The Supreme Court's thinking in this case—that state laws designed to protect workers rather than society as a whole violated due process—was repeated in many cases until 1937. Between 1897 and 1937, the Supreme Court frequently invalidated state and federal legislation that the court perceived to regulate economic activity.[55]

Corporations also used the Sherman Antitrust Act of 1890, passed to curb the monopolistic practices of large corporations, to sue unions, claiming that unions were "combinations" that restrained trade. This

practice continued until the passage of the Norris-LaGuardia Act of 1932, the later interpretation of which exempted labor unions from prosecution under the antitrust laws.[56]

The legacy of *Santa Clara County v. Southern Pacific Railroad* is that corporations have extended their powers far beyond those of individuals. As author Robert Sherrill observed, "The inequality between black and white that the 14th Amendment was supposed to overcome has instead been transformed into perhaps an even greater inequality between the corporate person and the natural person."[57] With their greater financial clout and power, corporations have successfully used the courts and Fourteenth Amendment protections to curb attempts to police their abuses.

Santa Clara County v. Southern Pacific Railroad isn't the only court decision or government action that has contributed to the growth of corporate power during the past century. One of the most important has been the U.S. government's perception that big businesses are needed to compete globally. This perception has permitted mergers, such as the 1999 merger between Exxon and Mobil, the nation's two largest oil companies, that would have been banned under antitrust laws in another era.[58] It has produced legislation such as the Telecommunication Act of 1995 that allowed large corporations like General Electric to grow even larger.

Part of the reason why legislation like the Telecommunication Act has been passed by Congress and state legislatures is that several Supreme Court decisions, particularly *Buckley v. Valeo*, have allowed corporations to become active in the political process, lobbying extensively and contributing money to candidates running for public office. The *Valeo* decision allowed corporations, through their political action committees (PACs), to donate money directly to political candidates and indirectly through unlimited "soft money" contributions to political parties. In federal elections, the largest contributions now come from corporate PACs. Corporate PACs contributed $48 million to Republican House candidates in 1998 and $23 million to Democratic candidates, more than any other group.[59] Corporate PACs also contributed the most money to political party organizations. For example, nearly half of the money flowing into

the National Republican Congressional Committee during the 1998 elections came from corporations.[60]

Political parties and elected officials dependent on these contributions lobby federal agencies on behalf of, or vote for legislation benefitting their contributors. An example of this is provided by Arizona Sen. John McCain, who campaigned in the 2000 Republican presidential primary against the corrupting influence of political contributions. Despite his campaign message, McCain lobbied extensively on behalf of his contributors. McCain wrote regulators on behalf of America West Airlines, Ameritech, BellSouth, Paxson Communications, and other financial backers. He asked the Federal Communications Commission to give "serious consideration" to BellSouth's proposal to offer long-distance telephone service, asked the FCC to approve Paxson Communication's request to buy a television station, and castigated the FCC in a letter for being unfair toward Ameritech's proposed merger with another regional telephone company.[61]

Not only have laws and regulations been adopted that have allowed corporations to expand their size and power, but U.S. tax policies during the last half-century have benefitted corporations at the expense of citizens. The federal tax burden has been shifted from corporations to individuals since the 1950s, giving corporations more money to use for acquisitions and to influence legislation. In 1952, corporate income taxes accounted for 32.1 percent of federal revenues. By 1970, federal revenues coming from corporate taxes dropped to 17 percent, and, by 1980, they had fallen to 6.6 percent.[62] Relieved of their tax responsibilities, corporate coffers have swelled, allowing them to evolve from multidivisional organizations to national conglomerates to multinational entities rivaling the size and power of many nation states.[63] Because they have more assets available to them than most governments and because they lack public accountability, corporations now wield immense power, which they often use to restrict speech or silence critics.

It is not just multinational conglomerates such as Philip Morris that act as censors. Small corporations often employ similar censorial strategies: forcing employees to sign nondisclosure agreements, filing SLAPP suits against critics, and pressuring the news media to kill or alter stories affecting their businesses. The most consistent sources of advertising pressure on newspapers and television stations are real estate companies and automobile dealers, not multinational corporations. Real estate companies and auto dealers are not content merely to pressure the news media; they have also tried to silence citizens who have criticized their business practices. For example, Thomason Ford & Toyota, Washington State's largest automobile dealership during the mid-1990s, sought to enjoin the Consumer League, an activist consumer group, from picketing and leafleting near its car lots. The dealership was accused by the Washington State Attorney General, auto buyers, and the Consumers League of engaging in unfair business practices, such as bait-and-switch advertising. Rather than agreeing to meet with the picketers, the dealership sought to enjoin them from gathering on public property in front of the dealership. The dealer accused the picketers of trespassing and defamation, and asked Superior Court Judge Liem Tuai to issue a restraining order halting the picketing. The judge refused to issue the order, ruling that there was no "evidence that would indicate that the picketing people were doing anything the court didn't allow."[64] With the help of Judge Tuai, the consumer activists eventually triumphed. Thomason was forced to sell its car lots and leave Washington.

Most of the daily occurring censorship is exercised by smaller corporations, such as Thomason Ford & Toyota. These companies can and usually do restrict citizens from gathering on their property; write civil contracts that strip citizens of their constitutional rights; or file lawsuits against citizens to punish them for speaking. Although most citizens do not realize it, every time they enter a mall or shopping center, they leave their free speech rights at the curb outside. Almost every resident in planned housing developments, such as condominiums and retirement communities, have signed leases or deeds restricting their free speech rights. And every citizen who complains about the produce or meat that they have purchased can be sued for product disparagement. This is the status of free speech in the United States.

PART 1

SPEAKING OF LABOR

U nlike many European countries, the United States has lacked a labor party and strong labor unions. Because of the political weakness of U.S. labor, employer-employee relations in the United States are governed by the "at-will employment" doctrine. The doctrine covers the vast majority of U.S. private sector employees, excluding only those who have individual employment contracts or are covered by collective bargaining agreements. The at-will employment doctrine views employers and employees as fictitious equals in the workplace, with employees selling their labor to employers for the highest wages. Because employers and employees are deemed to be equals by the doctrine, an employee is viewed as capable of injuring an employer by quitting at any time, and employers are viewed as having equal power—the power to discharge an employee at any time.[1]

Reality, of course, is far different. Employees are dependent upon their jobs for their livelihoods, but employers are seldom dependent on a single employee for the success of their firms. A large firm, particularly a corporation, can have hundreds or even thousands of employees, who individually exercise very little leverage over the firm by quitting.

Because the at-will employment doctrine gives employers the power to discharge employees at any time for any reason, including speech disliked by the employer, employers have tremendous power over employees, who often silence themselves fearing termination if they do not. Under the at-will employment doctrine, this threat is ubiquitous.

There are two government-imposed limitations on the at-will employment doctrine—those made by courts such as the public policy and implicit exceptions and those imposed by statutes such as the civil rights laws. Without these government-imposed limits, employers would be free to exercise totalitarian control over employees.

Of the public policy limitations, implied contracts usually impose the weakest restraints on employers. The limits imposed by implied contracts have evolved judicially, with courts interpreting company work rules as implied contracts. For example, if a company's personnel employment handbook requires employees to give two weeks' notice before quitting, the employer cannot immediately fire an employee who submits a two-week resignation notice because the company has implied two weeks of continued employment by its requirement.

However, if company policy does not explicitly require a two-week notice for resignations, the employer can immediately discharge an employee who submits a resignation. An employer who does not want a quitting employee to talk about the advantages of the new job or better pay and better working conditions elsewhere can immediately discharge an employee who has submitted a resignation. Under the at-will employment doctrine this is permitted.[2] For that reason, some attorneys representing employers recommend fewer rather than more requirements in employment handbooks because explicit requirements can be viewed as implied contracts limiting employers' abilities to immediately discharge employees. In addition, some employers put specific disclaimers in handbooks, and these probably prevent an employer from making an implicit contract claim.

By far the greatest limitations on the at-will employment doctrine have come from legislation. State and federal laws and regulations have limited the power of employers to discharge employees because of their support for unions; because of employees' participation in political campaigns; because of employees' physical disabilities, age, religion, gender, or ethnicity; and because employees have reported company wrongdoing to government agencies. The latter are referred to as "whistle-blower protection laws." This legislation is often the only protection that employees have from autocratic employers.

With these exceptions, at-will employment governs most employer-employee relations and therefore places significant limitations on free speech. Because employees can be discharged at any time for any reason, the at-will employment doctrine is perhaps the greatest impediment to free speech in the United States. Because employers' powers to limit speech in this way is so broad and pervasive, it will not be discussed much in the following chapters. It will be assumed to be present. The following chapters instead explore other tactics used by employers to curb the speech of employees, sometimes in clear violation of court rulings, legislation, and regulations. These tactics include blacklisting, using trumped-up charges to discharge protected employees, and the use of private security forces, whose presence are constant reminders to employees that they are not truly free to speak.

2
Coercing Workers:
Company Towns and Labor Camps

In American labor history, few events are as famous as the "coalfield wars"—the often bloody attempts of workers to unionize the Appalachian coalfields. The battles of this war are named for the areas where drawn-out strikes took place: Bloody Harlan, the Mingo War, the Blair Mountain Battle, the Paint Creek-Cabin Creek Conflict and the Matewan Massacre, which was dramatized in John Sayles's 1987 feature film, *Matewan*.[1]

A 1935 film, *Black Fury*, depicted life in a company-owned town, where miners were routinely brutalized by company guards. After a coal miner, portrayed by Paul Muni, is beaten and his friend killed, the miner barricades himself in a mine to protest the company's treatment of employees.

Black Fury portrayed a company town where the company owned and controlled the housing, retailing, social activities, and most other facets of their employees' existence. Company towns such as these were built in remote areas where streams provided power for textile mills, mountains could be excavated for their coal, or virgin trees felled and cut for lumber. To attract workers to these isolated areas, companies built housing, which they rented to their employees. To supply employees with food and clothing, companies operated retail stores, and to provide for employees' spiritual comfort, companies built churches.

Because the housing, land, retail outlets, and even roads were owned by the companies, these towns constituted private property over which the companies exercised total control. To assure their control wasn't challenged, the companies hired private police forces, banned literature and speech that challenged company dictates, and evicted employees who failed to be compliant.

In these towns, the companies were responsible for building and road maintenance, fire protection, and health services, functioning as private governments. By providing these services, rather than allowing bona fide governments to provide them, the companies were able to keep legitimate, democratic governments out. All policy decisions were made by the owners of the firms or their boards of directors. They were, in form and practice, autocracies.

Some were ruled by tyrants; others by benevolent despots. Captain Ellison Smyth was the owner and tyrant of Pelzer, South Carolina. In his fiefdom, Smyth banned after-dark activities and dogs, which he considered "worthless and troublesome." In contrast, George M. Pullman, whose company-owned Pullman, Illinois, referred to employees as his children.[2]

Company towns were built principally between 1830 and 1930, when approximately 2,500 were constructed.[3] A few were built prior to 1830 by textile manufacturers in New England, and some were built after 1930 in timber- and mineral-rich areas of the West. During the 1930s and 1940s, New Deal laws and court rulings sharply diminished companies' authority over employees. The biggest setbacks to the operation of traditional company towns were federal laws such as the Wagner Act that made it difficult for companies to stop their employees from organizing unions, and court decisions such as *Marsh v. Alabama* that ruled citizens have free speech rights on company owned streets and sidewalks.[4] Because these government actions severely curtailed companies' abilities to coerce employees, the rationale for operating traditional company towns evaporated.

After the Second World War, many traditional company towns evolved into company-dominated towns. Company-owned housing was sold to employees, infrastructure such as roads and social services like fire departments were turned over to local governments, and company-owned stores were sold or leased to retailers. The costs of fire protection and social services were shifted to employees and retailers, who paid taxes for the services formerly provided by the company. Although the local governments were not directly controlled by the companies, the companies learned that they could still exercise indirect control of political institutions.

One method used by companies to maintain control in these civil towns was restrictive covenants attached to deeds. When the houses were sold to employees, the deeds contained restrictions on what homeowners and retailers could do with the property.

In company-dominated towns, which exist in large numbers today, there is one large company or industry that dominates the local economy. In these towns, the company exercises indirect power through its employees, political and charitable contributions, and public relations. Such towns include Midland, Michigan, dominated by Dow Chemical; Newton, Iowa, dominated by Maytag; Rochester, New York, dominated by Eastman-Kodak; and Corning, New York, dominated by Corning, Inc. In these towns, the financial well-being of the company is viewed as synonymous with the financial well-being of the city, and public policies are usually adopted with the interests of the company in mind. For example, Newton, Iowa, schools for many years showed Maytag-produced documentary films that lauded the company's contributions to the city. The school board neither questioned the educational value of these propaganda films nor permitted contrary views to be presented in classrooms.[5]

Although companies cannot restrict speech in company-dominated towns in the same way that speech could be restricted in traditional company towns, there are still many private limitations on public discourse. In North Freeport, Maine, the town's largest employer and taxpayer, L.L. Bean, pressured the city into allowing it to expand its business into residential areas near schools and to give it a twenty-year, $3.4 million tax rebate in 1996. Although many residents privately opposed the company's requests, they were fearful to speak out publicly. As the *Portland Press Herald* reported, "Many residents [were] reluctant to criticize Bean. They didn't want to be ostracized by their neighbors, lose their jobs with the company, or get cut off from business contacts."[6]

When public relations campaigns, lobbying, and threats to lay off employees fail to achieve the company's policy objectives, SLAPP suits, media pressures, and other techniques are used to limit the expression of opposition viewpoints. For example, after the *Corning Leader*, which had long been a Corning company sycophant, published a story saying that Corning, Inc., was in a "state of emergency" resulting from a drop in demand for optical fibers, Corning took swift, stern action against the newspaper. Corning first denounced the newspaper for being "irresponsible" and then removed all of the newspaper's vending machines from its properties. Corning then dumped the vending machines in the *Leader*'s parking lot.[7]

Company-dominated towns like Corning are not the only vestiges of the old-style company towns. Company-owned housing continues to exist and has made a resurgence in many regions where property values prohibit wage workers from buying homes or renting apartments. In Aspen, Nantucket Island, and other resort areas, such as the Opryland Resort area of Memphis, employers have built housing for their workers. And, as in company towns, employees' shelter is dependent on their remaining in their employers' good graces. As a spokesperson for Opryland, which rents motel rooms to its service employees, said, "If they are not working out as an employee, they need to move out."[8] If employees are fired, they are also evicted, leaving them not only unemployed but homeless, making the employees very reluctant to speak out against employers' abuses.

Predictably, this power over employees has led to abuses, including the curtailment of employees' free speech rights. For example, the Opryland Hotel adopted a no-solicitation, no-talk rule that employees were required to follow on the job, but it was enforced primarily against union organizers, who were discharged for their advocacy of unionization. The National Labor Relations Board eventually declared the no-talk rule an unfair labor practice, because it was "applied only to union-related matters."[9]

The Origin of Company Towns

The rise of industrial capitalism and company towns in the United States are nearly synonymous. In New England, textile mills were built around rivers and waterfalls that turned the mill wheels. To attract workers, mill owners built housing for employees and operated stores that sold goods to the employees and neighboring small farmers. On some occasions, small farmers and their families became so indebted to company stores that they were forced to pay off their debts by working in the mills.[10]

In early New England, two types of company towns evolved. One was a small village employing poor farmers and their families, who worked part-time, and even poorer families and single men, who worked full-time. The workers lived in company tenements.

In these tenement villages, pay was poor and was sometimes given in scrip, and employees were forced to buy at the company store. Rent for the tenement housing was deducted from employees' pay, and evictions were used to punish those who failed to show up for work or violated company rules. In these mills, child labor was used extensively, and the children's wages were seldom enough to sustain life. Conditions in these villages were horrible, as Hiram Munger, who worked in the Benjamin Jenks & Co. mill in Massachusetts, wrote in his autobiography:

> Here is where I was made acquainted with American slavery in the second degree. The treatment of the help in those days was cruel, especially to poor children, of whom I was one. Although I was young, I recollect thinking that life must be a burden if I was obliged to work in a factory under such tyrants as the Jenks were then, and they never improved. . . .[11]

These family employees became a propertyless, exploited working class that often rebelled against the mill owners, who required their employees to attend church, remain silent during work hours, and keep their complaints to themselves. Failure to follow the rules could result in fines, lowered wages, or suspensions without pay, which made the hapless employees even more indebted to their employers.

The other type of mill town was populated by a large, temporary work force of young women, who worked in the mills for several years and then moved on to other employment. Because the young women worked in the mills to get out of their parents' homes, to make money for buying luxury goods, or to save for higher education, rather than from need, they were more free to quit their jobs and return to their families' homes and farms than were the propertyless families living in company tenements. The company towns populated by young women were touted during the early 1800s as models of industrial development.[12] However, this type of mill town eventually merged with the first type in the middle nineteenth century, as young women and recent immigrants became permanent rather than temporary mill employees.

The young mill women lived in cramped company-owned homes, slept two to a bed and six to a room. The homes were run by widows, who cleaned the homes and cooked for the employees, and saw to it the young women obeyed the company's rules in and out of the mill. The rules they were required to follow were very restrictive, governing morals, church attendance, speech, and even reading materials. A system of "mutual surveillance" was adopted, where mill girls were encouraged to report the transgressions of others, similar to the *Stasi* system developed in post–Second World War East Germany.

The rules were actually used by the mill companies as a recruiting tool. Religious, conservative families, aware that the behavior of their daughters were tightly controlled by the company, were willing to let their daughters move unchaperoned to the mill towns.

Although the mill companies promised to oversee their employees *in loco parentis*, their rules were far stricter than in the most authoritarian families. These rules were printed and given to employees with their work contracts. The work contracts specified the type of work the employee would do and the number of months the employee was obligated to work for the company. The employment contracts required employees to give two weeks' notice to the company before quitting, but employers could fire anyone at any time for any reason, making the contracts extremely one-sided.

The young women were prohibited from talking in the mills during the sunup to sundown working hours and were prohibited from bringing reading materials into the mill. In Lowell, where the mills were large and corporate-owned, employees could be fired for bringing newspapers, books, or even printed leaves to work with them.[13] Church attendance was mandatory, even though attendees had to pay pew rent; curfews and sleeping hours were company determined; and speech was tightly controlled. One contract stated that the company "will not continue to employ any person who shall smoke within the company premises, or be guilty of inebriety or other improper conduct."[14] Employees who were considered vulgar, complained about working conditions, or "conspired" to strike or form unions were immediately dismissed, blacklisted, and evicted.

Although employees' speech and behavior were severely curtailed, they were free—even encouraged—to spend their money on clothes, shoes, and other fashion items. In this respect, the mill towns resemble modern-day shopping malls, where consumers are free to spend money but not to exercise free speech.

In addition to establishing a pattern of paternalism that other company towns would copy, the mill towns of New England introduced two other innovations adopted by many companies. First, the textile companies introduced secrecy agreements into employment contracts. Mill mechanics, who constructed and maintained the looms and other mill equipment, were required to sign secrecy clauses forbidding them from disclosing any aspects of the mills' operations to others. For example, machinist Thomas Lyon signed a contract in 1812 containing a three thousand dollar forfeiture clause—a huge sum at the time—that stated, "I will not within the space of seven years herefrom in any way or manner directly or indirectly disclose, reveal or communicate to any person or persons the nature, construction, properties, operation, contrivance or peculiarities of the machinery of the said cotton manufactory as the same now is or hereafter."[15] Because the technical innovations at most mills were typically minimal, the major purpose of the secrecy contracts was to limit the mechanics' abilities to find employment at another mill for higher wages. In effect, mill owners could not only fire workers for any reason, but they could also prevent them from being hired elsewhere.

Another innovation of the mill towns was the company magazine. The most famous of the mill town magazines was the *Lowell Offering*. Although the magazine was written by employees, it was neither funded nor edited by them. The magazine was funded by the mill owners who used it to recruit employees. The *Lowell Offering* discussed cultural activities, such as lecture series and performances, available to the young mill employees and, by publishing their short stories, poems, and essays, suggested that mill employees were being culturally uplifted by their work experiences. Because literary achievements were highly prized in early-nineteenth-century New England, the magazine indicated to potential employees and their parents that mill work had many benefits when compared to other types of employment available to young women, such as child care and domestic work.

What the *Offering* did not discuss was the long working hours, cramped living conditions, or the wage cuts forced on employees. Sarah Bagley, a Lowell employee who tried to organize a mill workers' union, said that the magazine refused to publish articles that complained about "the abuses of oppressive rules or unreasonable hours" of mill work. After being attacked by Bagley as "a mouthpiece of the corporations," the magazine's propaganda value eroded and it was closed.[16]

The *Offering* served as a model for other in-house or industry publications. These are often distributed to employees by management to explain corporate decisions and to boost employee morale. Although they may allow some employees to grumble in their pages, they are nevertheless company controlled and highly censored.

By the late 1830s, the number of young women going to work in the mills had increased, producing a labor supply that exceeded demand. Taking advantage of this labor surplus, the mill owners and corporations cut wages and increased workloads, which led to spontaneous strikes and job actions by mill employees. Strike leaders and advocates were fired, evicted, and blacklisted. In the Waltham mills, striking employees were fired and Irish strikebreakers brought in.

The worsening conditions made mill work unattractive to all but the neediest New England women, who became permanent mill employees, dependent on their employment for survival rather than as an opportunity to save money. In the 1850s, these young women were joined in the mills by Irish immigrants, who came to the United States in large numbers to escape the potato famine of 1845–1847. Because the immigrant employees were accustomed to the ruthless European factory system and even more dependent on their jobs for survival than poor New England women, mill owners again imposed wages cuts and speedups, producing an even more exploitative system. Because of the exploitation, Irish immigrants eventually left the mills and were replaced by successive waves of Italian, Polish, Russian, and Greek immigrants. By 1912, when the Industrial Workers of the World led the now-famous Lawrence textile strike, immigrants representing twenty-five different nationalities were working in Lawrence mills.[17]

Immigrants are still hired for low-paying jobs in textiles and other industries. Like the nineteenth-century immigrants, they too are exploited because employers believe that immigrants are fearful of complaining to federal and state authorities about working conditions. As a consequence, these immigrants are often deprived of their economic and free speech rights.

There are numerous examples of illegal immigrants being inhumanely exploited. In California, illegal immigrants were forced to work seven days a week, fifty-two weeks a year for $1.60 an hour sewing garments for upscale clothing stores to pay off debts for their food, housing, and transportation from Thailand. The Thai immigrants were kept in virtual seclusion, so they could not complain about their treatment. In San Diego, eighty-seven illegal Mexican immigrants were kept in a boarded-up house, where they were forced to work to pay off the "coyotes" who smuggled them into the United States. And numerous illegal Chinese immigrants have been forced into virtual servitude, working in sweatshops and prostitution to pay off their debts to smugglers. These immigrants are not really free to complain about their treatment, as the case of the illegal Thai immigrants shows. After being rescued, the Thai workers were arrested by the Immigration and Naturalization Service (INS) and placed in a federal detention center.[18]

Although these are examples of extreme exploitation, debt peonage, in which people are forced to pay off debts by working, is common.

Large companies are rarely as heavy-handed as coyotes or sweatshop operators, but they also assume that illegal immigrants will be reluctant to speak out against their exploitation. For example, Gregorio Arista Lea was fired in 1999 for being an illegal immigrant after he suffered a back injury at Kenosha Beef International in Wisconsin. The company believed that by firing Lea it could avoid paying him disability payments, since he was an illegal immigrant who would be reluctant to file a claim against them. When Lea did file, the company claimed that he was not eligible for disability payments because, as an illegal immigrant, he was not eligible for employment.[19]

In Minneapolis, eight undocumented workers were turned into the INS by the manager of the Holiday Day Inn Express after they and other employees voted to join the Hotel Employees and Restaurant Employees Union. The manager claimed that he was fearful of being penalized for hiring undocumented workers, a fear that apparently arose only after the union vote. The AFL-CIO and the local union spoke up on behalf of the fired employees, successfully arguing to the INS that the employer's actions undermined federal agencies' abilities to enforce existing labor laws. On April 25, 2000, the INS agreed, allowing seven of the eight undocumented workers to remain in the United States.[20]

Coal Towns: From Exploitation to Paternalism

During the late nineteenth century, immigrants also moved to U.S. mining towns in the hopes of making and saving money. At the time, mining regions had very small populations, so workers were imported to work in the mines. Between 1861 and 1870, Irish, English, and German immigrants moved to the anthracite regions of Pennsylvania, where they constituted a majority of miners.

Because of the working conditions, these immigrants left the mines and were replaced by eastern and southern Europeans, who by 1900 constituted nearly 70 percent of miners in Pennsylvania and 30 percent in West Virginia.[21] They were joined in the mines by African-Americans, who migrated to the Appalachian coalfields to escape the horrid sharecropping and debt peonage system of the South, where tenants could be summarily evicted, beaten, and deprived of civil liberties. These African-American migrants discovered a similarly oppressive, but somewhat better paying, system in the mines. By 1900, African-Americans constituted about 20 percent of mine workers in Appalachia.

The remainder were white—mountain folk—who had lived for nearly a century in the Appalachian hills. In West Virgina, these hill people were forced into the mines after the railroad, iron, and coal companies used the courts to steal the deeds to their land. Most poor West Virginians lacked the money and knowledge to engage in protracted court battles, and lost their land and freedom to the Mellon, Morgan, and Guggenheim trusts.[22] The animosity generated by this theft is one reason why the West Virginia coalfield battles were the bloodiest of all.

Company towns were also built around the coal and iron mines of Alabama, where poor whites and African-Americans were treated to still worse indignities than were Appalachian miners. In Alabama, coal operators exploited racial hatred to keep wages down, paying blacks less than whites, and hiring blacks as strikebreakers when whites went on strike. Blacks were also forced into the mines when ill by guards called "shack rousters," who forcibly entered black miners' homes to force them into the mines. These shack rousters even molested black women when their husbands were in the mines. The Mine Workers Journal described these ordeals, writing that the "shack rouster rides from sunrise until [sunset] with his billy and his revolver hanging to his saddle, and if any negro opens his mouth in protest of his cowardly acts with their women they are either beaten almost to death or shot down like a dog." When blacks and whites united to fight this exploitation by unionizing, private armies of Klansmen were dispatched to the break the strikes.[23]

Coal mines were also opened in midwestern states such as Illinois and Iowa, but in these areas company towns rarely developed because land was plentiful, cheap, and productive, allowing workers to own their own homes, gardens, and small farms.[24] Overall, less than 10 percent of Illinois miners lived in company towns at the beginning of the 1900s, compared with 80 percent in West Virginia. In Alabama and Kentucky, as in West Virginia, a majority of miners lived in company towns, whereas the number in Pennsylvania was estimated at between 16 and 45 percent.[25]

In company towns, employees had little freedom at work or at home. What freedom they had was at the discretion of the company. Benevolent employers allowed their employees greater freedom, such as the right to buy at independent, rather than company, stores. In contrast, malevolent employers completely controlled miners' lives and made employment contingent on shopping at the company store. Some companies even barred traveling salesmen from entering their towns, and others barred independent merchants from delivering goods to workers living in company-owned houses. There were apparently so many malevolent coal operators in West Virginia, a state whose political and judicial systems were dominated by coal interests, that the state managed to pass a law barring operators from firing employees who shopped at non-company stores. However, most coal towns were distant from civil towns, making it difficult for miners to find alternatives to the company store.[26]

Some coal companies paid their miners in scrip or company currency that was redeemable only at the company store, or was discounted from face value by independent merchants. Although there is debate as to whether company stores charged higher prices than other retailers,[27] there is no debate that the stores were profitable operations for the coal companies. When coal prices dropped, the mining companies could still count on their stores to generate a profit for their firms.

After laws were passed prohibiting companies from paying employees in scrip, scrip continued to be used as an advance against wages, rather than in lieu of wages. As a result of these advances, rent for company housing, medical fees, charges for the use or sharpening of tools, black powder, and other deductions, miners living in company towns were seldom paid more than half their earnings.[28]

In many mining towns, speech, the availability of reading materials, and even postal communications were severely regulated. So severe was the control that not even Stalinist Russia could match it, despite capitalist exhortations that the free market and personal freedom are synonymous.

Virtually everyone residing in these coal towns was a company employee, including the clergy, postal clerks, and doctors, who were expected to act on behalf of their employer. The churches were built by the company, and the clergy served at the discretion of the company. Often, the coal companies built churches for the denominations preferred by the company owner, rather than the employees, and miners had to join that denomination or not attend church at all. As David Alan Corbin in *Life, Work and Rebellion in the Coal Fields* wrote, "In the company town, a miner's denomination became not a matter of personal preference or tradition, but was determined by the coal company, which selected the faith in the town."[29]

In larger company towns, several denominations were permitted, but the companies made sure that all members of the clergy gave pro-company, anti-union sermons. Ministers who preached the social gospel, advocating decent working conditions, equitable pay, and civil liberties, were forced out of town. Consequently, religion was just another method of social control exercised by the company.[30]

Company employees, usually a clerk in the company store, also served as town postmaster, and examined incoming and outgoing mail to make sure it did not contain pro-union materials. Mail sent to miners by unions was confiscated, and the mails were used to uncover miners holding pro-union sympathies, who were sacked. Newspapers, magazines, and political information mailed to miners were also examined.

Although the miners paid for medical services—typically $5 per month, which was deducted from their pay—the doctors in company towns were company employees who answered to the company rather than their patients. Rather than regarding the communications between them and miners as privileged, doctors were expected to inform on miners who complained about the company, faked illness, or expressed pro-union sympathies.

Schoolteachers, who were public employees but whose salaries were often supplemented by the coal companies (which sometimes deducted money from miners' wages to pay for these supplements), were also expected to give pro-company, anti-union lectures.[31] School administrators were expected to watch over their teachers and check with the coal companies before revising their curriculum.

To enforce their policies, the mining companies employed private guards, whose brutality was notorious. Some guards were employees of the coal companies, which was often the case in Alabama; some were employees of private policing firms such as the Baldwin-Felts and Pinkerton agencies, which had security contracts with the West Virginia and Pennsylvania coal companies; and some were county sheriffs, whose salaries were paid by the coal companies, despite their ostensibly being public employees. Because they were county sheriffs, these guards were able to accost and arrest union organizers for trespassing, vagrancy, and other trumped-up charges.[32] In some cases, union organizers were arrested for violating state blue laws barring meetings on Sunday, the one day that miners had off. In other cases, miners were virtually conscripted by the guards to help fight union organizers.[33]

Baldwin-Felts and Pinkerton agents were not only employed as guards but as union infiltrators and informers. Sometimes the agencies hired anti-union miners as informers. The informers identified pro-union miners, who were fired.

These private police also controlled who entered and left the company-owned towns and, in Alabama, even issued miners passes, which stated the roads that miners were permitted to use.[34] By tightly controlling entrance to the company towns, the guards could control access to political information, prohibit the entry of newspapers critical of company policies, and bar speakers who might denounce coal company actions.

The leases for houses that miners signed with coal companies invariably stripped miners of tenancy rights, even though the miners paid rent for the housing and the companies profited from the leases.[35] The contracts specified that occupancy was to end when employment ended and gave the company the right to enter the home and remove belongings of discharged employees. This could be done without regard to state land-lord-tenancy laws, because the companies claimed—and were upheld in this claim by state courts—that the relationship of miners to the company was a "master-servant" relationship rather than a "landlord-tenant" relationship. For example, in *Watt Angel v. Black Band Consolidated Coal Company*, the West Virginia Supreme Court of Appeals ruled that coal operators could evict striking workers from homes by force, if needed, because the homes were owned by the company, not the employee, and master-servant relationships prevailed.[36]

The leases were a major deterrent to union organizing and strikes. Evictions were common when employees spoke in favor of or joined a union, or went on strike. Eviction was even used as a tool against worker complaints about working conditions, such as short weighting. In Logan County, West Virginia a miner was discharged for asking the company to double-check the weights given by the company check-weighman, who weighed the amount of coal each employee mined, which determined how much miners were paid. After being discharged, the miner was evicted.[37]

Even after the passage of the Wagner Act, evictions from company-owned houses were used to break strikes, as in the village of Kohler, Wisconsin. There, Kohler, a manufacturer of sinks, faucets, and other kitchen and bathroom fixtures, evicted striking employees during a prolonged United Auto Workers strike during the 1950s.[38] Kohler Company still owns housing in the company-controlled village, over which it exercises control.

Not only could employees be evicted from company-owned housing without due process, but their rights to speech and association were severely curtailed in the houses that they rented. Many coal company leases had provisions giving the company the power to determine who could enter company-owned houses. In some company towns, "bunching"—the gathering of three or more miners together—was prohibited. These policies were adopted to keep union organizers from entering miners' homes to discuss the benefits of unionizing and to prevent miners from getting together to talk union.[39]

The employment contracts that companies had miners sign invariably contained clauses that severely limited the miners' rights of free association and freedom to advocate unionization.[40] These yellow dog contracts not only prohibited employees from joining unions, but also prohibited employees from advocating unionization or boycotting, picketing, and striking. These contracts stripped employees of their free speech and free association rights.

Although yellow dog contracts were outlawed by the Wagner Act, many employers still use provisions of employment contracts to restrict employees' freedom of action. Secrecy agreements imbedded in employment contracts are one example. Another commonly used clause in employment contracts requires employees and former employees to pursue complaints against the company through arbitration, rather than the courts, stripping employees of their right to have the case heard by a jury of peers.[41]

Conditions in western coal towns, particularly in southern Colorado, were not much better than in West Virginia. As in West Virginia, attempts to establish unions in the West resulted in bloody conflicts. The most infamous conflict, known as the "Ludlow Massacre," occurred in 1914, when a private militia operated by Colorado Fuel and Iron Corp. attacked a tent colony of strikers, killing 21 people, including 11 children.

Owners of western coal towns used company stores, scrip, and rigid controls to strip employees of their rights, as did coal companies in Appalachia. Speech in these communities was severely curtailed. Incoming mail was monitored for literature and letters that the companies considered hostile, and school teachers and ministers were policed and censored. Larger companies attempted to control information by publishing their own periodicals, such as *Camp and Plant*, published by Colorado Fuel and Iron. "Fault-finders, individual or collectively, were not tolerated in these closed camps. Intruders and malcontents were ferreted out by an intricate espionage system and treated by heavily armed guards to the kangaroo, the coal district term for a professional beating."[42]

After the bloody strikes of the 1910s and 1920s and the passage of federal laws that restricted companies' abilities to intimidate workers, many mining companies turned to paternalism as a method for controlling workers. Paternalism consisted of top-down control exercised with a velvet, rather than an iron, fist. The companies built YMCAs, operated bowling alleys, published company-controlled newspapers and magazines such as the *Stonegazette*, and sponsored sports leagues, social clubs, gardening, and other activities in an effort to keep workers focused on things other than their working conditions.[43]

Paternal Control

Although coal companies turned to paternalism relatively late, paternalism was practiced in many company towns during the late nineteenth century as part of the "welfare capitalism" movement. Probably the best known example of paternalism was the city of Pullman, Illinois, a company town built south of Chicago by the Pullman Palace Car Company, one of the nation's largest builders of rail cars. It was planned by the Pullman company's founder, George M. Pullman, who believed that a model company town would produce a placid, union-free work force. Pullman built a town for employees so that they would develop good work habits and avoid "baneful influences" such as liquor, gambling, and tobacco.[44]

Pullman, Illinois, wasn't created as a philanthropic attempt to placate workers; on the contrary, George Pullman opposed philanthropy, which he believed stifled individuals' initiative, a view that is similar to that of modern-day opponents to public assistance. The town was designed to be profitable—to generate a 6 percent annual return on investment. In order to maintain high occupancy and profit levels, the housing had many modern conveniences, including gas lighting and indoor plumbing. In return for these conveniences, residents paid higher than average rents and ceded many of their liberties to the Pullman Palace Car Company.

Unlike the coal towns, Pullman residents were free to come and go, had free access to information, and were generally free to express their opinions privately, something that coal miners were often reluctant to do.[45] The town had baseball diamonds, tennis courts, an athletic club, a

library, and even a theater, but fees were charged for the use of all facilities. The library had a large selection of books, but the majority were
nonfiction technical and scientific works that Pullman believed would
uplift his employees. The theater was run by the Pullman company, not
professional theater managers, because George Pullman wanted the
power to select "only such [plays] as he could invite his family to enjoy
with the utmost propriety."[46] Except during the famous Pullman Strike
of 1894, the camp was free of armed guards, and the city's managers
were benevolent, evicting residents at a far lower rate than in Chicago.

But there were also many subtle restraints on behavior and expression.
The town was built with just one bar, located in the hotel, to limit residents' access to alcoholic beverages. This was done because George
Pullman believed that alcohol reduced employee productivity and thrifti-
ness, virtues that he prized. Although alcoholic beverages were available in
Kensington, a town to the south, where many Pullman residents went to
imbibe, some residents felt compelled to leave Pullman walking north,
and then traveling south, lest they be seen heading to the bars. Such were
the pressures that Pullman exercised over employee behavior during non-
working hours.

In Pullman, the locations of stores were tightly controlled by the company. There were two shopping locations—the market hall, where prepared and fresh foods were sold, and the arcade, which was essentially the
world's first fully-enclosed mall. On the top floor of the market hall was
an assembly room that could accommodate six hundred folding chairs.
The arcade housed over thirty shops including dry goods, books, clothes,
and furniture on the first floor and a post office, professional offices, a
barber, and meeting halls on the second. And like modern-day malls,
access to the meeting and assembly rooms was controlled by George
Pullman and his company.[47]

During elections, the large meeting rooms were used for rallies for
candidates and issues supported by Pullman and his company. Opposition
voices had difficulty getting access to these facilities. The facilities were
also closed to union organizers, who were forced to meet in Kensington.

There were even reports that Pullman company foremen served as poll watchers and that employees were fired for signing petitions or expressing support for positions strongly opposed by George Pullman.[48]

Pullman had two periodicals, the *Pullman Journal* and the *Arcade Journal*, but these were essentially company organs, stressing social activities, scheduled events, and consumer news. They were not independent, community voices.

Although these social controls alienated residents from Pullman— some called living in Pullman "camping out"—it was not the social controls that led to the Pullman strike of 1894, it was economic issues. Faced with a decline in orders for railcars and falling revenues, the Pullman company cut employee wages rather than pay stockholders a reduced dividend.

The authoritarian Pullman would not negotiate with the employees over wage cuts, believing that employees should have no say in company decisions. Failing to get any relief from the Pullman Co., employees joined Eugene Debs' American Railway Union (ARU), which tried to negotiate with Pullman on their behalf. After rumors spread that ARU representatives were being discharged by Pullman, union members walked out, shutting down the plant. The strike quickly spread across the United States when union rail workers refused to attach or haul any Pullman cars, and, if Pullman cars were attached to trains, the trains were not moved.

The company responded by shutting down all of the stores in Pullman. The Pullman company also barred the union from meeting in the town and hired spies to report on union meetings. Using the information obtained from the spies, the company established a blacklist of union activists.

Just a few of the strikers were evicted from their homes. One reason why mass evictions were not used, as they were in coal towns, was that the company needed the renters for its bottom line, even if the rents weren't being paid immediately. At the beginning of the strike, some employees moved from the housing voluntarily to avoid the high rents, which produced an unexpectedly high vacancy rate that the company did not want to add to with evictions. When the Pullman Palace Car Co.

reopened its plant, strikebreakers started renting the vacant units, and their presence forced many of the striking employees not on the blacklist to go back to work.

Although the workers lost the strike, the state ordered the Pullman company to sell off its company-owned housing, because the state-granted corporate charter was for building railroad cars, not for operating a housing development. By 1909, the company had sold off all of the town property.

Despite the failure of paternalism in Pullman, it was adopted by many copper and chemical companies, including Phelps Dodge Corporation, Anaconda Copper Company, Kennecott Copper Corporation, Du Pont Corporation, and American Potash and Chemical Corporation, all of which operated mines in remote areas of the West. The paternalistic company towns included Ajo and Bisbee, Arizona, owned by Phelps Dodge; Conda, Idaho and Weed Heights, Nevada, owned by Anaconda Copper; Ray, Arizona, and Santa Rita, New Mexico, owned by Kennecott Copper; Du Pont, Washington, and Louviers, Colorado, owned by Du Pont; and Trona, California, owned by American Potash and Chemical. All were model cities, where the company built houses, recreational facilities, schools, stores, and medical facilities to attract family workers.

In all of these paternalistic company towns, persuasion and co-optation rather than force were used to maintain a docile work force. In many of these towns, the company operated a newspaper or other periodical that provided residents with the company's view of events. Although the companies usually controlled the colors that employees' houses could be painted, residents were given a choice of colors from which to select. Company unions were created to keep militant unions at bay, or the company quickly signed agreements with one union that represented everyone in town, thus avoiding potentially disruptive strikes called by different unions. For example, the McLeod River Lumber Company, which owned McLeod, California, signed three contracts with the International Woodworkers of America, covering plant, lumberjack, and town employees.[49]

When persuasion and co-optation failed, repression became the tool of last resort, as events in Bisbee, Arizona, during the summer of 1917 demonstrate. In late June and early July, the Phelps Dodge copper mine and processing plant in Bisbee were shut down by a strike called by the Industrial Workers of the World. Rather than negotiate a settlement to the strike, Phelps Dodge executives ordered the sheriff to deputize and arm pro-company employees, who arrested 1,250 strikers. The strikers were held in a baseball park under armed guard and then loaded into boxcars and deported to New Mexico, where they were released and ordered not to return to Bisbee. A federal inquiry into the events concluded that the order for the deportation came from Walter Douglas, president of Phelps Dodge, and it constituted a serious violation of the law and constitutional rights. Although others were indicted by the federal government for engaging in the unlawful deportations, the Phelps Dodge CEO was never prosecuted.[50]

Although not often used in paternalistic towns, most companies believed that they had the right to arrest and expel from company towns individuals who didn't have the company's permission to be there. This belief was shattered by the Supreme Court in 1945 in a case originating in Chickasaw, Alabama, a town owned by the Gulf Shipping Corporation. Except for the fact that Chickasaw was corporate owned, it resembled other towns in Alabama with streets and sidewalks linked to Mobile, of which Chickasaw appeared to be a suburb.

In 1945, a deputy arrested a Jehovah's Witness for distributing literature on a Chickasaw sidewalk. The Jehovah's Witness was prosecuted for, and convicted of trespassing, and the Alabama Supreme Court upheld the conviction, concluding that the sidewalk was private property even though publicly used.

The U.S. Supreme Court overturned the conviction in *Marsh v. Alabama*, deciding that company property was not like a home, where a homeowner has the right to regulate the conduct of guests.[51] "The more an owner, for his advantage, opens up his property for use by the public in general, the more do his rights become circumscribed by the statutory and constitutional rights of those who use it," the Court concluded. Rather than a home, the Court equated company towns with bridges, ferries, and railroads that are built and operated with a public function in mind and are therefore "subject to state regulation." The Court stated that residents of company towns remain free citizens and "as good citizens they must be informed. In order to enable them to be properly informed their information must be uncensored." More important, the Court concluded that "when we balance the Constitutional rights of property against those of the people to enjoy freedom of press and religion . . . the latter occupy a preferred position."[52]

Justice Frankfurter wrote a separate concurring opinion that more clearly distinguished between property rights and free speech rights. Frankfurter opposed the portion of the decision that concluded that free speech rights depended on "the extent of 'dedication' of private property to public purposes." According to Frankfurter, property rights are defined by state law and therefore "cannot control issues of civil liberties." In Frankfurter's view, free speech has protection that private property rights cannot supersede.

The *Marsh* decision was one of the final blows to traditional company towns. It eliminated one of the rationales for operating company towns— control over employees' speech. But it wasn't just *Marsh* that undermined traditional company towns. It was the encroachment of government and civil society into formerly remote areas that companies controlled. The discount chains that emerged after the Second World War made it difficult for company stores to remain competitive, and laws were passed curtailing companies' issuance of scrip. These took their toll on the profitability of company towns. Highways, telephones, and other developments made it impossible for companies to isolate their workers, so companies began selling off their towns.

Chickasaw was sold off shortly after the end of the Second World War when new ship orders declined. In the mid-1950s, Kennecott sold off its company towns, and many other companies followed. Today, former company towns like Bisbee and Ajo, where mining operations were closed down in the mid-1970s and mid-1980s, are mere tourist attractions. Scotia, California, a town owned by Pacific Lumber Company, remains company-owned, but it too is a tourist attraction. Others, like Kohler, Wisconsin, have become company-dominated towns with civil, rather than corporate, governments.[53]

Today, private colleges and universities most closely resemble traditional company towns, providing housing for students and sometimes faculty, operating restaurants and stores, having their own police forces, and creating rules of behavior that students and faculty are expected to follow. If students or faculty fail to abide by these rules, they can be expelled or fired.

Although universities pride themselves as centers of openness and free speech, this openness is due solely to the paternalism of university corporations. Freedom of speech on college campuses is not a matter of law, although several state court decisions, based on their state rather than the federal Consitution, have suggested that speech on private campuses should be broader than speech on other private property. In *Commonwealth of Pennsylvania v. Tate*, the Supreme Court of Pennsylvania ruled that Muhlenberg College had opened its doors to the public and controvery by inviting FBI chief Clarence Kelley to speak, and therefore could not bar leafleteers from its campus during the time of his appearance.[54] In *State of New Jersey v. Schmid*, the court ruled:

> Princeton has made its campus available as a forum for an open and robust exchange of political ideas and the Princeton community and the public generally . . . . Such a commitment of its facilities and properties constitutes a holding out of this property for a public use. As such, Princeton has assumed a public function . . . .[55]

Because of this, the court concluded, Princeton could not completely bar leafleting by nonstudents on its campus.

Nevertheless, private universities are private property, where the university corporation determines what behaviors and speech are acceptable. At many public universities, the bookstores, cafeterias, and student unions are operated by private entities or university-owned corporations, making these private rather than public facilities. Speech can be—and often is—restricted in these environments.

At many liberal arts colleges, "politically correct" speech codes were adopted during the 1990s that restricted students' speech about others' physical characteristics, sexual orientation, or ethnic heritage. At politically conservative universities, speech and behavior are also severely restricted. The most notorious restriction was at Bob Jones University in South Carolina, which barred interracial dating among students. Students violating the policy were disciplined. The restriction was reluctantly ended after GeorgeW. Bush visted the campus during his 2000 presidential campaign, which caused the media to examine and publicize Bob Jones University's racial policies.[56]

Most universities also have rules about the distribution or posting of literature, even for political candidates. At Marquette University, leaflets that are posted on bulletin boards or distributed to students must be approved by school officials. Otherwise, the literature will be taken down or confiscated. Policies such as these exist at most private universities.

Claiming that they are not truly public places, some state universities have adopted policies that limit free speech. At Arizona State University, Roger Axford, a seventy-six year-old professor emeritus was arrested in the student union building for collecting signatures on a political petition. Axford was arrested after being asked to leave, which he refused to do on First Amendment grounds. Floyd Land, the director of the union building, claimed that the union was private property and that Axford had no constitutional right to gather signatures there. "If our policy were based on the First Amendment, everyone could come in and express whatever they wanted," said Land about the union policy.[57]

The University of Texas at Austin has a policy of prohibiting anyone other than students, staff, or faculty from distributing leaflets on the campus. The university adopted the policy, according to administrator Lee Smith, because of crowding and safety issues and because off-campus groups can interfere with the university's educational mission. Using this as the rationale, the university ordered environmental activists to leave not just the campus but sidewalks outside the Erwin Center, a university-owned stadium where sporting events and concerts are held.[58] Activists challenged this policy in court. A federal district court judge upheld the university's right to ban leafleting on the campus in 1999, but ruled that the university could not ban leafleting in areas where many nonuniversity people travel, such as sidewalks near the Erwin Center.[59]

Farm Labor Camps

Similar to company towns, but on a far smaller scale, are farm labor camps that provide housing for, and sell supplies to, migrant farm laborers. These labor camps are operated by farmers' cooperatives, large farms, or farm labor contractors, who sign agreements with farmers to provide laborers during the harvesting season, relieving farmers of the responsibility of locating, hiring, and paying temporary laborers.

These labor camps first emerged in California, Florida, and other Sunbelt states where agribusinesses rather than family farmers dominated vegetable, cotton, and fruit production. As traditional family farms have been replaced by corporate farms in other states, migrant laborers have become the principal source of farm labor in these areas, too. And as the number of migrant laborers increased, so has the number of migrant labor camps.

These labor camps, almost since their inception, have deprived migrant farm laborers of their freedom to speak. As in company towns, migrant laborers have a right to housing only as long as they are working for the camp's owner. Since the labor camps are on private property, the property owners can and do restrict the types of literature carried onto the property. Information about unions or higher wages being paid elsewhere can be confiscated. Laborers who complain about working conditions or attempt to unionize are fired and immediately evicted from the camps.

Moreover, these camps are often located a considerable distance from public roads, so that they are hidden from view, and unauthorized visitors have to trespass to reach the camps. The trespassers can be arrested and evicted. In Washington, for example, a cherry grower called the county sheriff in 1997 to keep newspaper and television reporters from his property, where they went to examine conditions in a labor camp.[60]

The most abusive employers are farm labor contractors, who provide the laborers who work on large farms. The farms pay the contractor, and the contractor pays the laborers, freeing the farms of any responsibility toward the workers in their fields. The contractors have the responsibility of making social security payments for the migrant laborers, which they sometimes pocket; of transporting the laborers to the fields, for which they charge the laborers; and providing the laborers with food, housing, and other necessities. Because the labor contractor's income depends on the number of workers employed and the speed at which they work, the system encourages exploitation. Workers may be forced into the fields against their will and threatened when they fail to work at the pace demanded by the contractor.

During the past three decades, state and federal legislation has been passed that has marginally improved the working conditions of migratory farm laborers, but the laws have produced many unintended negative consequences. For example, after California adopted legislation fifteen years ago that set minimum sanitation and safety standards in farm labor camps, many farmers chose to close their camps rather than meet the standards. This forced laborers into substandard housing provided by third parties or into living in cars, tents, or under bridges.[61] In Washington State, the tree-fruit industry's farmers shut down their labor camps rather than provide up-to-code housing for migrant laborers. Dependent on picking apples and cherries for survival, the laborers resorted to living in woods, their cars, or shabby trailer parks.[62] Not surprisingly, trailer parks are considered private property, where speech can be regulated. In Nevada, Democratic assemblyman Mark Manendo introduced a bill that would permit trailer park tenants to post signs. Manendo reported cases where trailer park owners allowed some tenants to post political signs, but prohibited others.[63]

The one benefit of these mass evictions is that it deprived farmers and labor contractors of one threat that was often used to kept farm workers quiet—the threat of eviction. However, farmers still wield substantial power over migratory workers, because a majority of farm laborers in Florida, Texas, and California are illegal immigrants, who are afraid to join unions or complain about working conditions. A Miami business publication reported that legal residents constitute only 1 percent of farm laborers in many parts of south Florida.[64] Illegal immigrants are preferred to legal residents by farmers because they are more easily threatened and controlled.

Some farm laborers are foreign nationals brought to this country under the federal H-2A program. This program allows farmers to recruit workers from abroad when workers are not available locally. The H-2A workers sign contracts with farmers that specify pay, and the type, hours, and length of work. The contracts require the farmers to provide the H-2A worker with housing and transportation to the United States, which are paid back to the farmer in the form of wage deductions. H-2A workers whom employers discharge before midseason usually reimburse the farmer for the transportation costs, which eats up much of their savings.

The contracts that H-2A workers sign are similar to the "yellow dog" contracts. They are civil contracts that the employees are obligated to honor. If the workers complain about or refuse to accept the working conditions or pay, the laborers can be evicted, deported, and left without money.[65]

A study of Jamaican sugarcane cutters brought to the United States under the H-2A program found many living in overcrowded shacks, paid on the basis of a formula designed to evade Department of Labor rules on task work, and thoroughly insulated from the outside world, so that the immigrants' living and working conditions remained secret. The Florida Sugarcane League, a trade and lobby group, serves as the chief censor, giving or denying permission to those seeking access to sugarcane plantations. A researcher was told by the League that he would never meet any Jamaican cutters because they "didn't like being disturbed" and didn't like being photographed, so cameras were not allowed in the fields.[66]

The League's barriers to gaining access to the fields were made over a decade after the U.S. Court of Appeals for Florida ruled that labor camps on sugarcane farms constituted company towns because they provided housing, mess halls, and stores for employees. Moreover, the court held that third parties interested in, and investigating, the working conditions in these labor camps also had a right of access.[67] Clearly, the League pays no attention to that decision.

Ending the Coercion

Despite double-digit unemployment in many agricultural areas, agribusiness has lobbied for an extension of the H-2A program and, in 1999, the Senate passed a bill supported by agribusiness that extended the program, lowered already low wage rates and benefits, and eliminated the requirement that employers provide imported workers with housing. In practice, the bill would have stripped H-2A workers of all rights.[68]

Bruce Goldstein of the Farmworkers Justice Fund argues that political dynamics "favor the growers . . . [a] member of Congress has a choice: to support H-2A workers who will never vote, and who will most certainly never make a campaign contribution. Or, he or she can support the growers, who live in the district, vote, and donate to political campaigns. Even a liberal democrat might be inclined to support the growers, because H-2A workers have no political clout."[69]

The political clout that growers have compared to H-2A workers is greater than the clout that most employers have compared to their employees, but even in other industries there is not a level playing field: Employers have more money to contribute to political campaigns, have well-organized lobby and trade groups, and have the power to fire employees for any reason, except those covered by fair employment laws or by union contracts.

To obtain political clout, workers need to unionize. With a union, employees can collectively contribute to political campaigns, organize lobbying campaigns, and fight employers' arbitrary and retaliatory actions. However, many workers, and especially those who are undocumented, are easily intimidated and threatened with deportation if they exercise their First Amendment rights by joining a union.

As Service Employees International Union organizing director Tom Woodruss said, the real story about freedom of speech and association "is the millions of workers who were denied the right to choose a union because of employer intimidation. . . . We would not allow an employer to unduly influence an employee's political or religious choice, yet we allow employers to unduly influence his or her choice to join a union."[70]

To counter some of the employer coercion, the AFL-CIO has adopted new policies of dealing with undocumented immigrants, including organizing the undocumented, calling for amnesty for undocumented workers, and defending undocumented workers who have been intimidated or punished by employers for speaking out.[71] The defense includes lobbying the INS to allow undocumented workers to stay in the United States if they have been fingered by employers in an effort to silence the workers or to derail unionization efforts.

The same is true of H-2A workers: They need to have their rights protected, too, but recently-proposed legislation does the opposite. The Senate-passed bill strips H-2A workers of the few rights that they did have, such as the right to minimum wages.

As long as undocumented and H-2A workers enjoy fewer workplace rights than legal residents, exploitative employers will prefer to hire these easily silenced employees. The AFL-CIO's efforts to protect undocumented employees is clearly necessary, but not enough. Major changes are needed in federal and state employment laws. Employers must be prohibited from influencing employees' decisions on whether to join unions and from using the INS to impede efforts at unionization. Immigrant workers must be provided with the same protection that U.S. residents enjoy.

However, these ideals cannot be achieved as long as business groups, such as the Florida Sugarcane League, are able to lobby, contribute to political campaigns, and influence legislation.

3
Dirty Work:
Blacklisting and Silencing Employees

More attention has been paid to the post–Second World War blacklist era of Hollywood history than any other. Films such as *The Way We Were* and *Guilty by Suspicion,* books such as *Radical Innocence, Naming Names,* and *Tender Comrades* and autobiographies such as *Hollywood Exile, Inside Out,* and *Odd Man Out* describe the impact of the House Un-American Activities Committee (HUAC) hearings on Hollywood writers, directors, and performers who were named at the hearings as Communists.

The attention paid to this era by films and books has created several misconceptions. One is that the post–World War II blacklists are unique in U.S. history. Actually, they are almost as old as American industry. Throughout the nineteenth century, industrialists used blacklisting extensively to fight unions. When employers discovered that a worker was pro-union, the worker was usually fired and blacklisted to keep pro-union sympathies from being expressed on shop floors. Although blacklists were used to restrict employees' speech, business owners viewed their blacklists as constitutionally protected speech. blacklists were viewed as a legal form of information-sharing among employers.[1]

A second misconception is that blacklisting in Hollywood was confined to a brief period following World War II. This is far from the truth; Blacklisting has a long history in the film industry, dating from the earliest days of the industry. A third misconception is that the post-World War II Hollywood blacklists were imposed by the federal government, when in fact they were privately developed and maintained. A final misconception is that blacklisting no longer occurs. Quite the contrary, blacklisting is still used to silence union organizers and whistle-blowers.

Blacklisting Unionists

In the era when New England textile towns developed, traditional blacklists were difficult to maintain and enforce. Workers, mostly young women, moved back and forth between mills and their families' farms; factory wages were paid in cash, scrip, or goods rather than checks; social security numbers did not exist; and communications systems were rudimentary, so there were few methods available to employers to determine whether a prospective employee had been terminated by another employer for insolence, morals, or complaining about working conditions.

In lieu of a formal blacklist, a system of "working papers" evolved in early-nineteenth-century New England, whereby employees needed to present to prospective employers discharge papers from their previous employer. Discharge papers were issued to employees who had faithfully worked for the mill and did not commit acts found offensive by the employer. Without discharge papers, it was difficult to find work, so the papers substituted for a formal blacklist.[2]

As mill towns grew into cities and employers developed associations to lobby, fix wages, and discuss industrial developments, the associations became the means for maintaining formal blacklists. By the late 1830s, employer associations were well organized and, when labor strife developed, were used to suppress the strife. For example, after women struck against Middlesex Mill in Lowell, Massachusetts, in 1842 for being required to attend to four looms instead of three, the association blacklisted the strikers. As a result of this collusion by employers, state legislators created a committee to investigate blacklisting but never introduced legislation to ban the practice.[3]

In large urban areas, formal blacklists were possible even earlier because employers and their factories were geographically closer to each other. The blacklists were used primarily by master craftsmen to keep journeymen and apprentice wages down, and by factory owners to curb growing worker militancy. As industry developed in U.S. cities, working conditions began to more closely resemble those in Europe: pay was poor, working hours were long, and factory conditions harsh. The urban evils that Thomas Jefferson sought to avoid—pauperism, crime, and child labor—appeared in U.S. cities along with factories. The blacklists carried the names of workers who protested about their pay and working conditions, but they were not widely employed until workers began to organize unions. When unions began to organize in the nineteenth century, blacklists were used in combination with prosecutions of union organizers for "conspiracy" to injure trade.[4]

One of the earliest formal blacklists was developed in 1821 by Philadelphia master shoemakers, who met and agreed not to employ any journeymen who would not accept reduced wages. In 1830, merchant shippers in New York met in an effort to fight unionizing by journeyman shipbuilders. To coerce the journeymen into abandoning their attempts to unionize, the merchants' association publicly announced its intention to blacklist unionists.

A similar strategy was used by the master tailors of New York City in 1835, who published a declaration stating they would not employ members of unions who demanded a closed shop.[5]

Some employers and their associations were not just open about keeping blacklists—they even revealed their methods for maintaining them. The Iron Founders' and Machine Builders Association of the Falls of Ohio declared in 1863:

> Should the employees in any of our establishments stop work in order
> to force their employers to submit to unreasonable demands, the
> members of the Iron Founders' and Machine Builders' Association of
> the Fall of Ohio, and the members of the associations of other cities,
> or the establishments who have agreed to act in concert with these
> associations, shall not employ any men engaged in such strike. The
> names of the parties engaged in any attempt to force their employers
> to submit to unreasonable demands shall be sent in a circular at the

expense of the Association to all the other associations or establishments with which we are in correspondence, in order that they be prevented from getting employment.[6]

Blacklists were not just used to prevent employees from speaking in favor of, or organizing, unions, but were used to coerce workers into accepting employers' unfair employment practices. For example, in the era when the ten-hour day was being legislated in New England states, employers inserted clauses in employment contracts that required employees to work more than ten hours. The employers told workers that if they didn't sign the contracts, they would be fired and blacklisted.[7]

These contracts were precursors of modern-day employment contracts that pledge employees to secrecy, thereby preventing whistle-blowing, and "yellow dog" contracts that workers were forced to sign to gain employment, which were widely used to combat unions at the end of the nineteenth century. Yellow-dog contracts contained clauses prohibiting workers from engaging in speech injurious to their employers and from joining unions. Workers who violated these provisions could be fired or even sued.

Blacklists were used repeatedly and publicly to intimidate workers until states started outlawing them at the turn-of-the-century at the urging of the newly created labor unions. Wisconsin passed one of the first antiblacklisting laws in 1887. The law prohibited employers from circulating blacklists or cooperating in any way to block workers from gaining employment. A provision of the law also banned yellow-dog contracts.

The law was actually a bone thrown to labor unions. At the same time that the antiblacklisting law was passed, the Wisconsin legislature passed antipicketing and antiboycotting laws. The antiboycotting law prohibited "any two or more persons. . . [from] injuring another in his reputation, trade, business or profession by any means whatsoever, or for the purpose of compelling another to perform an act against his will."[8] The antipicketing and antiboycotting laws severely curtailed unions' abilities to publicly protest an employer's unfair labor practices or to effectively strike.

Proving that the antiblacklisting law was actually a bone, the state legislature modified and weakened the law in 1895. This law prohibited "any two or more persons, whether members a partnership or company or stockholders in a corporation, who are employers of labor" from threatening to or actually circulating blacklists, but allowed employers to make "truthful statement[s]" to others about a discharged employee This loosening of the law made it easier for employers to create blacklists.[9]

Utah passed an antiblacklisting law in 1898 that prohibited "any company, corporation, or individual" from blacklisting an employee. Violators were subject to a fine between $500 and $1,000 and imprisonment for 60 to 365 days. By 1905, 21 states had passed laws barring blacklisting by name, but few had the stiff penalties of Utah's law. Colorado's law fined blacklisters $10 to $250 and maximum imprisonment of 60 days.

The stiffest penalties were adopted in 1905 by Illinois, which developed powerful unions. Illinois's penalties for blacklisting consisted of a "fine not exceeding $2,000," maximum imprisonment of five years, or both, but allowed employers to make statements about employees that were neither fraudulent nor malicious, a loophole that allowed companies and their trade associations to maintain "truthful" blacklists. However, the majority of states did not prohibit blacklisting, even with loopholes, although some prohibited "interfering with lawful employment," as Rhode Island did. In 1901, the United States passed a similar law to Rhode Island's, prohibiting employers engaged in interstate or foreign transportation from conspiring to prevent a former employee from obtaining employment.[10]

Despite the antiblacklisting and anti-interference laws, blacklisting was common during the first decades of the 1900s, and little could be done to stop it. The existence of blacklists was hard to prove. Other reasons could be given for not employing blacklisted workers, and court decisions did "not recognize the illegality of blacklisting as clearly" as other outlawed acts, such as boycotting.[11] For example, shortly after the antiblacklisting and anti-interference laws were adopted, a court struck down a U.S. statute banning companies engaged in interstate commerce from firing employees because of union membership, and another ruled that an employer could legally maintain a list of employees fired for union membership and then invite other employers to study the list.[12]

Blacklisting and other coercive methods were used so extensively to silence workers during the Depression era that a subcommittee of the Senate Committee on Education and Labor headed by Senator Robert "Battling Bob" La Follette, Jr., spent five years between 1936 and 1940 researching and reporting on attempts to silence workers through spying, violence, firing, and blacklisting. La Follette and his colleagues were able to conduct an extensive inquiry, despite opposition lobbying from big business and an initial paltry budget of $15,000.[13] The hearings, which were published in annual, multivolume reports titled *Violations of Free Speech and Rights of Labor*,[14] showed that intimidation of workers was widespread and practiced by many large corporations, including Republic Steel and General Motors.

Testimony before La Follette's Senate subcommittee by E. C. Davison, the mayor of Alexandria, Virginia, and a former secretary-treasurer of the International Association of Machinists, provides some insight into how pervasive blacklisting was in the metal trades, where a strong, belligerent employers association maintained an industry blacklist at least into the mid-1930s. Davison was blacklisted after participating in a Richmond strike, and his name was sent to the National Metal Trades Association, which placed him on their blacklist. After being blacklisted, he could not find employment in his city, so he finally moved to Newport News, where he obtained work at the Newport News Shipbuilding and Drydock Co. using an alias. When his real identity was discovered, Davison was sacked. Davison testified:

> After leaving Newport News, I went to the western part of the State and later became a general foreman in a shop in Danvill, Va., and as a general foreman I became interested in the general manager and he supplied me with one of the [black]lists. . . . My name was on the list. In other words, I was supposed to blacklist myself though I was general manager at the time.[15]

Davison learned that metal workers needed to be certified by the National Metal Trades Association employment office, which kept "a card record and file, and when that file was turned over to the employer that signified the man was not to be employed." The blacklist turned many metal workers into unemployed, poverty-stricken tramps, Davison testified.

Workers in other industries also had to adopt aliases to circumvent the blacklists. High profile and vocal union activists had a very difficult time getting past the blacklists. They were sometimes barred from getting any work, and they, too, were forced into poverty.[16]

In 1935, Congress belatedly passed the National Labor Relations Act (or Wagner Act), which outlawed unfair labor practices and established the National Labor Relations Board (NLRB) to regulate and investigate labor practices. The Act, passed despite opposition by the National Association of Manufacturers, the United States Chamber of Commerce, the National Metal Trades Association, and other trade associations and businesses, barred blacklisting, yellow-dog contracts, and other anti-union activities, and created an agency where workers could appeal unfair employer actions.[17]

Within a decade and a half of the passage of the Wagner Act, about two-thirds of the states had similar laws protecting employees' rights, and some states passed other laws forbidding discrimination based on age or religion. Nearly half of the states passed laws prohibiting employers from interfering with an employee's right to vote or political activity.[18] A California law stated that "no employer shall make, adopt, or enforce any rule, regulation or policy forbidding or preventing employees from engaging or participating in politics or becoming candidates for public office." The law prohibited employers from attempting to politically influence employees by "threat of discharge or loss of employment."[19]

Although the Wagner Act and many state employee protection laws were adopted a half-century ago, an examination of complaints filed with the NLRB in recent years shows that many employers still try to silence workers, particularly when they speak in favor of, or try to organize, unions. Some examples include:

- At Fieldcrest Cannon, Inc., the large towel manufacturer that resisted unionization of its North Carolina plant, employees were told they would be suspended for singing union songs on the plant floor. The employees were told that the singing violated the company's rule against disrupting plant operations. The threat was made despite the plant's machines, which were noisier than the singing, other employees were not within earshot of the singing, and employees were paid on a piece-rate basis, so that the company wasn't financially affected even if the singing slowed down the workers' productivity.[20]
- Caterpillar, Inc., fired an employee who was a union representative because he spoke to other employees after being told not to. Before being fired, the union representative endured name-calling and threats that he would be fired. Caterpillar also suspended a union representative for wearing a button critical of company practices.[21]
- Grand Canyon Mining Corp. threatened employees that it would close if they voted for a union. The company also conducted surveillance of union meetings, and coerced employees to stop organizing by telling them that some employees were laid off because of their involvement with unions.[22]
- United Parcel Service, Inc., disciplined employees for distributing union materials during breaks in lounges and meeting rooms, where other employees were allowed to distribute materials on fishing contests, football pools, and golf tournaments.[23]

The situation for minority workers, who often work in service jobs such as at hotels, is even worse, as these examples suggest:

- At the Flamingo Hilton-Laughlin, employees were coercively interviewed about union activities, threatened that if they joined a union their wages would be reduced, and warned that they could be discharged and blacklisted for union activities.[24]
- At the Frontier Hotel and Casino in Las Vegas, pro-union employees were fired for pretextual reasons, told that bringing "union shit" into the

workplace would cause them trouble, warned that security would be watching those wearing union buttons, and videotaped while distributing pro-union leaflets in the parking lot.[25]

In each of these cases, the NLRB ruled against the companies' attempts to suppress employees' speech.

These cases represent the norm, rather than the exception. In 91 percent of union organizing drives, employers force employees to attend meetings where employees are urged to vote against unions. Three-quarters of the time, supervisors hold one-on-one meetings with employees to dissuade them from joining unions. About half of all companies threaten to shut their doors if employees vote for unions.[26]

In 31 percent of union campaigns, employers fire employees for being pro-union. That amounts to 10,000 firings each year. Of these attempts to silence unionists, Milwaukee County Labor Council president John Goldstein says, "This is one of the most blatant yet hidden examples of violations of free speech that exists in society today."[27]

State employment laws are violated as frequently as the federal laws. In fact, the post–Second World War Hollywood blacklists were imposed after California enacted its law prohibiting employers from attempting to politically influence employees by "threat of discharge or loss of employment." Despite this and antiblacklisting laws, the studio chiefs nevertheless imposed blacklists on the industry.

The Early Motion Picture Blacklists

Blacklisting was used almost from the inception of the film industry as a form of coercion, as a method for suppressing controversy and assuring profits, and as a method for eliminating militant unionists from the studios. Blacklisting was firmly entrenched in the film industry by the time the House Un-American Activities Committee (HUAC) opened its inquiries in 1947 into Communist subversion in Hollywood, when the "Hollywood Ten"—eight Communist and two ex-Communist screenwriters, directors, and producers—obdurately denounced the Committee during public hearings.

The early motion picture blacklists were based on economics, race, and morals, rather than speech and political association. The New York–based Motion Picture Patents Company, a trust created in 1908 by ten major motion picture companies to monopolize commercial film production, developed a set of rules for trust members, nickelodeon owners, and distributors. The rules blacklisted actors and directors who went to work for non-trust production companies and required nickelodeon owners and distributors to exclusively carry films produced by trust members. Exhibitors and distributors caught with films made by non-trust film companies had their trust-issued licenses to exhibit films revoked and were boycotted.[28]

The trust also established the National Board of Censorship that screened and approved films, ensuring that there would be fewer public complaints about the content of movies.[29] The Board was a predecessor of the Hays Office, the self-censorship bureau of the Motion Picture Producers and Distributors Association (MPPDA) that operated from the 1920s to the 1960s, and the Classification and Rating Administration of the MPPDA, which has assigned ratings to movies since 1968.

After the Motion Picture Patents Company collapsed and Hollywood became the filmmaking capital of the world with production controlled by Metro-Goldwyn-Mayer, Twentieth Century Fox, Paramount, and four other studios, informal blacklists were also kept. African Americans and stars accused of morals violations such as Roscoe (Fatty) Arbuckle and Mary Miles Minter were barred from the industry.[30]

During the 1930s and 1940s, blacklists were used to keep union militants out of the studios. The blacklists were maintained by mob-affiliated union bosses, who colluded with the studio owners to keep work slowdowns and strikes at a minimum. The crime syndicate moved into labor racketeering to make up for the profits it lost when Prohibition ended. Profits were made by taking bribes rather than negotiating better wages and by diverting union dues to mob bank accounts.

Fearing that the Wagner Act would hamper their ability to fight off militant unionism, the movie moguls turned to International Alliance of Theatrical and Stage Employees (IATSE) president George Browne, a Chicago mobster who promised worker complacency in return for bribes. At the end of 1935, with the support of the studio owners, IATSE moved quickly into the studios, ousting and replacing other unions. Opponents of the move were blacklisted by the union.[31]

After several years of enduring Browne's racketeering, a militant faction within IATSE called the "progressives" was organized. The progressives demanded local autonomy and an investigation of corruption within the union. To divert attention from his own crimes, Browne accused the progressives of being Communists, gave information about them to the FBI, and invited HUAC, referred to as the Dies Committee in that era, to investigate Communist activities in Hollywood.[32]

HUAC did come to Hollywood, but by that time Browne had stood trial for racketeering, was convicted, and sentenced to prison. Browne was replaced in 1941 by one of his vice presidents, Richard Walsh. Walsh appointed Roy Brewer as IATSE's West Coast representative in 1944. Brewer was charged with ridding the union of the progressive "troublemakers" and beating back the Conference of Studio Unions (CSU), a militant, left-leaning union group that threatened IATSE's supremacy in the studios. Brewer expelled and blacklisted the IATSE progressives, and his union assisted the studios in defeating CSU strikes in 1945.[33] Militants in the CSU were also blacklisted after that union was broken. Because these blacklists principally affected crafts and trade workers, rather than glamorous stars and screen writers, scant attention has been paid to them.[34]

"Glamorous" Blacklisting

One of the misconceptions fostered by the films and books about the post–World War II Hollywood blacklists is that they were developed and maintained by HUAC.[35] HUAC might have encouraged and even supported the blacklisting of Communist screenwriters and directors, but it was the studios, not the HUAC, that established the blacklists, and private groups such as the Motion Picture Alliance for the Preservation of American Ideals (MPA) that assisted the studios in determining who remained on, or was taken off, the blacklists.

The MPA was founded in February 1944 by director Sam Wood and other conservatives who felt that Communists had become powerful in the motion picture industry and were influencing casting and content. IATSE representative Roy Brewer, seeing the organization as a bastion of anti-Communism that could help fight the left-leaning CSU, joined the MPA in mid-1947. The MPA lobbied HUAC to investigate the Hollywood film industry, and when HUAC did investigate in 1947, provided "friendly witnesses," from whom the committee heard testimony. The testimony of the MPA members consisted principally of undocumented assertions, innuendo, and name-calling.[36]

Having failed to get any meaningful evidence or testimony from MPA members, HUAC turned to the FBI, which, unbeknown to HUAC, other government agencies, or the Communist Party, had been burglarizing the Hollywood offices of the Communist Party for years.[37] The FBI provided HUAC with evidence on the Communist Party memberships of ten directors, writers, and producers, whom HUAC called to testify. The "Hollywood Ten," dubbed "unfriendly witnesses" by HUAC because they refused to answer the committee's questions, were shown to be Communist or former Communist Party members during the hearings using the purloined evidence obtained from the FBI.[38] The evidence included photographs of Communist Party membership cards.[39] After exposing the Hollywood Ten as Communists, HUAC abruptly ended its investigation.

Less than a month after the HUAC hearings ended abruptly, representatives of the motion picture industry met at the Waldorf-Astoria Hotel in New York City and decided what action to take against the Hollywood Ten. There, the studio bosses settled on a strategy that had worked well for them in the past—blacklisting. At the end of the meeting, the industry chiefs issued a statement promising to immediately fire Communists in their employ. The statement, in part, said:

Members of the Association of Motion Picture Producers deplore the action of the ten Hollywood men who have been cited for contempt of the House of Representatives . . . . We will not knowingly employ a Communist or a member of any party or group which advocates the overthrow of the Government of the United States by force or by any illegal or unconstitutional methods.

The immediate effect of the new studio policy was negligible. The only proven Communists were the Hollywood Ten, who were fired and blacklisted primarily for their behavior before HUAC, which had embarrassed Hollywood and left it under a cloud of suspicion.

The studios discovered that their actions didn't appease anti-Communists like Roy Brewer, who complained that the studios had not purged their ranks of "pinkos." The studios responded by secretly blacklisting several well-known Communists and "graylisting" several high-profile non-Communist leftists like Edward G. Robinson. Because of the graylisting, Robinson received only one movie role in 1949.[40]

The Business of Anti-Communism

HUAC's accusations that Hollywood was riddled with Communists were soon repeated by other groups. Some, like the American Legion and the Catholic War Veterans, denounced Hollywood out of misplaced ideological conviction. Others, like American Business Consultants, Inc., and Aware, Inc., did it to make a profit.

American Business Consultants, Inc., was started by three ex-FBI agents who concluded that they could make more money operating a for-profit, anti-Communism business than working for J. Edgar Hoover. The three had previously published *Plain Talk*, an anti-Communist newsletter bankrolled by industrialist Alfred Kohlberg that never made money. With American Business Consultants, Inc., they finally struck black gold, charging $24 for a subscription to the biweekly *Counterattack*, a considerable sum back then, and charging fees running up to five figures for conducting background investigations on personnel for companies.[41]

Counterattack read and sounded like a gossip column but spread stories about people's Communist affiliations rather than their sex lives. For example, the publication reported:

> Actor WILL GEER, who has a feature role in the recent Universal-International release "Bright Victory," married HAROLD WARE's daughter, Herta. GEER has been identified as a Communist . . . . He sponsored CP's May Day Parades, entertained at benefits for the Daily Worker, etc.[42]

The information published in *Counterattack* was culled from Communist Party newspapers and HUAC and other government committee reports, which gave the publication a strong defense in court against libel suits, even when factually untrue, which was often.[43]

In late June 1950, just as the Korean War started, American Business Consultants, Inc. released *Red Channels*, a book listing the names of 151 individuals in entertainment industries who had lent "their names . . . to organizations espousing Communist causes." This list included musicians, television and radio performers, writers, and motion picture artists, and the organizations with which they were associated, many of which were left-leaning, but non-Communist.[44] The book claimed its intent was to "discourage actors and artists from naively lending their names to Communist organizations or causes."[45]

Promotional copies of *Red Channels* were sent to advertising agencies, advertisers, the broadcast networks, movie studios, the American Legion, and newspapers, which provided the scurrilous publication with publicity. The *New York Times* mentioned *Red Channels* over a dozen times during the last half of 1950—nine times in September alone.[46] *The Catholic World* carried an article by Vincent W. Hartnett, who wrote *Red Channel*'s introduction, that summarized the charges in the book.[47] This and similar articles incited the Catholic War Veterans and the American Legion into protesting the continued presence of "pinkos" in the entertainment industry.

Because of the ensuing publicity, individuals named in *Red Channels* were quickly moved from movie studio graylists to blacklists. Non-

Communists like Edward G. Robinson, who were named in *Red Channels*, quickly concluded that they needed to clear their names if they were to continue their careers. Robinson contacted HUAC and requested an opportunity to clear his name by testifying before the Committee. Robinson testified but had little to offer the HUAC, because he was never a Communist.[48]

Ex-Communists like director Edward Dmytryk and actor Sterling Hayden were also looking to get off the blacklist. To get off the blacklist, they named names during public HUAC hearings held during 1951. Among others, Dmytryk named directors Jules Dassin and Frank Tuttle; Hayden named Abraham Polonsky and Karen Morley.[49] Named individuals were then subpoenaed by the Committee, asked to confess, and name names.

This and subsequent hearings functioned like a chain letter or a pyramid scheme, ever enlarging the number of people involved. People who named others were removed from the blacklists by the studio bosses. Witnesses who took the Fifth Amendment had their names added to the blacklists. Many who were blacklisted never again worked in motion pictures. Some, like Abraham Polonsky, returned to filmmaking in the late 1960s.

Because HUAC uncovered more names than it had time for testimony, many people identified during the hearings were never called to testify. These were usually supporting actors and "B" directors, who were not glamorous enough for the committee to call. Some were former Communists who had broken with the CP years earlier; some had attended Communist Party functions but were never Communists. Most were immediately blacklisted by the studios and discovered that the only way they could clear their names was by going to the MPA or the American Legion's National Americanism Committee, which developed its own blacklist, published in *The Firing Line*.[50]

Brewer, actor Ward Bond, and other MPA members became members of a self-appointed clearance committee that determined the fate of these blacklisted souls.[51] If these vigilantes decided to "clear" an individual, they would contact the studios, the American Legion, and American Business Consultants, Inc., in an effort to get the person off the blacklist. If they chose not to clear an individual, the person continued to be banished from the studios. For individuals subjected to these private interrogations, the process was far more emotionally scarring than appearing before HUAC.

The Broadcast Blacklist

Blacklisting during the post–Second World War era was not confined to the film industry. Blacklists were used by advertising agencies, the television and radio networks, manufacturers, trade unions, and even schools and universities to keep out individuals expressing left-wing political views. In some industries, such as broadcasting, blacklisting was far more pervasive and insidious than in the film industry.

Private, non–industry groups such as American Business Consultants, Inc., Aware, Inc., and the American Legion played a much larger role in blacklisting in broadcasting than film. The reason was simple: They could easily persuade advertising agencies like BBDO and advertisers like Procter & Gamble, which sponsored network radio and television programs, to remove performers or writers from their shows.

The ease with which pressure groups could influence the broadcasting industry was demonstrated in 1949, when General Foods and Pepsi-Cola pressured William Sweets into resigning as director of two radio programs, *Gangbusters* and *Counterspy,* which they sponsored. The companies decided they wanted Sweets ousted after receiving letters complaining that Sweets was a Communist. The letters were based on unsubstantiated charges leveled against the director by *Counterattack*. Rather than disregarding the complaints, which were apparently few in number, or investigating the accuracy of them, the companies and their advertising agencies decided it was simply easier to fire Sweets. [52]

This sequence was repeated in 1950, after *Red Channels* was released. In August 1950, two months after being named in that publication, actress Jean Muir was fired from NBC's *The Aldrich Family* after General Foods, the show's sponsor, received a few complaints about Muir's political activities. The same month, Irene Wicker had her television show cancelled. She, too, had been listed in *Red Channels*. General Foods also received complaints about actor Philip Loeb, a star of CBS's *The Goldbergs*, who had also been named in *Red Channels*. General Foods initially decided that it would not act on the complaints, but later decided to withdraw its sponsorship of the show.[53]

To assure that their programs would remain noncontroversial—but also out of ideological conviction—the networks, advertising agencies, and large advertisers developed policies concerning program content and a system for screening stars, directors, and writers to assure that none hired could be accused of "subversive" activities.[54] The content policies determined what were acceptable storylines and character types. Procter & Gamble, one of the largest advertisers, had a policy of not sponsoring shows that depicted industrialists or members of the military in a bad light. The employee screening system consisted of checking the political backgrounds of people before they were hired, thereby avoiding any public controversies.[55]

To check on political backgrounds, the networks, agencies, and advertisers developed departments that screened prospective employees. These departments developed "whitelists" of people who could be hired and blacklists of people who could not. The blacklists used by the clearance departments included the published lists of American Business Consultants and Aware, Inc.; Vincent Hartnett's *File 13*; a list complied by supermarket chain owner Laurence Johnson, who was an influential member of the National Association of Retail Grocers; and the American Legion's *Firing Line*, most of which contained the names of liberals rather than Communists. Despite their inabilities to distinguish between Communists and liberals, Hartnett and American Business Consultants were even hired by some agencies and advertisers to screen individuals.[56]

Anyone who criticized these Red-baiters eventually wound up on their blacklists, as actor John Henry Faulk learned. Faulk was accused by Johnson, Hartnett, and Aware, Inc., of being a Communist and blacklisted after he opposed an Aware, Inc., faction in the American Federation of Television and Radio Artists (AFTRA). Faulk sued Johnson, Hartnett, and Aware, Inc., for libel, and, after being blacklisted for four years, won a $3.5 million judgment against them in 1962.[57]

Blacklisting in broadcasting was so institutionalized that it continued into the late 1960s, despite the demise of Senator Joseph McCarthy and groups like Aware, Inc. Folksinger Pete Seeger, who was named in *Red Channels* and blacklisted in 1950, never appeared on television until the late 1960s, when he finally appeared on *The Smothers Brothers*, whose contract gave them, not the CBS network, control of program content. Because the Smothers Brothers decided to include politically controversial content in their show, it was cancelled by CBS in midseason, despite high ratings, torpedoing the brothers' careers.[58]

Today, graylists rather than blacklists are used to punish individuals in broadcasting. Graylists are less formal than blacklists and make it possible for some companies to hire the graylisted individual, although being hired is the exception rather than the rule, as actor James Garner discovered. Garner, a popular television actor, discovered that demand for his acting talents virtually disappeared in Hollywood after he filed a lawsuit against Universal in 1981, claiming the corporation used shady bookkeeping to hide profits due him from the *Rockford Files* television program. His contract gave him 37.5 percent of the profits from *Rockford*, but Garner received less than $250,000 in profits, even though the program grossed more than $120 million from first-run, syndication, and foreign rentals.[59]

Garner eventually settled out of court with Universal, and signed an agreement that prohibits him from talking about the lawsuit. However, it was only after the case was settled that television production companies again hired Garner, who was clearly embittered by his experiences. In 1991, Garner complained, "I haven't done much work in the last nine, ten years. I've only done, what three Hallmarks [Hall of Fame presentations] and maybe one movie. I prefer to work more than that."[60]

Garner's situation isn't unique. Graylisting and blacklisting are most commonly used today to punish disloyalty to companies, rather than disloyalty to government. Whistle-blowing is viewed as the supreme form of disloyalty in such industries as nuclear power and stock trading, and whistle-blowers in these industries have been fired and blacklisted.[61]

Although limited, political blacklisting and graylisting still occurs. Ed Asner, who made a much publicized speech in 1982 opposing President Reagan's policies in Central America and advocating medical assistance for war-ravaged Salvadorans, had his popular television show, *Lou Grant*, cancelled after two advertisers withdrew their sponsorship. The advertisers, Vidal Sassoon, Inc., and Kimberly-Clark, informed CBS that they were troubled by Asner's political statements.[62] After *Lou Grant* was spiked, Asner discovered that his talents were no longer wanted in Hollywood. Asner's graylisting lasted for nearly a decade. Commenting on the situation in 1991, Asner said, "What I realized is that no blacklist works without the cooperation of people who call themselves liberal. There are many people, particularly in this town, who parade under the banner of being liberal, but who would never dream in a million years of committing that terrible sin of possibly offending a corporate sponsor or network head."[63]

The Academic Blacklist

In academia, ex-Communists, Communists, and other radicals were fired and blacklisted during the 1940s and 1950s. As in broadcasting, blacklisting in academia was stimulated in part by private, anti-Communist groups such as American Business Consultants, Inc., and the American Legion, which viewed universities as bastions of subversion. *Counterattack* accused members of the academy of being Communists at least as often as it accused members of the film industry.[64] *American Legion Magazine* asserted that "in any inventory of red-front supporters, professors always make up the single largest groups."[65] Like *Counterattack*, the *American Legion Magazine* and *Firing Line* usually named professors engaged in "pro-Communist" activities.[66] (They rarely accused the academicians of being Communists because this would have opened the organizations to libel suits.)

As part of its campaign against subversion on campuses, the Legion pressured universities to ban speakers and films, and many universities acquiesced. At Muhlenberg College, a small private school in Allentown, Pennsylvania, the Legion convinced the college president to cancel the showing of four Charlie Chaplin films scheduled as part of a "Great Films of Yesterday" series.[67] As the attack on Chaplin suggests, the American Legion was as likely to attack non-Communist leftists as genuine Communists.

The American Legion also encouraged its members to privately—but not publicly— complain to members of the board of trustees about the political activities of students and faculty. This approach allowed the Legion to make accusations in secret to board members, who were often business executives and who were more likely to share the Legion's point of view than were college administrators. *Firing Line* instructed Legionnaires to protest about left-wing activities "in the spirit of cooperation, and under no circumstances should advance publicity be given to a conference between a Legion delegation and representatives of a school's Board of Trustees."[68]

In several instances, the Legion's complaints were successful in getting board members to conduct inquiries into the political activities of faculty. At Indiana University, trustees held a hearing on the Legion's charges about Communist activities, but neither the Legion nor any witnesses presented any evidence to back up the charges.[69] In West Virginia, the Legion helped spread rumors that Luella Mundel, head of the art department at Fairmont State University, was a "security risk" after she publicly challenged some of the assertions made at a Legion-sponsored public forum on Communism. Although she was not a Communist, Mundel was fired by Fairmont's board for being an atheist, a security risk, and a poor teacher, despite objections of the college president.[70]

At Ohio State University, after the Legion protested the appearance of liberal economist Harold Rugg, Ohio State's president required all speakers invited to campus to be approved by his office. The Ohio State president used this power to ban former William Penn College president Cecil

Henshaw, a Quaker, not a Communist, from speaking, provoking a national outcry from civil libertarians.[71]

At most universities, pressure from the American Legion wasn't necessary to ban speakers or fire faculty radicals. Alumni, trustees, and wealthy donors independently pressured private universities into adopting policies requiring speakers to be approved by administrators, thoroughly trampling free speech on college campuses. Because of these pressures, Communists and other controversial speakers were barred from Cornell, Columbia, New York University, and many other colleges.[72] Many universities even adopted policies that expressly prohibited Communists from holding faculty appointments. Columbia University's board of trustees declared that it "would not countenance the presence of an avowed communist on the teaching staff." Cornell University's president declared that Communist Party membership "manifestly disqualified" individuals "for membership in a faculty of higher learning."[73]

As a consequence of such policies, universities fired professors who refused to cooperate with government investigations. Lyman Bradley, a professor of German and a longtime treasurer of the Modern Language Association, was fired by New York University after refusing to cooperate with a HUAC investigation of the Joint Anti-Fascist Refugee Committee. Blacklisted, Bradley was never able to find another job in academe. Temple University, a private university that received state funding, fired philosophy department chair Barrows Dunham after he took the Fifth Amendment at a 1953 HUAC inquiry. When he applied for other academic jobs, Temple's Board of Trustees sent copies of their statement dismissing Burrows to these universities, making it impossible for him to get hired. At Tulane University in New Orleans, Robert Hodes, a tenured professor of medicine, was harassed by the administration and then fired in 1953 after the university learned he was a Communist.[74]

The experiences of Bradley, Dunham, and Hodes were not unique. In No Ivory Tower and Cold War on Campus, Ellen Schrecker and Lionel Lewis document the cases of over 150 academic employees whose dismissals, blacklisting, or harassment became public during the decade following World War II. Many other terminations occurred but were kept silent by the universities and the fired employees.

Blacklisting in academia was not confined to the post–World War II era. It was also used during the late 1960s and early 1970s to curb unrest on campuses. Relatively few professors were involved in the Sixties protests; those that were, and were untenured, were often fired and black-listed, as Staughton Lynd discovered.

Staughton Lynd, a young Yale University professor, visited North Vietnam in 1965 with other antiwar activists, earning him the enmity of the U.S. government and, apparently, his employer. Soon after the visit, Lynd was denied tenure at Yale. "My personal feeling was that I was denied tenure for political reasons," says Lynd.[75]

After being dropped from Yale, Lynd applied for teaching positions in the Chicago area, where he moved, but was never hired, despite several teaching vacancies in the area. "I was offered five or six jobs and in each of these instances, the administration vetoed the decisions of their history departments," Lynd reports. At Roosevelt University, the president was honest about why he wouldn't hire Lynd: Lynd's presence could adversely effect the university's fund-raising. Unable to find a university job, Lynd attended law school. After graduating, he became a well-known labor lawyer.

At California State University Northridge (CSUN), Mel Standig, an untenured professor, was arrested for allegedly disrupting a speech during an anti-Vietnam War protest, but was subsequently acquitted of the charges. Despite the acquittal, CSUN would not rehire Standig, and when other colleges learned of the arrest, they would not hire him, either. He never found another job in the academy.[76] Several other untenured professors involved in political activities at CSUN were sacked the same year. One opened a restaurant but eventually returned to academe; another emigrated to Australia.

The academic blacklists—or more accurately, graylists—are far less formal than the blacklists in oligopolistic industries like broadcasting and motion pictures. In broadcasting, there are just a few major networks; in motion pictures there just a few major production companies, making enforcement of a blacklist easy. In contrast, there are thousands of colleges, which makes circulating a blacklist impossible.

Academic graylisting is carried out through the letters of recommendation given dismissed employees by administrators and former colleagues, which function like the working papers or discharge papers carried by textile mill workers in early-nineteenth-century New England. A quantitative study of university hiring practices found that letters of recommendations, not a prospective employee's accomplishments or potential, were the primary determinant of whether an individual was hired.[77] A weak recommendation or a discussion of an applicant's problems at a previous institution doom the applicant's job prospects.

Blacklisting Whistle-Blowers

Letters of recommendation are still used by universities to graylist employees, but graylists are primarily reserved for whistle-blowers, who expose research fraud and thereby impair a university's ability to bring in grants.[78] People are no longer blacklisted or graylisted for political reasons.

An example of this blacklisting is provided by Margot O'Toole, a postdoctoral researcher who observed errors in a *Cell* journal article by Thereza Imanishi-Kari of Tufts University and Nobel Prize–winner David Baltimore of the Massachussetts Institute of Technology (MIT). O'Toole was unable to replicate the paper's results and examined Imanishi-Kari's data to see why her study failed. She concluded that the data contradicted the published results, so she sought a clarification from Imanishi-Kari, who did not admit to the errors.

Because Imanishi-Kari begged rather than clarified the issue, O'Toole asked MIT and Tufts to investigate. The MIT and Tufts inquiries concluded that the discrepancies were a "difference in scientific interpretation." As a result of her whistle-blowing, O'Toole was dismissed by Imanishi-Kari, and Baltimore conducted a high-profile campaign to discredit her. O'Toole soon learned what whistle-blowing in academia gets you. She wound up answering telephones at her brother's moving company.[79]

A similar fate befell Michelle Rennie, a research assistant at the University of Minnesota, who blew the whistle on Dr. Barry Garfinkel, a professor of psychiatry. Garfinkel's fraud in a study of Anafranil, an antidepressant drug, was extensive, but an internal university investigation exonerated Garfinkel anyway. Instead of charging Garfinkel with fraud, the investigators charged Rennie with incompetence and dishonesty. In addition to this character assassination, Rennie was pressured into resigning her job at the university. Because of the univerity's charges against her, Rennie was unable to find another, comparable job.

Eventually, justice was meted out to Garfinkel, but not by the university. Garfinkel was tried and convicted in federal court of falsifying data in the Anafranil experiment.[80]

Higher education isn't the only industry that blacklists whistle-blowers. It is a common problem in the energy and power industries, even though these industries are regulated by the federal government. Commonwealth Edison (ComEd) punished several employees who complained about safety problems at the company's Zion nuclear power plant in Illinois. The company demoted six staffers who complained and transferred them to menial jobs at another facility. The company also lowered its performance evaluation and ended its promotion training for another employee who reported safety problems. It discharged another after he reported sixty problems at the Zion plant In the latter case, the employee reported being blacklisted by ComEd.[81]

Arnold Gunderson, a senior vice president at Nuclear Energy Services in Danbury, Connecticut, found radioactive materials in a company safe and reported the safety violation to the company president. After filing the report, Gunderson was discharged by the company, which claimed the dismissal was the result of staff reductions. Gunderson took his case to the public and to court, alleging the company retaliated against him for whistle-blowing. Faced with the lawsuit and publicity, the company settled with Gunderson out of court. The settlement included a gag clause prohibiting Gunderson from talking publicly about the case.

Gunderson's case didn't end there. The company later filed a $1.5 million lawsuit against him, claiming that he continued to talk about the company, violating the gag clause in the settlement. According to Gunderson, he was blacklisted by the company, which sent letters about him to 78 people. There is evidence to support Gunderson's charges of blacklisting. Despite his years of experience and a master's degree in nuclear engineering, the best job that Gunderson could find before turning to teaching was driving a dump truck.[82]

Gunderson and the ComEd employees represent just a handful of the cases in the nuclear power industry where employers retaliated against whistle-blowers. As of the beginning of 1995, 609 cases of retaliation had been filed with the Nuclear Power Commission, but the U.S. Department of Labor investigated just 44, despite there being a federal whistle-blower protection program for that industry. The situation suggests a need for more strenuous regulation and enforcement, rather than deregulation.[83]

Even though states and industries have antiblacklisting and whistle-blower protection laws, these laws often fail to protect employees because the companies use other pretexts to discharge whistle-blowers. One example is the securities industry, where the Security and Exchange Commission (SEC) adopted a whistle-blower protection regulation to protect brokers who report such acts as account churning, which produce profits for brokers at the expense of clients.

> After broker Ronald Brown reported sales violations at his firm to the SEC, Brown was fired. The company's excuse for discharging Brown was that he was not generating enough business, even though he was outperforming other employees. After being discharged, Brown was unable to find another brokerage job. He discovered that he had been blacklisted.

Because the blacklisting violated SEC regulations, Brown filed for arbitration, which is mandatory in the securities industry. He won the arbitration case, allowing him to file a civil suit against his employer.[84] The suit has not yet gone to trial, but it is the first to test the SEC's whistle-blower protection policy.

Blacklisting and retaliation against whistle-blowers also occur in the construction industry. For example, Ben Pate was fired and blacklisted by Parsons-Dillingham construction company after he complained about safety violations in tunnel construction for the Pasadena MetroRail system. Because Pate's revelations caused the *Los Angeles Times* to write several articles about safety problems with the construction job and eventually led to a congressional investigation of the project, Pate was able to secure an attorney who would represent him in a suit against the company, something that most whistle-blowers—who are without money and lack proof that they were blacklisted—have a difficult time finding. Pate won the suit and the jury awarded him $460,000 for back and future salary losses, which were trebled under the state's labor law prohibiting blacklisting.[85]

Retaliation doesn't just occur against whistle-blowers, an investigation of the managed health care industry by the *Boston Globe* discovered. The newspaper discovered that some health care companies limited patients' access to mental health care in an effort to keep costs down and profits up. Therapists who requested additional services for patients were sacked and blacklisted, suggesting that any form of advocacy that impinges on companies' bottom lines can result in retaliation.[86]

The cases show why laws, regulations, and vigorous enforcement are needed to protect employees from companies, which are often more interested in profits than the public's or employees' welfare. While companies lobby for fewer laws and more deregulation, claiming that blacklisting and retaliation against whistle-blowers are rare, the opposite is the truth. Companies have a long tradition of silencing employees, which is why government supervision of labor policies is needed.

PART II
UNCIVIL ACTIONS

When authoritarian public officials abridge free speech, citizens and organizations often turn to the courts for relief. In New York City, groups disfavored by former Mayor Rudolph Giuliani repeatedly turned to the courts to obtain parade permits, to stop the harassment of speakers on public property and street corners, and to obtain permission to hold press conferences and assemblies at City Hall, which the mayor, citing the potential of terrorism, closed to public speech in 1998.

In the last half of 1998, federal judges ruled against Giuliani three times, decreeing that an AIDs demonstration should be allowed to assemble near City Hall; that taxi drivers should be granted a permit to hold a rally; and, in a case involving the Million Marijuana March Organization, that the police and mayor's office had used the city's parade permit ordinance to stifle speech.[1] A federal court finally struck down the city's parade permit ordinance as an arbitrarily applied abridgement of speech.[2] New York City officials were also forced into a settlement with the Black Israelites near the end of 1998, after the American Civil Liberties Union filed a suit against the city for harassing members of the religious sect, prohibiting sect members from speaking in Times Square, and denying them sound amplification permits.[3]

Although citizens and organizations look to courts for relief against abridgements of their speech by governments, corporations use courts to abridge speech. Corporations often go to court to obtain gag orders, restricting speech about matters being litigated; to seal records and files in cases that have been litigated; to silence former employees; and to punish critics, whom companies often sue, claiming that the criticism constitutes defamation, copyright infringement, tortious interference with business contracts, or some other imagined harm. Chapter 4 examines how companies use civil lawsuits to silence their critics. These speech-stifling lawsuits are called Strategic Lawsuits Against Public Participation, or SLAPPs, which is why the process of suing critics has become known as "SLAPPing."

Civil lawsuits brought under food disparagement statutes, which have been adopted in a number of states during the last decade, are closely related to SLAPPs. As Fiona Donson wrote in *Legal Intimidation*, "The idea of the food disparagement law is to give a statutory basis to a key legal claim that may then be used in a SLAPP context."[4] Thus, product disparagement statutes represent standing, codified threats to critics of agribusiness, warning critics not to speak about agricultural products unless the speaker has irrefutable scientific evidence to back up the criticism, which, of course, can never exist. If agricritics cannot scientifically prove their claims, they can be held liable for damages under product disparagement statutes. These statutes and some of the lawsuits that they have spawned are discussed in chapter 5, "Hog-Tying Critics."

Although chapters 4 and 5 focus on SLAPPs and product disparagement lawsuits, these are not the only types of lawsuits that businesses file to stifle criticism or prevent the release of information. If there is a tort or a court precedent, corporate attorneys will latch on to it in an effort to curb speech, as the actions of Universal Foods Corporation demonstrate. Universal Foods represents an example of a company engaging in a SLAPP, then sealing documents in the case, and then trying to enjoin a magazine from publishing an article about the company and the SLAPP it filed. It also provides an example of how a SLAPP can actually give the filing company a black eye.

Executives at Universal Foods, a Milwaukee-based food manufacturer now called Sensient, were angered by messages posted on Yahoo! in July 1998, claiming that the company was being sued for sex discrimination and suffered from "poor management, poor morale, [and] poor ethics." Universal sued, attempting to block Yahoo! from posting the messages, and it then filed a defamation suit against the message writer, Elizabeth Zande, a former Universal employee.

In her defense, Zande introduced several documents in court to support her contention that Universal Food executives were unethical, including a document showing that Universal had been contacted by the U.S. Department of Justice about price fixing in the yeast industry. Universal quickly sought and received a court order sealing the documents.

Although the documents were sealed, they were never marked as such, and a reporter for the *Milwaukee Business Journal* was given permission to examine them. The reporter discovered the information about the price fixing inquiry and included it in a story about the company.[5]

After executives at Universal Foods learned about the forthcoming article, they went to court, seeking an injunction to prohibit the story's release. The company's rationale for seeking an injunction sounded eerily like the Nixon administration's rationale for seeking an injunction in the 1971 Pentagon Papers case. The company claimed that publication should be enjoined because the report was based on court documents that were sealed. In the Pentagon Papers case, the Nixon administration argued that the documents were classified and therefore should not be published. Universal Foods also argued that the company would suffer "irreparable harm" if the story were published; similarly, the Nixon administration argued that disclosure of the Pentagon Papers would "endanger the national security" of the country. Like the Supreme Court in the Pentagon Paper's case, Milwaukee Circuit Court Judge Thomas Donegan refused to restrain publication of the *Milwaukee Business Journal*. The parallels suggest that government and corporate infringements of speech can be very similar.

Finally, three months after Universal Foods failed to enjoin the *Milwaukee Business Journal*, the suit against against Zande was dismissed, suggesting that it was a meritless SLAPP.[6] The judge, as often occurs in civil cases, sealed the court file, keeping the public ignorant of the case's details.

Because Universal Foods' attempts to suppress information and speech for the most part failed, the case is an anomaly. Attempts by companies to suppress speech often succeed rather than fail, as the following chapters suggest.

4

SLAPPing Speakers

In 1991, Washington, D.C. real estate developer Dominic Antonelli, Jr., facing $260 million in debts, filed for bankruptcy, and his company, Franklin Point Associates, Ltd., liquidated assets, including 477 acres on the Shady Side peninsula along Maryland's Chesapeake Bay, to help settle the debts. Franklin Point Associates sold the Shady Side acreage for $500,000 to Pointe Properties, Inc., another company in which Antonelli was a director and shareholder. Four years later, Antonelli proposed building 152 upscale homes in a development called Baldwin's Choice on the 477-acre parcel.[1]

Antonelli's plans were vehemently opposed by a citizens group called South Arundel Citizens for Responsible Development (SACReD), headed by Michael Bevenour and Brett Joseph. The group claimed that the development would destroy wetlands, crowd schools, and produce traffic congestion, but county officials nevertheless gave Antonelli waivers to move forward with the project. In an effort to derail the development plan, SACReD members poured through Antonelli's bankruptcy filing and concluded that the fair market price of the 477 acres was over $1 million, not $500,000. The group deduced that the sale was a "sweetheart deal" that violated bankruptcy laws, and sent letters to this effect in October 1996 to government officials, including the U.S. Department of Justice and the financial officers overseeing Antonelli's bankruptcy.[2]

Antonelli's attorney, after hearing of the letters, wrote SACReD's leaders that "your actions have caused my clients many millions of dollars in damages, as well as serious damage to their reputations." The letter warned,

"You would be making a grave mistake if you underestimate their outrage and determination to seek legal recompense if your apology and retraction are not timely and forthcoming."[3] The SACReD members replied that their actions were constitutionally protected and asked that the letters' inaccuracies be identified.

Antonelli and another Pointe Properties executive responded by filing a $50.2 million defamation suit in December 1997 against SACReD and its leaders, claiming that the group's allegations were malicious, false, and injurious. In contrast, an attorney for SACReD characterized the suit as "not about vindicating the truth, it is about the naked use of political power to scare off political enemies."[4] According to the attorney, the lawsuit was filed to punish the group and its leaders for opposing Antonelli's development plans.

The attorneys for SACReD filed a motion to dismiss the suit, arguing that it was a punitive, not substantive, defamation suit. The judge refused on the grounds that Washington, D.C., where the lawsuit was filed, had no laws barring or even defining such suits. Consequently, the suit went to trial in May 1998. After hearing testimony for two-and-a-half weeks, the jury reached a verdict in favor of SACReD, concluding that while some of the group's allegations against Antonelli, whom the jury considered a public figure, were false, they were not made with malice, a precondition for a finding of libel. The jury reached similar conclusions about the other Pointe Property executive, finding that some statements were false, but that SACReD was not negligent in making them.[5]

The same year that Antonelli filed for bankruptcy, Nancy Hsu Fleming and other residents of North Kingstown, Rhode Island, learned at a town council meeting that groundwater samples obtained from test wells adjacent to a landfill owned by Hometown Properties, Inc. were polluted.[6] Alarmed by the report, Fleming and a number of other North Kingstown residents met with Rhode Island Department of Environmental Management (DEM) officials to discuss the contamination. During the meeting, the DEM officials suggested that interested residents comment on groundwater regulations that the department was proposing.

On April 12, 1992, Fleming wrote a four-page letter to the DEM director commenting on the proposed regulations. In her letter, Fleming stated that the proposed regulations would hamper efforts to close the landfill and reiterated points made during her meetings with DEM officials— that Hometown's landfill contained hazardous waste exceeding allowable contamination levels, and that the company had resisted the DEM's attempts to monitor the landfill. Fleming sent copies of her letter to the governor, the state's congressional delegation, and the Environmental Protection Agency.[7]

Fleming received a letter from Hometown Properties' attorney five months later, warning that the company "would have no alternative but to pursue the formal legal remedies available to them" unless Fleming either substantiated or retracted her statements. The attorney threateningly enclosed a retraction for Fleming to sign.[8]

Believing that the Constitution protected her activities, Fleming refused to sign the retraction. She wrote back, defending her assertions and her right to complain to government officials, noting, "The U.S. Constitution grants me the right to petition government. In this instance, I am petitioning state government to close and clean up your client's dump."[9]

Unmoved by Fleming's assertions of her constitutional rights, Hometown Properties filed a lawsuit on December 2, 1992, against Fleming alleging defamation and tortious interference with its contractual relations.[10] A few months later, Fleming's lawyer—an ACLU volunteer—moved to dismiss the lawsuit, but the motion was denied, allowing the case to drag on for three more years.[11]

Although the suit against Fleming was eventually dismissed, the landfill got what it wanted: "They silenced Nancy for four years," says Fleming's attorney.[12]

In 1998, toy manufacturer Mattel, Inc., maker of the Barbie doll, filed a trademark infringement lawsuit against Seal Press, a small

Seattle-based publishing house that produced a book titled *Adios, Barbie*, which showed Barbie in high heels on the front cover. *Adios, Barbie* consisted of feminist essays criticizing Barbie's "tall, thin, and white" body image. Few, if any, readers could possibly have thought that *Adios, Barbie* was published by Mattel, but the toy company nevertheless claimed that the cover caused trademark confusion. Lacking the financial resources to defend itself in court, Seal Press settled with Mattel, agreeing to retitle the book and redesign the cover for subsequent printings.[13]

SACReD, Nancy Hsu Fleming, and Seal Press are but three among hundreds, perhaps thousands, of organizations, citizens, publishers, and media threatened with lawsuits or actually sued by corporations and business executives intent on suppressing criticism of their business operations. Many corporations have filed frivolous, vexatious lawsuits, alleging copyright violations, patent infringement, defamation, business torts, process violations, civil rights violations, and a laundry list of other alleged injuries, not expecting to win the suits but seeking simply to silence their critics. As attorney Mark A. Chertok, who defended the Nature Conservancy against a suit filed by a developer, observed, these lawsuits "scare the hell out of a lot of people. . . . Citizens see a million-dollar lawsuit and they just want to go run and hide. People have disappeared into the woodwork."[14] These lawsuits that intimidate and silence critics are called Strategic Lawsuits Against Public Participation, or SLAPPs.

The term "SLAPP" was developed in the 1980s by Professors George W. Pring and Penelope Canan of the University of Denver to describe civil lawsuits brought against private citizens or groups because they had petitioned some branch of government. Today the term is used much more broadly by attorneys, activists, courts, and legislators to describe civil suits lacking merit, but which are nevertheless filed against speakers and the press for criticizing corporations, executives, and even public officials.[15]

According to Pring and Canan, SLAPPs transform public debates in three major ways. First, what was a public policy controversy—about zoning, the environment, or consumer protection—becomes a private legal dispute. Second, the dispute moves from a public arena to a private, judicial forum. Third, the focus of the debate shifts from the corporation's wrongdoing to the defendant's actions.[16] Overall, the transformation places a burden on the defendant—the financial burden of defending oneself in court and the burden of demonstrating the accuracy of one's words. As New York Justice Nicholas Colabella observed in his decision in the SLAPP filed against the Nature Conservancy:

> SLAPP suits function by forcing the target into the judicial arena where the SLAPP filer foists upon the target the expenses of a defense. The ripple effect of such suits in our society is enormous. Persons who have been outspoken on issues of public importance targeted in such suits or have witnessed such suits will often choose to stay silent. . . . Those who lack the financial resources and emotional stamina to play out the "game" face the difficult choice of defaulting despite meritorious defenses or being brought to their knees to settle. . . . Short of a gun to the head, a greater threat to First Amendment expression can scarcely be imagined.[17]

Not only have many citizens been sued into silence, but many have ceased to speak out when threatened with lawsuits by deep-pocketed companies and CEO. The threat of a lawsuit often suffices to silence public criticism at a fraction of the cost of actually bringing a lawsuit. Faced with millions of dollars in potential damages and thousands of dollars in legal costs, even the most outspoken critic may decide to retract whatever "objectionable" statements he or she made.

These threats to sue can occasionally backfire, as the case of Professor Sut Jhally at the University of Massachusetts shows. MTV, the music cable network, threatened to file a copyright infringement lawsuit against Jhally in 1991, because Jhally used excerpts from MTV music videos in *Dreamworlds*, a video critique of the use of sex and violence in music videos.

Rather than knuckling under to the threat, Jhally continued to distribute copies of *Dreamworlds* and informed newspapers and other media about MTV's actions. In a letter to MTV, which he also released to the media, Jhally urged the cable network to be consistent in its defense of freedom of speech, writing, "I have noted with interest MTV's much publicized recent stress on 'anti-censorship' and would hope that you would want to support free and open expression of important social issues and First Amendment speech rights."[18]

Jhally's release of the letters to the press effectively diluted the SLAPP threat by making the threat a public issue, turning attention to the harm that MTV posed to Jhally, not the harm that Jhally posed to MTV—the opposite of what SLAPPs intend to do. Because of the negative publicity, MTV never followed up its threat by filing a suit.

Many times, companies file SLAPPs expecting to drop them before they go to trial. When companies enter into agreements to drop their lawsuits, these agreements can include secrecy provisions, which also silence critics. Ed Dienhart, who was hit with a million-dollar SLAPP, learned that even settlement agreements that result in the dropping of SLAPPs can effectively deter speech.

Dienhart bought a house in a subdivision of Oswego, Illinois, developed by Property Concepts, Inc. Several months after moving in, he found sewage coming up the basement floor drain, so he contacted the Fox Metro Water Reclamation District, the local agency responsible for sewage treatment. Fox Metro found that the sewage pipes had sunk six to eight inches due to faulty installation and ordered the subcontractor to correct the problem.[19]

Dienhart learned that his neighbors had similar problems, and during an Oswego Village Board meeting urged them to complain to Fox Metro and the developer. After that, Dienhart received a letter from Property Concepts, Inc., threatening him with a defamation lawsuit if he did not stop publicly complaining about the sewage problems. Ignoring the threat, Dienhart brought up the problems at a later Board meeting.

A few weeks later, Property Concepts filed suit, claiming defamation because Dienhart overstated the costs of repairs and accused the company of violating building codes. The suit was filed despite Oswego and Fox Metro officials' conclusions that many installations had not met code requirements.

Four months later, the lawsuit was settled on secret terms that prohibited Dienhart from commenting on the case. However, the court records showed that the "suit was settled 'without costs to either party.'"[20] Although the company did not win the lawsuit, it nevertheless succeeded in silencing Dienhart.

SLAPPs are brought by all kinds of corporations, but real estate developers, as Dienhart's and SACReD's experiences show, are among the most frequent SLAPP filers. Energy, logging, and mining companies, two of the major sources of environmental damage and rural pollution, are also notorious SLAPP filers.

An example of an egregious SLAPP filed by an energy company is provided by Western Fuels Association, a coal-buying cooperative and lobby group that filed a "commercial defamation" suit against six environmental groups, including Friends of the Earth, Public Citizen, and Ozone Action. The suit was filed in federal court in Wyoming in 2000, a state that has no laws barring SLAPPs, alleging that the environmental groups violated section 43 of the Lanham Act by making "false and misleading statements about the impact of burning fossil fuels." The association claimed that the organizations' statements linking coal burning and global warming, which were published in a *New York Times* advertisement and on a website, damaged its business and advocacy abilities. The rationale of filing under the Lanham Act, which addresses unfair business practices, was that the environmental groups received funding from the renewable energy industry, which competes with coal as an energy source.[21]

The suit was dismissed by U.S. District Judge William Downes ten months after it was filed because it should not have been filed in Wyoming. The proper venues, the judge noted, were either California, where several of the environmental groups were headquartered, or Washington, D.C., where the coal lobby group was based.[22]

A Case of Fury

After SLAPPs are filed against them, defendants often file motions to dismiss the suits for failure to state adequate legal claims. This is routinely done in SLAPP cases, but such motions are rarely granted, as the Fleming and SACReD cases show, because courts traditionally assume that at least some facts stated by the plaintiffs are true, and courts generally conclude that the facts and merits of the case should be decided in trials rather than in hearings. As an article in *New York University Law Review* pointed out, motions to dismiss are difficult to win because "SLAPP filers usually sue on ordinary tort actions and generally are able to allege the prima facie elements necessary to make out various tort claims."[23] Generally speaking, a motion to dismiss or for summary judgment is granted only when "it appears beyond doubt that the plaintiff can prove no set of facts in support of his claim."[24]

Because traditional procedures do little to prevent the speech-stifling effect of SLAPPs, several state supreme courts have crafted procedural rules that assure the early dismissal of SLAPPs. The West Virginia Supreme Court of Appeals did so two decades ago in *Webb v. Fury.*[25]

Webb v. Fury arose from a lawsuit filed against environmental activist Rick Webb by DLM Coal Corporation. Webb filed an administrative complaint against DLM with the U. S. Department of Interior's Office of Surface Mining (OSM) on September 13, 1979, and with the Environmental Protection Agency on October 12, 1979, charging that the company had polluted nearby watersheds. In an article in the newsletter of Mountain Stream Monitor, a West Virginia–based environmental group, Webb made the same charges, although DLM was not mentioned by name.[26] An investigation of Webb's charges by government inspectors found that seepage in areas near DLM's mines contained illegally high amounts of acid or iron, but they could not conclusively establish that the water pollution was caused by DLM.

In July 1980, DLM filed a defamation suit against Webb, alleging that Webb's communications to the OSM, to the EPA, and in the newsletter were "made maliciously, with knowledge of their falsity, in order to harass DLM and to damage its business relations." Webb's lawyers filed a motion to dismiss the lawsuit on the grounds that communications with the OSM and the EPA are constitutionally protected forms of petitioning. Circuit court judge William Fury denied the motion. Webb's attorneys then appealed to the West Virginia Supreme Court to prevent the defamation suit from continuing.[27]

A year after DLM filed its lawsuit, the West Virginia Supreme Court acted on Webb's appeal. Relying on several U.S. Supreme Court rulings that developed the *Noerr-Pennington* doctrine, which exempted companies from being sued for petitions they filed with the federal government unless they were "shams," the West Virginia Supreme Court declared petitioning activity to be immune from tort claims under both the U.S. and the West Virginia constitutions unless the activity was a "mere sham." Applying that standard, the court held that Webb's communications with OSM and the EPA were protected petitioning activity. The court also found that the allegedly defamatory statements made in the newsletter were also protected because they were part of the petitioning process. The court concluded:

> As a final note, we shudder to think of the chill our ruling would have on the exercise of the freedom of speech and the right to petition were we to allow this lawsuit to proceed. The cost to society in terms of the threat to our liberty and freedom is beyond calculation. . . . To prohibit robust debate on these questions would deprive society of the benefit of its collective thinking and in the process destroy the free exchange of ideas which is the adhesive of our democracy. Our democratic system is designed to do the will of the people, and when the people express cannot express their will, the system fails. It is exactly this type of debate which our federal and state constitutions protect. . . . We see this dispute between the parties as a vigorous exchange of ideas which

is more properly within the political arena than in the courthouse. To hold otherwise would be to isolate ourselves in ignorance and to deprive society of the collective genius upon which our civilization depends. This we must never allow.[28]

West Virginia Justice Richard Neely dissented, but nevertheless concluded that the majority decision was "well reasoned and written." He dissented in part because he felt the majority failed to "adequately explore appropriate procedures for cases of this sort." Instead of offering defendants blanket immunity for their statements, Neely proposed a "screening device," whereby trial judges hold preliminary hearings to determine whether the lawsuits are "brought in good faith" and "supported by reasonable cause."[29]

In 1984, the Colorado Supreme Court adopted a rule similar to that proposed by Neely. The rule was enunciated in *Protect Our Mountain Environment, Inc. v. District Court for County of Jefferson*, a SLAPP brought by the Gayno Corp. against Protect Our Mountain Environment (POME). A local environmental group, POME opposed Gayno's plan to develop 507 acres of wilderness at the base of the Rocky Mountains. Gayno charged the organization with abuse of process and conspiracy for its efforts opposing the development, and sought $10 million in compensatory damages and $30 million in punitive damages. POME was virtually destroyed by the SLAPP.[30]

Although lower courts refused to dismiss the lawsuit, the Colorado Supreme Court, also invoking the *Noerr-Pennington* doctrine, ruled that when a defendant moves to dismiss a lawsuit based on the First Amendment right to petition government, "the burden shifts to the plaintiff to make a sufficient showing to permit the court to reasonably conclude that the defendant's petitioning activities were not immunized from liability under the First Amendment." To make such a showing, the plaintiff must demonstrate three things: "(1) the defendant's administrative or judicial claims were devoid of reasonable factual support, or, if so supportable, lacked any cognizable basis in law of their assertion; and (2) the primary purpose of the defendants's petitioning activity was to harass the plaintiff or to effectuate some other improper objective; and (3) the defendant's petitioning activity had the capacity to adversely affect a legal interest of the plaintiff."[31]

Despite the Supreme Court decision, it took another year for the case against POME to get dismissed. Overall, the most positive outcome of the case is that the Colorado court's criteria have since been adopted as statutes in several states, which have tried to lessen the threats to speech by passing anti-SLAPP statutes.

Anti-SLAPP Laws

Recognizing that most legal procedures are inadequate in deterring SLAPPs, nineteen states have enacted anti-SLAPP laws. Washington was the first in 1989, followed by California, Delaware, New York, Rhode Island, Nevada, Massachusetts, Minnesota, Nebraska, Maine, Georgia, Tennessee, Indiana, Louisiana, Florida, Pennsylvania, Utah, New Mexico, and Oregon.[32] The laws provide varying degrees of protection against SLAPPs. Minnesota's and California's law provide substantial protection, whereas Pennsylvania's and Florida's law provide negligible protection.

While these anti-SLAPP laws were enacted because of the growing number of SLAPPs, several were enacted in response to particularly irritating SLAPPs. For example, the Rhode Island anti-SLAPP law was introduced in part because of the publicity surrounding the lawsuit brought by Hometown Properties against Nancy Hsu Fleming.[33]

The Florida anti-SLAPP law, adopted in 2000, was also passed in response to a particularly egregious SLAPP—this one filed by Pinellas County against the Coalition of Lake Association (COLA), a citizens group that contended Pinellas County's overpumping of county-owned well fields threatened lakes and wetlands. When COLA's members publicly threatened to bring a class action to stop the overpumping, Pinellas County sued them instead.

Although the citizens' group ultimately prevailed in court, it disbanded, mainly because of the lawsuit. Indignant state legislators responded by passing a law protecting Floridians from SLAPPs by state and local government bodies.[34]

Unfortunately, the new Florida anti-SLAPP law provides no protection from SLAPPs filed by the private sector, even though more vexatious suits have been filed by Florida businesses than by governments. For example, a mining company sued a Florida couple for publicly complaining about the company's blasting operations, which blew rocks onto the couple's house, and the head of the Florida Petroleum Marketers Association filed a lawsuit against an environmental magazine that declared the association and its head to be "Public Enemy Number One." A study done by the Florida Attorney General's Office found that nearly all SLAPPs filed in Florida between 1985 and 1993 were filed by private entities, which succeeded in tying up their critics in court for an average of ten months.[35]

After hearing from lobbyists from the real estate and other industries, the legislature disregarded the evidence about the dangers of private sector SLAPPs and adopted a law that merely barred public sector SLAPPs.[36] The legislators' capitulation to business lobbyists demonstrates the unhealthy influence that businesses often have on public policy.

Similar pressure in Pennsylvania resulted in the gutting of a proposed, far-reaching anti-SLAPP statute. The final, gutted bill protected individuals speaking about a single issue: "state and local environmental policy and . . . the implementation and enforcement of environmental law and regulation." Because the law is limited to speech addressing environmental regulation, particularly those affecting the coal industry, the Pennsylvania statute theoretically offers protection to speakers such as Rick Webb, but not Ed Dienhart, the Seal Press, or Professor Jhally.

Georgia state's legislature also enacted an anti-SLAPP law in response to a highly publicized SLAPP. The SLAPP was brought by Brock Construction Co., which sued Joe Nairon and two other DeKalb County residents after they spoke at a County Planning Commission meeting against Brock's petition to rezone property. When the Commission refused Brock's rezoning request, the developer sued Nairon and the others, claiming that their misstatements about which street Brock planned to use as an entrance to the property constituted defamation. A year later, the Superior Court of DeKalb County dismissed the suit, ruling that a mere misstatement of fact was not defamation. Moreover, the court concluded that "any communication which is made with the ultimate goal of supporting or opposing legislative action by the government must be protected by the petition clause of the state and federal constitutions."[37]

Two years after the Superior Court ruling, the Georgia legislature codified the court's decision by passing an anti-SLAPP statute prohibiting suits against individuals who have made written or oral statements "to a legislative, executive, or judicial proceeding, or any other official proceeding authorized by law" or who have made statements about issues being considered by a legislative, executive, or judicial body.

Anti-SLAPPs law might deter but do not stop the filing of SLAPPS. Just months after Georgia adopted its anti-SLAPP statute in 1996, developer Ron Leventhal filed a lawsuit against six homeowners who publicly opposed his plan to build a high-density development on sixteen acres adjacent to their properties in Cobb County, Georgia. Leventhal characterized his lawsuit as a "contractual dispute," claiming that the homeowners violated restrictive covenants attached to their properties by speaking against his proposed development. Immediately after Leventhal filed the suit, five of the homeowners, fearful of losing in court, reached agreements with Leventhal not to oppose his development, leaving just one defendant, Dave Bauer.[38]

Citing the state's anti-SLAPP statute, Cobb County Superior Court Judge Mary Staley dismissed the suit against Bauer. Judge Staley concluded that the suit "was filed in a clear attempt to chill the defendants' expected future opposition to the rezoning application . . . and to deter others from joining the opposition."[39] Although the suit was dismissed within forty-five days of being filed, Bauer nevertheless ran up $3,000 in legal defense bills, and Leventhal succeeded in silencing five of his six opponents.

And in 1997, the year following adoption of the anti-SLAPP statute, Matria Healthcare, Inc., a Marietta, Georgia–based company, filed a lawsuit against the National Women's Heath Network, charging that the Network interfered with its business relations and conspired to commit deceptive trade practices by urging the U.S. Food and Drug Administration (FDA) to stop Matria from distributing the terbutaline pump, used by pregnant women at risk of premature delivery.

Rather than capitulating to Matria's pressure tactic, the National Women's Health Network publicized the suit, labeling it a SLAPP, and continued pressuring the FDA to ban the pump because it had never been approved as a pregnancy device.[40] In October 1997, the FDA finally warned doctors that the pump could be dangerous, which led Matria to quickly drop its suit. Because Matria dropped its suit rather than having it dismissed or having lost in court, the company argued that it should not be required to reimburse the Network for the $18,000 legal fees that the Network incurred defending itself against the SLAPP, as provided by Georgia's anti-SLAPP statute.[41] Matria's tactic shows how companies are willing to exploit loopholes in laws in their efforts to suppress speech.

Comparing the Statutes

Most anti-SLAPP laws are similar to Georgia's, granting qualified immunity against tort claims to individuals involved in the petitioning process. As in Georgia, California's anti-SLAPP law provides immunity to

> any written or oral statement or writing made before a legislative, executive, or judicial proceedings, or any other official proceeding authorized by law; any written or oral statement or writing made in connection with an issue under consideration or review by a legislative, executive, or judicial body, or any other proceeding authorized by law.[42]

Although the statute appears similar to Georgia's, it also immunizes "any written or oral statement or writing made in a place open to the public or a public forum in connection with an issue of public interest," making it much broader than Georgia's. The California anti-SLAPP law protects virtually any statement concerning an issue of public interest, and has been successfully invoked by the news media as a defense against defamation.

Like California's, Rhode Island's statute provides immunity to "any written or oral statement made in connection with an issue of public concern." It is therefore written broadly enough to protect most statements about public issues, but exempts from immunity any statements that "are not genuininely aimed at procuring favorable government action, result, or outcome, regardless of ulterior motive or purpose," which is essentially the "sham" standard of the *Noerr-Pennington* doctrine.

In contrast, the New York anti-SLAPP law immunizes some petitioning activity from claims unless it is done with "knowledge of its falsity or with reckless disregard of whether it was false."

The New York statute, like the Delaware and Nebraska statutes, only protects certain petitioning activities, making them far narrower than the Georgia, Rhode Island, and California statutes. For example, New York's law can be invoked only when a "public applicant"—someone who has applied for or obtained government approval for some purpose—asserts a claim against someone who has commented on or opposed the application. However, the law covers a range of activities, as long as they are "materially related" to the application process. Despite this "materially related" extension, the act nevertheless excludes most citizen complaints to regulatory bodies, which usually do not challenge the granting of an application. However, New York courts have been willing to broadly interpret the definition of public permittees and applicants. For example, Manhattan Supreme Court Justice Sheila Abdus-Salaam concluded that Street Beat Sportswear, a clothing manufacturer, was a public permittee because it registered as an employer with the Commissioner of Labor. Justice Abdus-Salaam therefore declared a $75 million business interference lawsuit brought by Street Beat Sportswear against anti-sweatshop activists to be a SLAPP and dismissed it. Street Beat filed the suit because the activists asked retailers to stop carrying the company's sweatshop-made garments. As a result of the dismissal, the clothing manufacturer agreed to pay the activists $85,000 in damages.[43]

Other features of anti-SLAPP laws include requiring courts to expedite the resolution of the suits, slowing or staying discovery until motions to dismiss have been heard, and allowing SLAPP defendants to recover damages incurred as a result of the SLAPP. Almost all of the statutes implicitly or explicitly allow a "speedy hearing by a judge and a quick dismissal where applicable."[44] For example, the Georgia and California statutes require courts to hear within thirty days motions to dismiss under the statutes "unless the emergency matters before the court require a later hearing." The Rhode Island statute states that the "court shall advance and special motion [to dismiss] so that it may be heard and determined with as little delay as possible."

Procedural Elements. Many anti-SLAPP laws facilitate the early dismissal of SLAPPs by authorizing special motions to dismiss; some shift the burden of proof from the party moving for dismissal (i.e., the SLAPP defendant) to the party opposing dismissal (i.e., the SLAPP plaintiff). In New York, motions to dismiss under the anti-SLAPP statute must be granted unless the non-moving party (i.e., the SLAPP plaintiff) demonstrates that the claim "has a substantial basis in law or fact or is supported by a substantial argument for an extension, modification or reversal of existing law."[45] Nebraska's statute is similarly worded. If the motion to dismiss is granted by a court in either state, the court may award attorney's fees and other costs to the SLAPP defendant.

The Massachusetts anti-SLAPP law provides for the filing of a "special motion to dismiss" based on the right to petition. The motion must be granted unless the non-moving party (i.e., the SLAPP plaintiff) shows that the petitioning activity was (1) "devoid of any reasonable factual support or any arguable basis in law" and (2) "caused actual injury" to the non-moving party (the SLAPP plaintiff). While the motion is pending, all discovery is stayed.[46]

California's anti-SLAPP law provides for the filing of a "special motion to strike" SLAPP claims. The motion must be granted unless the SLAPP plaintiff demonstrates a "probability" of prevailing on the claim at trial, which is an easier burden to demonstrate than that in Massachusetts. While the motion is pending, all discovery is stayed unless the SLAPP plaintiff can demonstrate "good cause" why discovery should continue. [47] Similarly, the Rhode Island statute requires courts to "stay all discovery proceedings in the action upon the filing of a motion [to dismiss] . . . [and] the stay of discovery shall remain in effect" under the court rules on the motion.

Sanctions. Nevada's anti-SLAPP law permits the attorney general and other legal representatives to defend petitioners who have been hit with SLAPPs because of their petitioning activity. Rather ingenious, the statute shifts the costs of a SLAPP defense from a petitioner to government, which is better equipped and financed to battle SLAPPs than most ordinary citizens or activists' groups. The possibility that government may come to the aid of SLAPP defendents undoubtedly acts as a deterent to would-be SLAPPers. Moreover, the Nevada statute allows the government to recover its costs if it prevails. The plaintiff is likewise entitled to "reasonable costs and attorney's fees" if he or she prevails.

A number of state anti-SLAPP laws provide for the SLAPP defendant to recover damages from the SLAPP plaintiff. In Massachsetts, a SLAPP defendant who prevails in the special motion to dismiss is entitled to "costs and reasonable attorney's fees, including those incurred for the special motion and any related discovery matters." In California, SLAPP defendants who prevail in a special motion to dismiss are also entitled to "attorney's fees and costs."[48]

Nebraska's statute allows prevailing SLAPP defendents to recover "costs and attorney's fees" but allows for the recovery of other compensatory damages if the SLAPP was filed for "the purpose of harassing, intimidating, punishing, or otherwise maliciously inhibiting" protected speech.

Under Minnesota's anti-SLAPP statute, a defendant who successfully defends against a SLAPP may recover compensatory damages and even punitive damages from the SLAPP plaintiff if the lawsuit was filed "for the purpose of harassment, to inhibit the moving party's public participation, to interfere with the moving party's exercise of protected constitutional rights, or otherwise wrongfully injure the moving party." The Minnesota anti-SLAPP law also allows a SLAPP defendant who has been sued in federal court to file a lawsuit in state court to recover damages and attorney's fees.[49]

As the Minnesota statute suggests, SLAPPs may be filed in federal court, in addition to state court. When a SLAPP is filed in federal court, most state anti-SLAPP laws probably have limited applicability, although a recent court decision suggests that state anti-SLAPP laws may also offer protection from federal suits. In *United States v. Lockheed Missiles & Space Co.*, the Ninth Circuit ruled that when a SLAPP plaintiff asserts claims under California law in federal court, a SLAPP defendant may file a special motion to strike and seek attorney's fees and costs under the California anti-SLAPP law. The Ninth Circuit concluded that invoking the California anti-SLAPP law to this extent would not conflict with the Federal Rules of Civil Procedure, which govern the conduct of proceedings in federal district courts. The circuit court also reasoned that if SLAPP defendants could not invoke the California anti-SLAPP law in federal court, SLAPP plaintiffs would have a significant incentive to bring their meritless SLAPP claims in federal, rather than state, court.[50]

SLAPPback Suits

Citizens who have been SLAPPed have increasingly responded by filing "SLAPPback suits" against those who SLAPPed them. SLAPPback suits are filed to compensate SLAPP victims for monetary and emotional injuries incurred from the SLAPP; to punish SLAPP filers for having trampled on others' constitutional rights; and to deter other, would-be SLAPPers.[51] Because SLAPPs are viewed by most citizens as extemely vindictive acts, juries sometimes award substantial damages in successful SLAPPback suits, such as one brought by Jo Ann Baglini and her husband, who were originally SLAPPed by developer Frank Lauletta.

Lauletta filed his SLAPP after Baglini and two neighbors filed a lawsuit against Washington Township in July 1990, challenging the township's decision to rezone Lauletta's property from residential to commercial, allowing him to build office condominiums on the property. A month later, Lauletta sued Baglini, her husband, and several neighbors who actively opposed the zoning change for $10 million, claiming defamation, tortious interference with contractual relations, and emotional distress.[52]

During court proceedings, Baglini's lawyers confirmed what they had suspected from the beginning: Lauletta had sued Baglini and the others for one reason only—to punish them for filing the lawsuit against Washington Township. Despite this, Lauletta's lawyer during settlement negotiations offered to drop the lawsuit if Baglini and the others dropped their suit against Washington Township. Baglini and the others indignantly rejected the offer out of hand.[53] Although they continued to fight the lawsuit, the defendants virtually dropped out of public activism, as did nearly half of the forty-member citizens group that had formed to oppose the township's rezoning of Lauletta's property.

In April 1992, the New Jersey Superior Court overturned Washington Township's rezoning of Lauletta's property and dismissed Lauletta's SLAPP.[54] Three months after Lauletta's lawsuit was dismissed, the Baglinis sued him and his lawyer for malicious prosecution and abuse of process. In July 1998, six years after the series of lawsuits began, a jury found in their favor, awarding them nearly $1.5 million in damages.[55]

Although substantial, the Baglinis' award was nowhere near the largest award in a SLAPPback suit. A hospital employee won an $86.5 million award from a jury after an infectious-waste disposal company sued him for defamation for criticizing their operations.[56] In 1989, Shell Oil Co. was hit with a $5.1 million jury verdict for suing a consumer advocate who complained to a state health agency about a Shell home plumbing product.[57] The same year, a jury ordered the J. G. Boswell Company, a large Southern California–based agrifirm, to pay three family farmers $13.5 million, because of a malicious SLAPP the company had filed against them. Boswell's SLAPP falsely alleged that the farmers defamed the company with a newspaper advertisement supporting a proposition to build a new water pipeline. The advertisement stated that the pipeline would strengthen small farmers, noting that "if the small farmers go out of business, Boswell and [other big agrifirms] will be able to totally dominate California agriculture."[58] In its SLAPP, Boswell claimed that this fairly innocuous statement constituted defamation.

SLAPP defendants who have brought SLAPPback suits have principally claimed that the orginial SLAPPs constituted "malicious prosecution" in state courts or civil rights violations in federal court. However, winning a "malicious prosecution" suit is quite difficult.[59] A SLAPP defendant must prove that the SLAPP plaintiff filed the lawsuit "without probable cause" and "with malice," something that SLAPP plaintiffs rarely, if ever, admit. The filer of a SLAPPback suit must establish these using circumstantial evidence such as internal company documents or other, similar evidence, which can be obtained only through costly, time-consuming discovery. Proving civil rights violations is similarly difficult.

Demonstrating malice and lack of probable cause are not the only obstacles to winning a malicious prosecution SLAPPback suit. Several states require plaintiffs asserting malicious prosecution claims to prove that they were injured by the lawsuit, but also suffered "special damages" beyond those typically arising from lawsuits. Although some state courts have held that interference with one's freedom of speech and freedom of petition, as SLAPPs do, qualifies as "special damages," other state courts have rejected this position.[60]

Although there have been substantial damage awards in SLAPPback suits, SLAPP defendants who bring such suits often face many obstacles, making SLAPPback suits a poor method for either deterring SLAPPs or punishing SLAPP filers.

Many SLAPP defendants, weary of being involved in another court case, are also disinclined to bring SLAPPback suits. "The thought of protracting the original SLAPP suit, only to come back to court and counter-sue, may not appeal to a risk-averse [SLAPP defendant] who never dreamed of being dragged into court in the first place," a study of SLAPPs concluded.[61] Consequently, other remedies—such as federal anti-SLAPP laws—are needed to deter companies and well-heeled, malicious businessmen from filing SLAPPs.

SLAPPing the Media

Not surprisingly, the mass media have been frequent targets of SLAPPs for exposing companies' unseemly business practices, executives' dastardly deeds, and even the derelictions of public employees. Because of the impediments that public figures face in winning libel suits against the mass media, having to prove not only the falsity of the statements but actual malice, most SLAPPs filed against the mass media allege other torts.

SLAPPs have been filed against small, medium, and even large media companies, despite the public knowledge that most media firms have legal teams that are prepared and able to fight such suits. Here is an example of a SLAPP filed against a small medium:

• *The MacArthur Metro*, a community newspaper in Northern California, was sued by an auto repair shop owner after a columnist described the repair shop as an "eyesore," a term also used by city officials. A judge concluded that the suit was baseless and quickly dismissed it under California's anti-SLAPP law, and ordered the repair shop owner to pay the newspaper's legal bills.[62]

An example of a SLAPP filed against a medium-sized media company is:

• A $12.5 million lawsuit filed against San Francisco–based *Mother Jones* magazine because it revealed that Republican political consultant Donald Sipple, who advised California Governor Pete Wilson, Texas Governor George W. Bush, and 1996 presidential candidate Bob Dole, had been accused of battering his ex-wives. Although Sipple often advised political candidates to run on morality issues, Sipple contended that the abuse allegations were of purely private concern, despite being based on public court documents and despite his high political profile. The court disagreed, dismissing his suit under the state's anti-SLAPP statute.[63]

The final example of a SLAPP is one against a large media company:

• A lawsuit brought by Glamour Models, Inc., a modeling agency, against Paramount Pictures' *Hard Copy* television program, claiming that a story about how the agency made false promises and overcharged clients for services constituted defamation and trespassing. The trespassing claim arose from the *Hard Copy* reporters' unannounced appearance at the modeling agency's offices with cameras rolling. Although Paramount's lawyers filed a special motion to dismiss under California's anti-SLAPP law shortly after the suit was filed in December 1996, the presiding judge denied the motion, allowing the case to linger on for several years. The lawsuit was eventually dismissed by the California Court of Appeals in 2000.[64]

Many times SLAPPs filed against the news media are little more than public relations efforts designed to counter the negative publicity generated by news reports. For example, Isuzu company memos referred to their lawsuit as an effective "PR tool" and predicted that Consumers Union would knuckle under after being sued.[65]

Another public relations SLAPP was filed in 1999 against Boston television station WCVB-TV by San Diego–based Metabolife, Inc., after the station aired a two-part report on Metabolife 356, the company's big-selling dietary supplement. Metabolife 356's primary ingredient, a heart stimulant called ephedrine, or *ma huang,* is considered a food not a drug by the U.S. Food and Drug Administration and was therefore never subjected to FDA drug testing.[66]

WCVB-TV reporter Susan Wornick questioned the effectiveness and safety of Metabolife 356, stating that "every expert we asked said Metabolife [356] is not safe because of its main ingredient *ma huang.*" Her report included a brief interview with Harvard Medical School doctor George Blackburn, who said, "You can die by taking this product."[67]

Metabolife, Inc., responded with a full-page advertisement in the *Boston Globe* that rebutted the broadcast, falsely accused Blackburn of having endorsed a competitor's dietary supplement, and warned that it would "see Ms. Wornick and WCVB-TV in court."[68] Two weeks later, the company filed a suit against WCVB-TV owner Hearst-Argyle, Inc., Wornick, and Blackburn in federal court in California, alleging defamation, slander, and trade libel.

The defendants filed a motion to dismiss. U.S. District Judge John S. Rhoades granted that motion because Metabolife no scientific evidence invalidating Wornick's and Blackburn's statements. In issuing his decision, Judge Rhoades stated that Metabolife had "sued [the] defendants for their contributions to th[e] debate" about drug safety.[69]

Unlike the Metabolife case, which was quickly dismissed, a $30 million defamation and invasion of privacy lawsuit filed in federal district court in Wisconsin against the *National Catholic Reporter* by Briggs & Stratton Co. executives, a Milwaukee-area manufacturer of small engines, lingered on for years. The lawsuit arose from a December 1994 *Reporter* article critical of Briggs & Stratton's decision to move 2,000 jobs from the Midwest to Mexico and the South, even though the company was quite profitable. The article, "Adios American Dream," quoted a union activist who asked whether high-level Briggs executives, several of whom were Catholic, had "strayed from the social teachings of the Church." Although the *Reporter* had on several occasions attempted to interview Briggs executives for the article, each time they were rebuffed.[70]

Briggs & Stratton demanded that the newspaper print a 3,000-word, unedited rebuttal to the article, which the editor refused. Two years later, in 1996, Briggs & Stratton and three company executives filed suit against the paper, claiming that they had been defamed, publicly embarrassed by the accusations about the conflicts between their religion and business ethics, and that their children had been taunted.[71]

In October 1997, the trial court judge dismissed most of the suit challenging the *Reporter*'s interpretation of Catholic doctrine but allowed the libel suit about the company's business ethics to proceed. In December 1997, Briggs & Stratton and two executives dropped their suits, leaving one plaintiff, George Thompson III, Briggs' director of corporate communication. Thompson tried to persuade the judge that he was a private citizen not a public figure; was a religious man but perhaps was not a Catholic; and had had his privacy invaded by the newspaper. Apparently unmoved by Thompson's contradictory assertions, the judge dismissed the remaining claims in April 1998, ruling that the *Reporter* had "thoroughly investigated the facts underlying the articles" and that the plaintiff had not presented any evidence "that anyone had been misquoted."[72]

The contrast between the quick dismissals of most of the California SLAPPs when compared to the drawn-out *National Catholic Reporter* lawsuit demonstrates one of the benefits that SLAPP defendants receive from anti-SLAPP laws.

Another drawn-out, irritating SLAPP was filed against the ABC television network in North Carolina, which also lacks an anti-SLAPP law, by the 1,100-store supermarket chain, Food Lion, Inc. The suit was filed because of a undercover exposé broadcast by *PrimeTime Live* about Food Lion stores' nauseating meat-handling practices, which included washing, bleaching, and grinding up dated and rotten meat and then offering it for sale to an unsuspecting public.

After hearing reports about these practices from former Food Lion employees, two *PrimeTime Live* reporters, Lynne Dale and Susan Barnett, secured employment at Food Lion stores using false resumés and—with lipstick-size lenses concealed in wigs and with hidden microphones—videotaped three stores' meat-handling practices. The findings were detailed in a November 5, 1992, broadcast, shortly after which the supermarket chain's profits and stocks tumbled. The food chain's stock dropped 25 percent; 84 stores became unprofitable and were closed; and the company faced a $174 million income drop in 1993.[73]

Food Lion publicly disputed the accuracy of the broadcast, but instead of filing a defamation suit that would have required Food Lion to prove that the broadcast was false, instead sued Capital Cities/ABC, *PrimeTime Live* producers Richard Kaplan and Ira Rosen, and the two reporters for fraud, breach of loyalty, trespass, and unfair trade practices, alleging that the methods used for obtaining the video footage were unfair. Food Lion sought million of dollars in damages.[74] The food chain simultaneously launched a public relations campaign claiming that the company had been defamed and would be vindicated in court, even though the suit never challenged the accuracy of the broadcast. In fact, when the case finally went to trial, the judge told the jury to assume that the broadcast was true.[75]

In their defense, ABC and the *PrimeTime Live* journalists presented affadavits from former employees attesting to the accuracy of story. The affidavits were dismissed by Food Lion's "good ole boy" attorneys, who characterized them as coming from disgruntled union organizers. "Reporters all over the country need to know that when you cross the line, you're going to get punished," Food Lion's attorney stated.[76]

The jury of six men and six women decided in the local company's favor, finding the defendants liable for fraud and violation of the North Carolina Unfair and Deceptive Trade Practices Act, and the two reporters liable for breach of loyalty and trespass. However, U.S. District Court Judge Carlton Tilley, Jr., ruled that Food Lion could not recover damages for the company's lost sales, reduced stock prices, or closed stores because these were not directly caused by the investigative techniques but by the broadcast itself, the content of which Food Lion did not challenge.

Overall, compensatory damages in the case amounted to a paltry $1,400 for the fraud and $2 for the breach of loyalty.

Apparently angered at the investigative practices of ABC's out-of-town reporters, the jury also awarded Food Lion $5,545,750 in punitive damages—an amount later reduced to $315,000 by the trial judge.[77] The juror most adamant about socking ABC with a large punitive judgement was a white, sixty-four-year-old juror, Lois Marie Bozman, a loyal Food Lion shopper who argued that she had "never seen anything nasty or dirty in Food Lion."

ABC appealed the reduced judgment to the Fourth Circuit Court of Appeals. The appeals court upheld the jury's breach of loyalty finding, and decided that Food Lion was entitled to the two dollars in nominal compensatory damages, but reversed the judgment on the fraud claims and its attendant $1,400 compensatory and $315,000 punitive damages awards. The court also upheld the Judge Tilley's ruling that Food Lion could not recover damages resulting from the broadcast, and described Food Lion's attempt to recover such damages as "an end-run around First Amendment strictures."[78]

The Food Lion suit, and the jury's willingness to award a local corporation damages in a far-fetched suit underscores the need for adopting a federal anti-SLAPP law, as well as the need to adopt anti-SLAPP statutes in states that currently lack them.

5
"Hog-tying" Critics:
Agricultural Disparagement Statutes

On February 26, 1989, CBS's investigative news program, *60 Minutes*, aired a segment titled "'A' Is for Apple'" about the dangers of daminozide, a chemical sprayed on red apples to improve their marketability. Daminozide, sold under the trade name Alar by Uniroyal, Inc., retarded premature falling, increased apple size and color, and boosted storage life, allowing apples to be stored for up to a year instead of six months before being sold. However, laboratory studies showed that the chemical was a potent carcinogen that was absorbed into apples and therefore could not be washed off by canners, bottlers, or consumers. The Environmental Protection Agency (EPA) was aware that daminozide produced cancer in laboratory test animals but was reluctant to recall the chemical because it was already on the market and was widely used by apple growers, who claimed that banning Alar would hurt them financially.

The *60 Minutes* segment drew heavily on a report titled *Intolerable Risk: Pesticides in Our Children's Food*, issued by the Natural Resources Defense Council (NRDC). The report examined several carcinogenic chemicals used in farming, including daminozide, and received substantial publicity thanks to the NRDC's public relations agency, Fenton Communications, even before the *60 Minutes* segment aired.[1]

The segment began with reporter Ed Bradley saying, "The most potent cancer-causing agent in our food supply is a substance sprayed on apples to keep them on the trees longer and make them look better . . . . And who is most at risk? Children, who may someday develop cancer from this one chemical called daminozide." Bradley's statements were followed by an interview with Environmental Protection Agency administrator Dr. Jack Moore, who said that if daminozide were "a new chemical, not yet on the market, and it was brought to the agency to be evaluated, that it would not get on the market, based on the data that are available." Moore explained that the burden of proof showing the chemical to be dangerous was now on the government because the product was already approved for sale, and that Uniroyal could sue if the EPA banned Alar. Also appearing in the segment was Janet Hathaway of the NRDC, who spoke about the EPA's timidity in banning carcinogens, and Dr. John Graef, a Harvard Medical School pediatrician, who concluded that "children clearly are subject to very large exposures to these chemicals, that they are at significant risk, that they are at greater risk than adults."[2]

After the *60 Minutes* segment aired, school boards pulled apples and apple products from lunch menus; parents pulled them from breakfast tables and lunch boxes; and health-conscious eaters boycotted the fruit, producing an estimated $75 million loss for Washington State apple growers, the largest group of red apple producers in the United States.[3]

The industry responded in three ways. First, Uniroyal withdrew Alar from the domestic market three months later, claiming that sales for the chemical in the United States had dried up, but that the chemical was safe and would continue to be exported to other apple-growing countries. At the beginning of September 1989, six months after " 'A' Is for Apples" aired, the EPA banned Alar, even though Uniroyal had already withdrawn the product.[4]

Second, the industry launched a public relations campaign claiming that the reports about Alar's dangers were "overblown." The campaign was spearheaded by the American Council on Science and Health, a public relations front group, funded in part by Uniroyal and other chemical producers such as Dow, Dupont, and Union Carbide.[5] The American Council on Science and Health successfully planted many stories in the mass media, including one in the *New York Times*, claiming that Alar was "a scare that turned out to be overblown."[6]

Third, Washington apple growers filed a lawsuit alleging "trade libel" or product disparagement against CBS, the NRDC, Fenton Communications, and three Washington television stations that aired *60 Minutes*. Trade libel alleges "an intentional disparagement" of a product that results in "pecuniary damage," rather than injury to a person's character. Accordingly, the apple growers sought damages from CBS and the other defendants for losses incurred as a result of the broadcast.

The suit against the three television stations was dismissed because there was no evidence that the stations knew about the "defamatory character" of the program before airing it—a requirement for proving trade libel.[7] The suit against the NRDC and Fenton Communications was also dismissed because the NRDC's *Intolerable Risk* was a scientific study about a variety of carcinogens, not just daminozide or apples, addressed to government officials and scientists, not the general public, and therefore could not have caused damage to Washington apple growers.[8]

The case against CBS turned out to be as feeble as the cases against the television stations and the NRDC. The growers argued that *60 Minutes'* assertions that daminozide was a carcinogenic to humans was false and defamatory because it was based on tests of laboratory animals rather than humans, even though scientists routinely conduct laboratory tests on animals and generalize these to humans. The growers provided no other evidence challenging these scientific studies linking daminozide to cancer.

The growers also claimed that the assertion that children were at the greatest risk from daminozide exposure was false because no scientific studies had been conducted on children. However, they could not disprove that children consumed proportionately more apple products than adults or that children absorb into their bodies more of what they ingest than do adults. In effect, the growers had no evidence that the broadcast was false or defamatory. Because the burden of proof in trade libel cases is on the plaintiffs, who must prove not only "the falsity of the disparaging statements" but that the false statements were knowingly made, the suit against CBS was dismissed.[9]

The court decision demonstrated to agribusiness that it was vulnerable to environmentalist and mass media revelations about the safety of the food supply. Publicity about the potential hazards of chemicals, food-spread bacteria, and even the products themselves could negatively impact industry sales and profitability, but there was no recourse available against these revelations unless the industry could demonstrate "the falsity of the disparaging statements." Because court decisions placed the burden of proof on agribusinesses rather than environmentalists and the media, the industry began looking for ways to shift the burden of proof from themselves to potential defendants. By shifting the burden, the industry hoped to silence critics, who would have to prove their assertions or face legal sanctions, not the other way around.

One step taken by agribusiness in its effort to shift the burden of proof was to increase funding for, or establish new organizations and so-called think tanks such as the American Council on Science and Health that pose as neutral scientific organizations but exist in large part to discredit the research of environmental and health organizations. These organizations take the offensive against research that is profit-threatening, branding it as "hype" rather than science. After these think tanks have impugned the validity of research, agrifirms are in a stronger legal position to claim that research is "junk science" and therefore defamatory, something the Washington apple growers were unable to do.

Oftentimes these industry-funded groups work with public relations firms that publicize the groups' efforts to discredit research. For example, the Advancement of Sound Science Coalition (ASSC) is officed at APCO Associates, a Washington, D.C.–based public relations firm, that conducts "stealth campaigns" for its corporate clients.[10] The ASSC, which attacks much environmental and health research as "politically motivated," is funded by a variety of industry groups and corporation including Dow Chemical and Chevron. It has been especially vociferous in branding research about chemicals in the food supply as "junk science." By using front groups such as the ASSC, public relations firms and their clients give the appearance that others, not they, are responsible for the attacks.

An example of how the attack campaigns are conducted is provided by the American Council on Science and Health, the ASSC, and the American Crop Protection Association, which mounted a campaign to discredit *Our Stolen Future* by Dr. Theo Colborn of the World Wildlife Fund. The American Council branded the book, which linked chlorine-based synthetic chemicals with reproduction problems, as "innuendo on top of hypothesis on top of theory." The ASSC held a press conference denouncing the book as fiction, and American Crop Protection Association claimed the book indicted "modern society since World War II."[11]

Through campaigns such as these, agrifirms and allied industries, such as the chemical and biotech industries, have been successful in discrediting books addressing environmental, food, and health issues, keeping them out of bookstores and their authors off radio and television talk shows. *May All Be Fed*, a book advocating strict vegetarianism; *Diet for a Poisoned Plant*, a book about contaminants in the food chain; and *Beyond Beef*, a book about the environmental and health problems associated with beef, were undermined by behind-the-scenes, industry-sponsored public relations campaigns. The campaigns included calls to talk show producers cancelling scheduled interviews, campaigns to impugn the integrity of the authors, and enlisting government officials to criticize the books.[12]

The other, closely related approach to shift the burden of proof from agribusiness to activists and environmentalists has been to lobby for changes in laws, making it easier for agrifirms to win in court. As Emory University law professor David Bederman put it, agribusiness sought "to achieve by statute what had eluded them under the common law: the creation of a tailor-made cause of action for agricultural disparagement."[13]

With changes in laws shifting the burden of proof to speakers rather than industry, and with "think tanks" poised to discredit research about the dangers of food products, agribusiness concluded that it would be in a strong position to muzzle critics.

Changing the Burden of Proof

In 1992, the year that Washington apple growers saw their suit against the CBS affiliates and the NRDC dismissed, the American Feed Industry Association (AFIA), a Washington, D.C.–based lobby group for the livestock feed and pet food industries, which had been assailed by People for the Ethical Treatment of Animals (PETA) and other animal rights groups, asked the Washington law firm of Olsson, Frank & Weeda to draft a model statute on product disparagement that would make it easier for agrifirms and industries to sue critics like PETA.[14]

According to the AFIA, consumer confidence has been eroded by "animal rights activists and consumer activist 'food police,'" whom the industry needed to counter.[15]

The model statute was drawn up by Dennis Johnson, a member of the Olsson, Frank & Weeda law firm, who says he drafted the statute to protect small farmers and time-sensitive, perishable products. The food disparagement statutes are "aimed at protecting small farmers, who can spend a year growing a product, have only a window of a couple of weeks to market it, and then be left in the lurch if there's an unjustified food scare caused by some liar," says Johnson.[16]

This and similar statutes have been humorously referred to as "veggie libel laws," "banana bills," and "sirloin slander statutes," but their content and purpose aren't funny.

Of their model statute, AFIA spokesperson Steve Kopperud says, "Our model [statute] does not say though shalt not speak ill of meat, milk, and eggs. It says, if you are going to say it, you have every right to say it. If you do so in one of the states where there are some hoops to jump through, prove it."[17]

The "hoops" created by disparagement laws often include requiring critics to prove their statements, rather than requiring plaintiffs to demonstrate that the disputed statements are false. This is a clear shift in the burden of proof.[18]

As Kopperud's statement suggests, the statutes serve an invitation for agrifirms to sue critics, who can be bankrupted by defense costs, even when victorious in court. Conversely, the statutes permit agrifirms to pool their resources to sue a critic, cutting down legal costs for agrifirms, but leaving critics in the unenviable position of having to pay legal defense costs by themselves. Using the Washington State Alar lawsuit as an example, where 4,700 growers claimed to have been affected by the *60 Minutes* broadcast, the growers would have a legal war chest of $4.7 million if each grower contributed just $1,000 toward a legal fund. Even a large corporation like CBS would find a war chest of this size intimidating.

The AFIA 's model statute was distributed to farm lobby groups such as the American Farm Bureau Federation, which distributed it to state legislators and lobbied for its introduction. As the statute's author, Dennis Johnson, says, "They asked me to draft a model statute . . . . I built a product and [the AFIA] merchandised it."[19]

One of the first states to adopt a food disparagement statute was Washington's neighbor, Idaho, which like Washington, is the nation's largest producer of a single crop—potatoes. Because the Idaho statute was introduced early on—in 1992—and was critiqued by the state's attorney general before being adopted, it differs from statutes adopted later in other states.[20] The Idaho statute, called the "Disparagement of Agricultural Food Products," states that product disparagement occurs when a defendant "intended" the disparaging remarks "to cause harm to the plaintiff's pecuniary interest," and when the remarks were "made with actual malice, that is, he knew that the statement was false or acted in reckless disregard of its truth or falsity."[21] The statute allows the producer of "perishable agricultural food products who suffers actual damages" from disparagement to recover the actual damages, providing the producer can "prove that each element [or remark] by clear and convincing evidence" is false.[22] The act specifically places the burden of proof on agrifirms, and therefore merely restates the rulings of courts in past trade libel cases. For this reason, the statute represents far less of a threat to free speech than do other statutes, even though it was introduced specifically to promote the interests of agrifirms.

Statutes adopted subsequently shift the burden of proof from agrifirms to critics. The Georgia product disparagement statute, adopted in 1993 primarily at the urging of peach growers, asserts that it was adopted "to protect the vitality of the agricultural and aquacultural economy for the citizens of the state," thereby suggesting that the statute serves all citizens—including auto mechanics, writers, teachers, and environmental activists—not just peach growers.[23] The statute, which applies only to perishable products, describes disparagement as a willful "dissemination . . . of false information that a food product or commodity is not safe for human consumption." False information is defined as statements "not based on reasonable and reliable scientific inquiry, facts, or data," a clear shift in the burden of proof.[24] The statute places the burden of proof on speakers, who must demonstrate that their statements are based on "reliable" scientific research. Under the wording of the statute, a speaker may be held liable for accurate statements that are not backed up by sufficiently reliable scientific evidence. Under this statute, the Washington apple growers could conceivably have won in court, because neither CBS nor the NRDC had "reliable" scientific research demonstrating that daminozide produced cancer in children.

The Georgia statute also increased the liability for speakers, increasing damages from the "actual damages" stated in the Idaho statute, to "damages and for any other relief a court of competent jurisdiction deems appropriate, including but not limited to compensatory and punitive damages." Although allowing agrifirms to seek damages beyond those actually incurred as a result of the defamation, the statute does not provide defendants with any relief, even when victorious in court. The statute is a one-sided law, giving agrifirms a club that can be used to punish critics, who have been stripped of their traditional common law defenses.

Because the Georgia statute was shabbily written and one-sided, the American Civil Liberties Union challenged its constitutionality in 1995, but the suit was dismissed by the Georgia Court of Appeals because no one had yet been sued under it.[25]

Other Product Disparagement Statutes

Product disparagement statutes were introduced and quickly passed in several states, including North Dakota and Texas, after mass media reports about agricultural products and practices placed agrifirms on the defensive. Of the statutes, the one adopted in North Dakota is the most speech-deterring, allowing trade associations, in addition to actual agrifirms, to sue, and is directed at disparaging remarks about all agricultural goods and practices, not just perishable goods. The law also specifies "injunctive relief" as remedy for product defamation, allowing courts to prohibit critics from again leveling their charges against agrifirms.

As with the Georgia statute, it prohibits the dissemination of "false statements," which are defined as those "not based upon reasonable and reliable scientific inquiry, data, or facts." However, the statute covers any statement that expressly "includes a fact or implies a fact as justification for an opinion," making it much broader than Georgia's.[26] Under the law, agrifirms can presumably decide that certain expressed opinions imply facts, and sue on that basis.

Although the original justification for product disparagement laws was that false statements create huge losses for producers of perishable products, which decay and become worthless if not sold quickly, the wording of the North Dakota statute and a similar statute in South Dakota shows that they are designed to curb criticism of agribusiness, not just to protect perishable products. The statutes apply to livestock and agricultural practices, not just fruits and vegetables, and because the laws allow agricultural producers to win treble damages, they provide a monetary incentive for using—and abusing—the law.[27] Agrifirms filing suit under these statutes can win treble damages, but face no explicit penalties if they lose.

The fact that product disparagement laws were extended in North Dakota from perishable products to all agricultural products to agricultural practices reveals the dangers these statutes pose to free speech: Other industries, using these laws as a precedent, can demand that disparagement laws also be enacted to protect their products and practices. Chemical, pharmaceutical, energy, and a myriad of other industries can, like the North Dakota urine collectors discussed later in this chapter, claim that their industries' sales are hurt by disparaging remarks.

Finally, the statutes do not limit suits to false statements made in North Dakota or South Dakota or to losses incurred in these states, creating a labyrinth of possible suits. Under the law, agrifirms can sue for damages when statements are uttered in other states or for damages sustained in other states.

The labyrinthine potential of product disparagement laws is demonstrated by the much-publicized suit filed in Texas against talk show host Oprah Winfrey and Humane Society representative Howard Lyman. The suit alleged that a drop in beef prices on the Chicago commodities exchange was attributable to comments made on Oprah's Chicago-based talk show. The suit was based in part on Texas' "False Disparagement of Perishable Food Products" statute and an assortment of other common law defamation charges.

As in North Dakota, the bad publicity sustained by one of the state's agricultural products became a pretext for passing the Texas law. In this case, the bad publicity originated with the U.S. Centers for Disease Control in Atlanta, which issued a warning in 1991 that salmonella food poisoning was linked to Texas cantaloupe. The health advisory and media reports of it caused a boycott of cantaloupes and a $12 million loss for Texas cantaloupe growers. As it turned out, the salmonella was spread by food handlers, who used infected knives to slice the melons, not by the cantaloupes.[28]

Citing cantaloupe as an example of the damage caused to farmers by false food scares, Texas state representative Bob Turner, a rancher from Voss, Texas, introduced the product disparagement statute as House Bill 772 in 1995, which makes speakers liable for knowingly disseminating false information about a "perishable food product."[29] Like other food disparagement statutes, the burden of proof is placed on the speaker, who can be held liable if the statements are not "based on reasonable and reliable scientific inquiry, facts, or data."[30]

In introducing the legislation, Turner said that the law would hold the mass media responsible for disseminating false information. Turner claimed that he came up with the legislation himself, but the *San Antonio Express-News* reported that "several agricultural groups, including the Texas Farm Bureau, gave him information and research." *Texas Lawyer* reported that Turner was "backed by a handful of agricultural and livestock lobby groups."[31]

A nearly identical bill was introduced in the Texas state senate. After some debate, which included humorous amendments written by representatives Kevin Bailey and Harold Dutton, which exempted comedians with incomes under $17,000, French chefs, chefs with French-sounding accents, and former presidents, the bill passed.[32]

The Cattlemen's Beef

What precipitated the lawsuit against Oprah Winfrey, Howard Lyman, and Winfrey's production company was a sharp drop in beef commodity prices on April 16, 1996, the day the *Oprah Winfrey Show* titled "Dangerous Food" aired. But beef prices had been declining prior to the show, probably because of reports about the spread of mad cow disease in England, where the government was initially reluctant to admit that a fatal disease known as "new variant Creutzfeldt-Jakob Disease" was a form of bovine spongiform encephalopathy, spread by eating beef. The disease, which infects human and animal brains, was spread by cattle which had ingested "rendered" animal protein, a cheap source of animal feed created by recycling dead animal parts.[33]

Less than a month after the British government concluded that eating tainted beef was the cause of "new variant Creutzfeldt-Jakob Disease," former Montana rancher and executive director of the Humane Society's Eating with a Conscience Campaign, Howard Lyman, and guests representing the National Cattlemen's Beef Association and the U.S. Department of Agriculture appeared on the *Oprah Winfrey Show*. Lyman asserted that "one hundred thousand cows are fine at night, dead in the morning. The majority of those cows are rounded up, ground up, fed back to other cows. If only one of them had mad cow disease, it has the potential to infect thousands. Remember, today, in the United States, fourteen percent of all cows by volume are ground up, turned into feed and fed back to other animals."[34]

Lyman criticized the practice of feeding rendered animal parts to cows, saying, "We should have them eating grass, not other cows. We've not only turned them into carnivores, we've turned them into cannibals." Winfrey reponded, "Now, doesn't that concern you-all a little bit right there, hearing that? It has just stopped me from eating another burger. I'm stopped."

The representatives of the National Cattlemen's Beef Association and the U.S. Department of Agriculture countered Lyman's assertions about the potential perils of feeding rendered animal parts to cattle, but a segment of the Beef Association spokesperson's comments were edited out because, according to Winfrey, he was boring. Because of this and complaints from the beef industry that the program was one-sided, Winfrey allowed the beef industry to present an unedited rebuttal on a later program. (In June 1997, a year later, the U. S. D. A. banned the practice of using rendered cattle for cattle feed.[35])

After cattle prices plummeted on the Chicago Mercantile Exchange, beef ranchers blamed Lyman and Winfrey. They called the price drop the "Oprah Crash," complaining that her comments cost them millions of dollars. Paul Engler, owner of Cactus Feeders, which sells about $650 million worth of cattle yearly, and five other cattlemen filed suit against Winfrey and Lyman in Amarillo, Texas, claiming that the comments made during "Dangerous Food" cost them $10 million in losses.[36] The cattlemen based their suit in part on Texas's product disparagement statute, which creates liability for defaming "perishable food products," even though the alleged losses concerned 1,500-pound, cud-chewing steers, not die-on-the-vine fruits or vegetables.

The fall in beef prices was just one of the reasons for bringing the lawsuit, the *Texas Monthly* reported. According to the magazine, "Engler knew that if he won his lawsuit, he would be considered as one of the greatest cattlemen in Texas history, next to Charles Goodnight." However, instead of generating positive publicity for Engler and Texas cattlemen, the lawsuit turned into a public relations nightmare. Oprah went to Amarillo, taped her show there during the trial, and wooed residents, who lined up to get into the show. They paraded around the courthouse with posters and t-shirts reading, "Amarillo Loves Oprah."[37] Rather than "creating a groundswell of support for cattlemen, the industry's practices were being scrutinized more closely than ever by the media. . . . The *Dallas Morning News* received letters calling Engler and his supporters 'crybaby cowboys' and 'spoiled children,' " *Texas Monthly* reported.

Not only did the cattlemen lose the public relations war, but they also lost in court. After the cattlemen presented their case, U.S. District judge Mary Lou Robinson dismissed those portions of the suit based on the product disparagement statute, leaving only the harder-to-prove lawsuit under the common law.[38] Judge Robinson did not rule on the constitutionality of the food disparagement statute; she dismissed the suit because the plaintiffs failed to prove intent and because cattle are not perishable products. A week and a half later, the jury cleared Lyman, Winfrey, and her production company of the remaining charges.[39]

Although winning, the lawsuit was nevertheless costly for Oprah Winfrey. According to one attorney, her legal expenses amounted to over a half-million dollars.[40] The high costs of defending against these suits demonstrates why they function as deterrents to free speech—even winning can be extremely expensive.

The dismissal of the product disparagement suit against Winfrey did not eliminate the threat to free speech posed by the Texas product disparagement statute. It remains on the books, although several Texas lawmakers tried repealing the law in 1999. The repeal failed by a vote of 80–57.[41]

Despite the failure of the cattlemen's lawsuit, two even more far-fetched suits were filed claiming damages under the Texas product disparagment statute. One was filed by emu ranchers, the other by a grass farm. The emu lawsuit originated with a Honda automobile commercial that aired between September 1996 and August 1997 that featured a young man named "Joe," who drove his Honda Civic from one fictional job opportunity to another. One job was as a salesman at Big Al's Awning and Siding; another, unspecified job was with a man who insists, "Joe, let's not call it a pyramid scheme"; and yet another was with a toothless emu rancher at Fowl Technologies, who says, "Emu, Joe, it's the pork of the future." The commercial, produced by Honda's longtime advertising agency, Rubin Postaer & Associates, devoted less than six seconds to emus.[42]

"Basically, Honda made people stop and look at emu meat, emu products, and the emu business as a joke," said one emu rancher about the commercial. According to the ranchers and their attorneys, the price of an emu fell from $25,000 to $30,000 in the early 1990s to $1,000 or less in the late 1990s, and part of the drop was attributable to the Honda commercial. Ten emu ranchers filed suit under Texas's product disparagement act, seeking $75,000 each, saying that the commercial depicted emus "in a false light by depicting it as a scam whose properties are those of pork. When, in fact, emu is the antithesis of pork."[43] The suit was eventually dismissed, but not until Rubin Postaer & Associates dispatched a team of Chicago-based attorneys to Texas to defend itself and Honda.[44]

The other case arose from a report by state agricultural agent James McFee, who concluded that a type of sod sold by A-1 Turf Farms wasn't suited to some Texas soil. His conclusions were included in a 1996 state news release. A-1 Turf Farms sued for over a million dollars in damages. The suit was eventually dismissed because the courts concluded that McFee, as a state employee engaged in state business, was immune from prosecution.[45]

Other States: Other Statutes, Other Threats

In addition to Idaho, Georgia, North Dakota, South Dakota, and Texas, eight other states have adopted product disparagement laws, and in seventeen other states disparagement statutes were introduced but not adopted.[46] In some states where the statutes were beaten back by coalitions of civil liberties groups, media, environmentalists, and unions, they will in all likelihood be reintroduced because of continued lobbying by the state's agrifirms, which in the case of Iowa and California, constitute large and powerful lobby groups.[47]

The statutes of most states are fairly similar, shifting the burden of proof from the agricultural industry to the defendant. Ohio's "Disparagement of Perishable Agricultural or Aquacultural Food Product" defines "false information" as information "not based upon reasonable and reliable scientific inquiry, facts, or data."[48] Alabama's statute defines false information as that "not based upon reasonable and reliable scientific inquiry, facts, or data"; Arizona's statute defines false information as that "not based on reliable scientific facts and reliable scientific data"; and Oklahoma's statute defines false information as that "not based on reliable scientific facts and scientific data."

The Ohio statute was used by AgriGeneral, a corporate egg producer with seven million hens in central Ohio, to sue the Ohio Public Interest Research Group (PIRG) and its state director, Amy Simpson. Like the Texas cattlemen's suit, AgriGeneral's suit was filed by a huge company rather than by a small farmer, for whom model statute author Dennis Johnson said it was intended.

At a press conference, Simpson announced that PIRG and the Equal Justice Foundation were suing AgriGeneral because it took returned eggs with expired dates, mixed them in with new eggs, and then shipped them back to supermarkets. "We have no idea how many, if any, have been made ill from these eggs," Simpson said.[49] The PIRG's charges were based on the statements of twenty-five current and former AgriGeneral employees, who were ordered to mix the eggs together.[50]

The suit was part of an ongoing conflict between AgriGeneral and several groups over its labor and business practices, which included refusals to pay employees overtime and using underage workers.

AgriGeneral responded by filing a countersuit against PIRG under the Ohio product disparagement statute, claiming that PIRG "intended to cast doubt on the quality and safety of AgriGeneral's egg products." AgriGeneral president Duke Goranites said, "We will not tolerate false or misleading statements about our products."[51] AgriGeneral's attorney said that the suit was filed because "it's difficult to defend against sound bites." He added that the disparagement statute "at least balance[s] the scales a bit and make people more responsible before they make remarks."[52]

In reality, AgriGeneral's suit amounted to a SLAPP against PIRG using the product disparagement statute as subterfuge. The suit nevertheless dragged on for over a year. It ended soon after NBC's *Dateline* aired an episode that included a hidden camera and an AgriGeneral memo showing that dated eggs were repackaged, as PIRG had asserted. The hidden camera showed workers opening dated cartons, removing the eggs, and placing them on a conveyor belt for washing and repackaging. The company memo told employees to reprocess eggs up to 29 days old. When asked about the *Dateline* report by *Columbus Dispatch* reporter Brian Williams, the company's new president responded, "Even if they were doing what the memo says, they were doing everything within regulations," because federal regulations allow eggs up to 30 days old to be repackaged.[53] A few months later, the suit against PIRG was dropped.[54]

About the suit, Simpson said she considered it "a form of intimida-tion." She said, "I fear that suits like this will continue to be filed against people without the resources to defend against them. It's enormously time-consuming and a terrible psychological drain."[55]

The possibility of being sued, even falsely as PIRG and Simpson were, for product disparagement is apparently intimidating publishers and broadcasters, who fear that reports about pesticides, fertilizers, and even genetically altered products can open them up to lawsuits. The problem is particularly vexing to smaller publishers, which cannot afford to defend themselves against lawsuits. Vital Health Publishing of Bloomingdale, Illinois, was in the process of obtaining libel insurance and bringing out *Against the Grain: Biotechnology and the Corporate Takeover of Your Food*, when it received a letter from the Monsanto Corp., sent originally to Marc Lappe and Britt Bailey of the Center for Ethics and Toxics in North California, the book's authors. The book questioned the safety of genetically altered foods and the widespread used of pesticides. The letter, written by a cor-porate attorney, suggested that the book included false statements dis-paraging Monsanto's herbicide, Roundup. The letter was sent even though Monsanto apparently had never seen the manuscript, although they had seen an excerpt in *Coast* magazine, and the publisher's attorney had reviewed and approved the manuscript for publication. Monsanto's letter suggested that the publishing company could be held liable for damages under state product disparagement statutes if it published *Against the Grain*, which the publisher's attorney concluded could happen.

Because of the letter, Vital Health Publishing owner David Richard said he "was scared. As soon as I told my insurance agent about the letter, he would not return any of my calls." Monsanto's letter apparently stopped the insurance company from issuing a libel policy, so "I had no choice. I had to let the book go," said Richard.[56]

Monsanto asserts that it was not interested in killing the book but merely wanted the inaccuracies corrected. "We're respectful of differing points of view," said a company representative about the incident.

However, the book was eventually published by left-leaning Common Courage Press, which shrugged off Monsanto's threats.

According to J. Robert Hatherill, a research scientist at the University of California at Santa Barbara (UCSB) and author of *Eat to Beat Cancer*, Renaissance Books purged long passages about the dangers of foods such as dairy and meat products from his manuscript before publishing it. "The problem had nothing to do with whether there was sufficient evidence to support the claims —there is," reports Hatherill. "It came down to fear of litigation. I was told we could win the lawsuit, but it would cost us millions, and it's just not worth it." According to Hatherill, the mere existence of food disparagement laws "is forbidding. They can entangle one in costly litigation, regardless of who wins the suits."[57]

The speech-deterring effects of food libel laws are not restricted to book publishing. Actor Alec Baldwin attempted to interest "every major" television network, including the Discovery Channel, the History Channel, and public broadcasting stations, in a documentary, *The History of Food*, examining the political and economic determinants of food consumption. What Baldwin learned was that every producer was "intrigued by the ideas of the show. But all these outlets, they're like, 'Oh God! We can't do that because of the Oprah Winfrey lawsuit.' I mean, this is what I'm getting from the History Channel."[58]

The food industry is not just threatening critics with lawsuits to stifle debates about the safety of food products; some are also threatening to lobby for food disparagement laws in an effort to silence critics. In 1995, a representative of the food irradiation industry sent a copy of Florida's food disparagement statute to a representative of Hawaii's Department of Agriculture, suggesting that Hawaii should consider adopting a similar law. The suggestion was made because of protests against a food irradiation plant in Hawaii by Food & Water, an activist group, which said that irradiated foods could be unsafe.

Olsson, Frank & Weeda, the law firm that wrote the model food disparagement statute, also sent a letter to Food & Water on behalf of the

United Fresh Fruit and Agricultural Association, a lobby group representing Dole, Sunkist, and other producers. The letter ordered the group to end its campaign against irradiated food, writing, "As you are no doubt aware, nearly 30 state legislatures have passed or are considering legislation which codifies a cause of action against persons who disseminate false statements regarding agricultural products." The intimidating letter stated that "Food & Water could be subjecting itself to substantial liability."[59]

Food & Water continued its campaign, despite the letter. The group's executive director Michael Colby welcomed the threat, saying, "We'd love to show [in court] how ridiculous the FDA approval was for some of these things."[60]

Discussion

The introduction or adoption of product disparagement statutes in thirty of the fifty states serve as reminders that businesses and industries are often willing to put their profits before public welfare and the Constitution, and that politicians are willing to assist them in doing this. Through their lobbying campaign to shift the burden of proof from themselves to speakers, agribusinesses demonstrate that they are willing to risk the public health by silencing those who are wish to publicly debate the issues of pesticides, genetic engineering, and commonly used but nevertheless controversial methods of agricultural production.

Industry lobbyists claim that the statutes are intended to protect small farmers who produce perishable products, but the statutes and suits arising from them go far beyond these stated intentions. Large companies such as AgriGeneral and Cactus Feeders have been the most persistent and successful invokers of the statutes, not small farmers. Moreover, the statutes have been expanded in some states to protect nonperishable products and even agricultural practices, demonstrating that they are designed to protect industry from criticism, not perishable products from spoilage.

Proponents of product disparagement statutes also claim that they are only attempting to hold "liars" accountable for their statements, but the food disparagement statutes do something very different—they require speakers to present "reliable scientific evidence" to support their contentions, which is often difficult if not impossible to do. Scientific evidence is cumulative, not definitive; it is ever-changing and designed to be open and public One or even several scientific studies cannot be considered reliable (because reliability and replicability are often used as synonyms in science), and the conclusions drawn from even multiple studies are subject to change and revision based on subsequent research. For this reason, the reliability and validity of scientific evidence is best reserved for scientific journals, books, and the marketplace of ideas, not courtrooms, where judges and jurors become the arbiters of scientific reliability under the statutes, something they are ill-equipped to be. As the federal district court in the CBS-Washington State apple growers case observed, "The skills which go with law and lawyering do not readily lend themselves to critiquing [scientific] studies . . . ."[61] Despite this admission, the statutes intentionally shift scientific debate to the courtroom, where true debates cannot take place.

Had food disparagement statutes been used to sue the NRDC and CBS for the statements made in *Intolerable Risk* and "'A' Is for Apple," the Washington apple growers and even Uniroyal may well have triumphed in court because the NRDC and CBS had no direct "scientific data" demonstrating that daminozide posed a threat to children. Their conclusions were largely deductive. Although deductive, they nevertheless proved sufficient for the EPA to conclude that long-term ingestion of daminozide was hazardous, even if short-term ingestion wasn't, and therefore barred the chemical from use in the U.S.

Similarly, had food disparagement statutes been on the books in 1962 when Rachel Carson published *Silent Spring*, a book about the hazards posed by DDT, she too could have been dragged into court, sued, and probably have been silenced, because at the time there was little direct scientific evidence about the dangers of DDT. Much of the scientific evidence about DDT was published later.

Even when scientific evidence exists for statements, the food disparagement statutes and the suits that they spawn can serve as deterrents to publicizing the evidence, because speakers are forced to weigh the benefits of speaking against the costs of defending themselves in court, which can oftentimes be huge, as Oprah Winfrey's defense demonstrates. While Oprah Winfrey can afford to spend a half million or even a million dollars defending herself and her show, most people cannot. That is what the agricultural industry counts on when it lobbies for the passage of food disparagement laws. This is what the industry counts on when it sends out letters threatening activists, writers, and publishers with lawsuits based on the product disparagement statutes. The industry also counts on writers, publishers, and broadcasters censoring themselves out of fear of being sued, which is what Renaissance Books engaged in when it excised portions of J. Robert Hatherill's *Eat to Beat Cancer*.

Some product disparagement laws, such as the one adopted in North Dakota, were adopted with the specific purpose of silencing critics. One reason why the North Dakota statute was adopted was to curb criticisms of horse urine farmers by PETA activists. The statute requires speakers to present "reasonable and reliable scientific inquiry, data or facts" for any statement that expressly "includes a fact or implies a fact as justification for an opinion," even when scientifically-collected data are impossible to obtain.

The wording of the statute makes it very difficult for critics of agricultural practices to defend themselves. The example of the horse urine protests provides an example of how a group like PETA can be "hogtied" by the statute. PETA activists' statements about the treatment of horses are necessarily either deductive—based on the fact that urine collection requires pregnant horses to be kept nearly immobile—or are based on the unsystematic and unscientific observations of a few PETA members who have sneaked onto horse farms to observe the treatment of horses. (Because horse farms are private property, PETA activists can be, and have been, barred by owners from entering the farms.) However, the statute requires PETA to produce impossible-to-obtain evidence as their defense. Although PETA activists are barred by horse farmers from systematically studying the treatment of horses, keeping them from demonstrating that certain practices, such as keeping water from the horses, are done, the statute nevertheless requires the activists to affirmatively and systematically prove that the practice is done and is widespread. Clearly, the statute can punish speakers for making true statements that simply can't be proven or for making speculative statements that have yet to be tested.

It is hoped that these statutes will be quickly and decisively overturned in court, but even this is questionable, because agrifirms have a vested interest in keeping them on the books, even if no suits have been filed under them. By themselves, the statutes pose a threat of costly litigation, which can produces self-censorship, giving agrifirms a strong motivation for either not filing suits in cases where the constitutionality of the statutes will be challenged, as in the case of Food & Water, or dropping the suits before a court can rule on the constitutionality of the statutes, as was done in the suit against PIRG in Ohio. This strategy could keep the statutes around for another decade.

Another option is to lobby against the statutes when proposed in states that do not already have them, or to lobby for their repeal in states that have already adopted them. The former approach has proved successful when broad coalitions of labor, environmental, civil liberties, and consumer groups have worked and lobbied together against the proposed statutes. Clearly, a broad coalition that includes labor, consumer, and environmental groups is needed, not just to discourage the passage of food disparagement laws but to protect free speech rights in a society that is increasingly private.

The latter approach—lobbying for the repeal of already adopted food disparagement statutes—may prove to be futile, as the attempted repeal in Texas shows. In states where agrifirms have a major lobbying presence, they are also major contributors to political campaigns, giving them substantial clout with politicians. Only substantive campaign finance reform, such as public funding of campaigns, can reduce the political clout of these large campaign contributors.

Part III
PRIVATE PROPERTY, PUBLIC SILENCE

As corporate power increased during the last decades of the twentieth century and the power and size of organized labor ebbed, freedom of speech also ebbed. In 1946, a year of unprecedented labor strikes and union activism, Justice Hugo Black wrote in *Marsh v. Alabama* that "the more an owner, for his advantage, opens up his property for use by the public in general, the more do his rights become circumscribed by the statutory and constitutional rights of those who use it."[1] In that landmark case, the Supreme Court concluded that free speech trumped property rights when the public was invited onto property by an owner. To a great degree, the court decision reflected the power of organized labor, whose ideas shaped American thinking during that era, including the thinking of the Supreme Court.

In 1968, when over 30 percent of private sector employees were union members, down from a peak of 37 percent in 1960, the Supreme Court reaffirmed the right of the public to exercise free speech rights on private property open "for use by the public." In *Food Employees Union Local 590 v. Logan Valley Plaza, Inc.*, the Supreme Court concluded that shopping malls and company towns, the focus of *Marsh v. Alabama*, were functional equivalents, and that union organizers had a right to be, and to speak, on shopping center property. The decision dramatically extended free speech rights.

Knowing that property, not knowledge, is power, business owners were not about to let these court decisions stand. Claiming that the *Marsh* and

Logan Valley decisions undermined their Fifth and Fourteenth Amendment rights, owners of shopping centers, malls, and other businesses repeatedly challenged the rights of citizens to speak on their property. Their argument was that the Supreme Court decisions had deprived them of their property rights. Of course, the owners still owned their properties, generated incomes from them, and could sell the properties at any time, so they were actually never deprived any property rights. However, the owners could not censor speech on their properties, something they sought to do.

In 1976, after union membership had dropped to around one-fourth of the private sector work force, the Supreme Court, by then dominated by pro-business Nixon appointees, finally reversed *Marsh* and *Logan Valley* in *Hudgens v. National Labor Relations Board*. That decision limited the rights of union organizers to picket on shopping center property. *Hudgens* and an earlier decision, *Lloyd Corp. v. Tanner,* effectively ended First Amendment protection for speech at malls and other business centers. As a consequence of these decisions, shoppers entering malls today leave their First Amendment rights outside.

The decisions have also made it difficult for unions to boycott, picket, and organize, a goal long sought by anti-union businesses. These restrictions on labor's right to speak have led to an erosion of labor union membership. Today, only 9 percent of private sector employees are union members. In contrast, over 25 percent of public sector employees are in unions. The difference in membership is due in part to the freedom to speak and organize on public property, and the barriers to speech on private property.

Chapter 6 analyzes the court decisions that have expanded and contracted free speech rights in malls. The chapter suggests that the battle for free speech is to be fought within states, which can extend protections to citizens that are not granted by the U.S. Bill of Rights. Although citizens in most states are deprived of their right to speak in malls and shopping centers, some citizens are also deprived of their right to publicly speak in their neighborhoods. The speech of residents in planned housing developments is often curtailed by deed restrictions and housing association rules that ban the display of yard signs, door-to-door solicitation, and even the collecting of signatures on petitions at commonly owned properties, such as golf courses and lakefronts. These restrictions on residential properties are discussed in chapter 7.

Although chapter 7 focuses on deed restrictions in residential areas, readers should be aware that restrictive covenants are used by businesses in a variety of ways to curb speech and economic competition. An example of how restrictive covenants are used by businesses is provided by the Marcus Corp., a real estate and entertainment corporation in the Midwest. Among other properties, the corporation owns and operates more than 160 Baymont Inns, 30 Kentucky Fried Chicken franchises, and over 400 theater screens, most of which are in multiplex theaters located in malls and shopping centers.

In 1996, the Marcus Corp. dumped an unprofitable, 173-seat, single-screen theater in Wauwatosa, a Milwaukee suburb, but placed a restriction in the theater's deed prohibiting the new owner from showing "first-run" films. The deed was designed to curb competition, although the competition presented to the Marcus Corp. theater chain by a small, single-screen neighborhood theater was negligible. In addition to curbing competition, the deed restriction also impinged on the theater operator's freedom to screen films. This is a free speech issue, not just an issue of business competition, because the Supreme Court has ruled that films are a form of expression that merit First Amendment protection.

The purchaser of the Wauwatosa theater went bankrupt in 1996, and the theater was eventually purchased by Jay Hollis at a sheriff's auction in 1999. Hollis refurbished the theater, replacing its seats with sofas and tables, and he received a license from the city allowing beer and wine to be sold at the theater during screenings. Hollis started exhibiting first-run, independent "art house" movies, such as *American Movie*, *Pollock*, and *Shadow of the Vampire*—films that received only limited screenings at Marcus Corp. theaters. Marcus, like other large theater chains, shows mass appeal, star-studded features, not limited appeal art house films.

The Marcus Corp., through its B&G Realty subsidiary, nevertheless sued Hollis, claiming that the art house screenings violated the restrictions it had placed in the theater's deed. The corporation sought an injunction from the court, prohibiting Hollis from screening any first-run films. In a small victory for the "little guy" and free speech, the judge refused to issue an injunction before the suit went to trial.[2]

In addition to restrictive covenants, the Marcus Corp. suit raises another free speech issue that is addressed in greater detail in chapter 8: the dominance of nearly all forms of mass communications by large corporations. When large corporations dominate the mass media, as is the case today in book publishing, television, and motion pictures, there are very few independent distribution outlets available to small producers, publishers, and filmmakers. At present, there are only one or two theaters in most metropolitan areas that exhibit independent films. If a corporation like Marcus, claiming deed restrictions or any other excuse, can shut one down, it drastically reduces the venues available for independent film exhibition. If the Marcus Corp. wins in court, independent filmmakers and their audiences will be the biggest losers. They face having yet another forum for independent expression closed down.

6

Freedom to Buy, Not Speak

Like other malls, Bayshore Mall in north suburban Milwaukee is filled with placards, posters, and advertising leaflets. A placard at The Athlete's Foot seemingly implores shoppers to exercise, declaring "Get Fit (Wear It)." At Rocky Rococo's pizza parlor, a red, white, and blue poster with a presidential flair declares, "Rococo '00—The Heavyweight of Candidates." In the mall's center, a triangular sign suggests that readers "Take a Stand!" The fine print states that the mall will lease to aspiring entrepreneurs specialty carts for selling soap, candles, jewelry, or other small items "on a short- or long-term basis." At the Lady Foot Locker, a poster announces "30% to 50% off selected items." At first glance, it appears that the free marketplace of ideas is alive and well at the mall.

Events at Bayshore Mall on the afternoon of December 23, 1995, however, reveal the real nature of free speech there. That day, twenty-three members of the Wisconsin Fair Trade Campaign entered the mall to urge consumers not to buy apparel made in foreign sweatshops. They leafleted near The Gap clothing store, and some leafleted near The Foot Locker store. The mall's security staff quickly called the police, then approached the leafletters, told them to stop leafletting, and demanded that they hand over their leaflets. A few of the protesters surrendered their leaflets. Others refused but nevertheless exited the mall.

The only African-American leafletter among the group, Ural Campbell, refused to surrender his leaflets as he left the building. The police entered the parking lot and noticed Campbell outside the mall building but still on mall property. Approaching Campell, they ordered him to surrender his leaflets. When he refused, Campbell was handcuffed and arrested for trespassing.

Of his arrest, Campbell said, "I've done this before and I know how to act. . . . It was just harassment and intimidation on their part." He described his arrest as a product of his being black. "They see every black as a troublemaker," he said.[1]

A mall spokesperson denied any racism in Campbell's arrest, adding that she felt "badly about this because we have a good public access policy."

Within days, Campbell's arrest became the focus of newspaper opinion articles, radio talk shows, and news stories emphasizing the role that race played in Campbell's arrest. The media coverage embarrassed the police, the prosecutor, and the mall. As a result, the charges against Campbell were dropped.[2]

The following year, ex-appellate court judge R. Eugene Pincham, an African-American and independent candidate for state attorney general, was distributing leaflets in the parking lot of the Old Orchard Mall in Skokie, Illinois, an older suburb of Chicago, when police and mall security guards threatened him with arrest if he did not leave. Although tempted to defy the order to leave, Pincham left, later saying that he "didn't want to create an incident." The former judge called the threat of arrest "an unconstitutional interference of my rights of free speech," adding that the mall was "a public space because the public has free access."[3]

On April 18, 1998, twenty-five activists associated with the American Friends Service Committee, a pacifist religious group, entered the 800,000-square-foot Mall of New Hampshire to educate shoppers about foreign sweatshops. They passed out leaflets describing the inhumane working conditions in Third World clothing and shoe factories. By disseminating their political views in the mall, the Quaker-led protestors were merely doing what Republican candidates Lamar Alexander and Steve Forbes did during the during their unsuccessful 1996 presidential bids, and mayoral candidate Raymond Wieczorek did in 1997.

Manchester police, called by mall management, viewed it differently. They ordered the leafletters to leave. When eight who were leafleting near the Foot Locker outlet refused, they were arrested for trespassing. The arrestees became known as the "Foot Locker Eight."[4]

Defending the arrest, Nancy Sterling, spokesperson for the Wells Park Group, which owned the mall, stated, "We can prevent political leafleting and we do not allow it." When asked why the mall allowed Lamar Alexander and Steve Forbes to campaign there in 1996, Ms. Sterling asserted that they merely came to the mall to eat and shop, not stump for votes. Arnold Albert, one of the Foot Locker Eight, disputed Ms. Sterling's implausible explanation, stating "Steve Forbes wasn't there shopping. He was doing what politicians do. And he went there, to the mall, because that's where the people are—which is the same reason why we went there."[5]

Albert was correct in saying that people are now found in malls. Approximately 70 percent of the U.S. adult population shops at malls during any given week. And malls now account for more than half of nonautomotive retail sales.

In most states, mall owners pick and choose whom they will allow to speak, leaflet, or set up tables. At Bayshore Mall, which claims to have "a good public access policy," the mall has no written policy on access and decisions are made on a case-by-case basis, with Corrigan Properties, Inc., the mall's manager, serving as the sole arbiter of speech. In effect, the First Amendment at this Wisconsin shopping center has been replaced by corporate decision-making. The marketplace is alive in the mall, but the marketplace of ideas is not.

Malled America

In *Marsh v. Alabama*, the U.S. Supreme Court overturned the 1945 trespass conviction of a Jehovah's Witness for distributing religious literature on the sidewalks of Chickasaw, a company-owned town near Mobile, Alabama. The Court concluded that if Chickasaw had been a traditional municipality, rather than one owned by the Gulf Shipping Corporation, citizens would unquestionably have had a First Amendment right to distribute literature on the sidewalks. Because "residents use[d] the business block as their regular shopping center" and because "its shopping districts [we]re accessible to and freely used by the public in general," the Court reasoned that the property functioned as public property, and that the public therefore had First Amendment rights there, too. The Court also stressed that private property rights were limited and did not provide for "absolute dominion. The more an owner, for his advantage, opens up his property for use by the public in general, the more do his rights become circumscribed by the statutory and constitutional rights of those who use it," the Court concluded.[6]

The *Marsh* decision affected judicial thinking about malls and shopping centers until the 1970s, even though malls and shopping centers did not even exist in 1946 when the Supreme Court reached its decision.

In 1946, the outlying suburbs (or exurbs) of large cities and the suburban "cities" of the Sunbelt that gave rise to the modern, private shopping center and mall, were yet to develop. The Milwaukee suburbs of Glendale and Brookfield, where Bayshore Mall and Brookfield Square Mall are today found, did not exist. They were unincorporated rural areas until 1950 and 1957.[7] Phoenix, San Jose, Albuquerque, and Las Vegas, which in 1998 had combined populations of nearly 3 million, had combined populations of 323,509 in 1950.[8] These Sunbelt "cities" and exurbs, with their dispersed populations, developed enclosed malls and strip malls as they expanded, rather than developing downtown shopping districts.

By 1950, there were still fewer than 100 privately owned shopping centers of any size in the United States.[9] By 1960, there were 3,000, and by the late 1980s, there were over 30,000. Today, there are over 40,000 privately owned shopping centers.[10]

The retailing and real estate industries classify shopping centers by their size, store numbers, and service areas. Regional shopping centers, which range in size from 300,000 to more than a million square feet, are built around one or more large department stores and sell a full array of merchandise, apparel, and home furnishings. They are typically described as "enclosed malls" and attract shoppers from outside the immediate community. Community shopping centers lack the variety of merchandise sold by, and are smaller than, regional malls. They are built around a variety or discount store such as Kmart, and usually include a supermarket and specialty stores. They range in size from 100,000 to 300,000 square feet. Smaller than these are strip malls, which lack either the anchoring discount store or the speciality shops.[11]

As the exurbs and suburban cities expanded, the older cities and their downtowns contracted. Minneapolis, which had a population of 521,718 in 1950, had a population of 351,731 in 1998. Washington, D.C., which had 802,108 residents in 1950, had 523,124 residents in 1998.[12] In these and other cities, the population declines were caused by the exodus to exurbs and to the Sunbelt. Southdale Mall, the first, fully-enclosed, climate-controlled mall built in the United States in 1956, is in the Minneapolis suburb of Edina. Columbia, Maryland, one of the largest planned suburban communities, complete with privately owned shopping centers, was built outside of Washington, D.C. in the 1960s.

As the suburbs and their malls developed, cities attempted to lure shoppers and residents back by building urban malls, such as the City Center Mall in Minneapolis and the Grand Avenue Mall in Milwaukee. Because city-based malls were just another gamble to lure residents and shoppers back, cities often provided these malls with public subsidies. The city of Milwaukee donated a public street to the Grand Avenue Mall project, floated $10 million in city bonds, and created a special tax district to help subsidize its building and operation.[13] Although built in the 1980s, the mall was still receiving subsidies two decades later. To keep the mall open and solvent, the state of Wisconsin in 2001 offered the mall $4.7 million in tax credits, a $1 million forgivable loan, and a $250,000 environmental cleanup grant.[14]

Milwaukee wasn't the only city providing subsidies for downtown retail developments. A survey of U.S. cities found that public subsidies to retail developments amounted to one-third the cost of the projects during the 1980s, and the percentage has risen since then.[15] However, subsidies are not restricted to urban malls. The Mall of America in the Minneapolis suburb of Bloomington, the largest mall in the United States, received public subsidies. The Bloomington Port Authority and the city of Bloomington issued nearly $200 million in bonds to finance street, walkway, and highway construction around the mall. Thus, between 20 and 30 percent of total development costs came from public monies, although the Mall of America Corp. was obligated to eventually repay these costs.[16]

Malls also receive many indirect public subsidies. A survey of malls found that over half have municipal police located on-site in stations or substations, and nearly 40 percent have postal stations. Many house other government offices, including armed forces recuiters, city and state officials, and even a congressional representative.[17] Most malls also have public buses routed to them, which is another indirect public subsidy.

With their array of retail shops, restaurants, government services, and public subsidies, malls appear to be the functional equivalent of town squares, an idea that the mall industry encourages. "In the regional mall business, the idea of serving as the town square has been foremost in our minds," says Bob Sorenson of the Hahn Corp., a mall builder.[18]

Although they invite the public to enter, browse, and even exercise; accept public subsidies; and claim to be town squares, mall owners nevertheless claim that malls are private property, where free speech can be curtailed. Mall owners have vigorously fought off efforts by community groups seeking to open common areas of malls to free speech, and mall owners have generously lobbied lawmakers to kill proposed legislation that would open up malls to free speech.

Federal Court Fights

Two decades after deciding *Marsh*, the Supreme Court finally considered whether the principles enunciated in that decision applied to privately owned shopping centers rather than just company towns, which by the 1960s had nearly vanished from the American landscape. The high court initially concluded that the *Marsh* standards indeed prevailed in shopping center cases, but an increasingly conservative Supreme Court revisited and then reversed the earlier decision, finally declaring malls to be private property rather than the functional equivalent of public property.[19] The conservative justices refused to admit that public subsidies, the presence of government offices, and even the granting of police powers to many malls constituted "state action."

The first case to reach the Supreme Court involved Logan Valley Plaza near Altoona, Pennsylvania. The mall was situated at the intersection of a heavily traveled highway and a boulevard, but the mall itself was separated from public thoroughfares by 12- to 15-foot-wide earthen berms. In early December 1965, a Sears department store and a Weis Supermarket opened for business in the newly built mall, with Weis employing non-union employees. Just a week after the Weis market opened, members of the Amalgamated Food Employees Union Local 590 began picketing the store from the parking lot and parcel pickup area with signs stating that Weis employees were not "receiving union wages or other benefits."[20]

The picketing was peaceful, but Logan Valley Plaza, Inc., the mall's owner, and Weis Markets nevertheless sought and obtained an injunction from the county court prohibiting the union from picketing on mall property, including the parking lot and "all entrances and exits leading to said parking area."[21] On appeal, the Pennsylvania Supreme Court affirmed the injunction. The court rejected the union's claim that its members had a First Amendment right to picket on mall property, concluding instead that the picketers were trespassing.

The union appealed these decisions, and the case reached the U. S. Supreme Court in 1967. In *Amalgamated Food Employees Union Local 590 v. Logan Valley Plaza, Inc.*, the Supreme Court reversed the Pennsylvania court decisions by a 6–3 margin, holding that the union had a First Amendment right to picket in Logan Valley Plaza.[22] The Court majority concluded that the "similarities between the business block in *Marsh* and the shopping center in the present case are striking," observing that the roadways and parking lots "within the mall and the sidewalks leading from building to building are the functional equivalents of the streets and sidewalks of a normal municipal business district." For that reason, the court found no reason why access to the business district of a company town was constitutionally protected, but access to property functioning as a business district was not. Quoting *Marsh*, the court concluded that the union members had a First Amendment right to picket in front of the Weis supermarket.

The Court decision left open the question whether picketing and leafleting for other purposes, such as political campaigning, would be protected in malls by the First Amendment. The Court wrote, "All we decide here is that because the shopping center serves as the community business block and is freely accessible and open to the people in the area and those passing through, the State may not delegate the power, through the use of its trespass laws, wholly to exclude those members of the public wishing to exercise their First Amendment rights on the premises in a manner and for a purpose generally consonant with the use to which the property is actually put."[23]

In ruling that Local 590 members had a First Amendment right to peacefully picket in front of the Weis supermarket, Justice Marshall stressed that the picketers would likely not reach their intended audience—Weis supermarket shoppers—if they had to stand on the berms surrounding Logan Valley Mall, the nearest public property, where passing motorists would have great difficulty reading the picketers' placards and could not easily stop to receive leaflets from the picketers.[24]

Justice Marshall also observed that private shopping centers in the United States and Canada accounted for 37 percent of retail sales. He concluded "businesses situated in the suburb[an malls] could largely immunize themselves from . . . criticism by creating a *cordon sanitaire* of parking lots around their stores," if picketing and protests were prohibited on mall property. Marshall warned of some of the possible dangers that could result from limiting free speech in malls: substandard working conditions and pay for mall employees, shoddy merchandise for shoppers, and even discrimination against minorities. Without a right to picket stores at shopping centers, it would be difficult to oppose such malevolent business practices.

Justices Hugo Black, John Harlan, and Byron White dissented. Quoting the Fifth Amendment's prohibition against taking private property "for public use, without just compensation," Black concluded that the majority's decision unconstitutionally deprived Weis Markets, Inc., of their property rights. Contentiously, Black wrote:

> If this Court is going to arrogate to itself the power to act as the Government agent to take part of Weis's property to give to the pickets for their use, the Court should also award Weis just compensation for the property taken.[25]

The fallacy of Black's argument, of course, is that Weis Markets' property was never taken without compensation: Weis continued to own the property, could operate the market with non-union employees, and could even sell the property whenever it wished.

Justice White concluded that the public is invited to malls for one purpose only—to shop—and that there is no invitation for other purposes. White wrote that the "public is invited to [shopping centers], but only in order to do business with those who maintain business establishments there. The invitation is to shop for products that are sold." Because of this limited invitation, White conclude that shopping centers were not the same as company towns.[26]

Although they were a dissenting minority in *Logan Valley*, Black's and White's arguments were used by a more conservative Supreme Court a few years later to conclude that shopping malls are purely private property, allowing mall owners to prohibit speech on their property.

Even though *Logan* addressed the narrow issue of union picketing in a private shopping center, it had a wider impact on speech in malls. In California, the state supreme court relied heavily on *Logan Valley* when it decided *Diamond v. Bland* in 1970. In that case, the People's Lobby, a nonprofit environmental group, was denied permission to collect signatures on two antipollution ballot initiatives by Inland Center in San Bernadino. Inland Center, an enclosed mall with three department stores and seventy other retail outlets, threatened members of the People's Lobby with arrest if they collected signatures in the mall or on the mall-owned sidewalks outside. After being expelled from the mall, the People's Lobby sued. The case reached the California Supreme Court, which concluded:

> *Logan* [*Valley*] is persuasive authority for the proposition that the right toengage in peaceful and orderly First Amendment activities on the premises of shopping centers should be protected.... The implication is clear from *Logan* that modern-day shopping centers, serving as the business districts for the surrounding residential communities, have important public functions, and they may not rely on their private ownership to justify blanket prohibitions on First Amendment activities that could lawfully be conducted on public property.[27]

The California Supreme Court therefore ordered Inland Center to allow the signature gathering on its property.

The U.S. Supreme Court addressed the issue of free speech in shopping centers again in *Lloyd Corp. v. Tanner*. By 1972, when the case was decided, there were four new justices on the Supreme Court—Harry Blackmun, Warren Burger, Lewis Powell, and William Rehnquist—all of whom were appointed by President Richard Nixon.[28] Like the president who appointed them, the new justices were political conservatives who were less inclined to protect speech than property.[29]

Lloyd Corp. v. Tanner addressed the rights of anti-Vietnam war activists to distribute leaflets in a multi level, fifty-acre mall in downtown Portland, Oregon, of which thirty acres were devoted to retail stores and twenty acres to parking. Like most malls, Lloyd Center was bordered by public streets and sidewalks, but most retail stores were accessible only from the mall's interior walkways. The Lloyd Center permitted speakers to deliver addresses about the valor of U.S. soldiers on Veterans Day, allowed presidential candidates to speak in the mall's auditorium, and even permitted the right-wing American Legion to solicit monies inside the mall. Despite these and other activities, the Lloyd Corporation, which owned the mall, claimed that it was off-limits to political activity. To buttress its claim, the Lloyd Corp. had imbedded in several places in the mall's sidewalk the following statement:

> Areas in Lloyd Center Used By The Public Are Not Public Ways But Are For The Use of Lloyd Center Tenants And The Public Transacting Business With Them. Permission To Use Said Areas May Be Revoked At Any Time.[30]

On November 14, 1968, a handful of antiwar protesters entered the mall and distributed leaflets announcing an antiwar protest. Security guards approached the leafletteers and asked them to leave, threatening them with arrest if they did not. Wishing to avoid arrest, the leafletteers left, but subsequently filed a federal lawsuit challenging the mall's action.

The Federal District Court ruled in the activists' favor. Citing *Marsh* and *Logan Valley* as precedents, the court concluded that the mall was "open to the general public" and was "the functional equivalent of a public business district."[31]

The court of appeals affirmed the district court decision, but the Supreme Court reversed it.[32] By a narrow 5–4 decision, with all four Nixon appointees voting with the majority, the court decided to narrowly interpret *Marsh* and *Logan Valley*.

The new majority suggested that *Marsh* and the company towns it described were "anachronism[s] long prevalent in some southern states and now rarely found." As for *Logan Valley*, the Court stressed that it was limited to activities related to the shopping center's purpose. In this case, the court concluded, "the handbilling . . . in the malls of Lloyd Center had no relation to any purpose for which the center was built and being used." Finally, the majority noted that the antiwar activists had the opportunity to distribute their messages elsewhere, whereas the union picketers at Logan Valley Center needed to assemble there, and only there. Consequently, the Court reversed the appellate and district court decisions.[33]

The majority decision also deferentially quoted Justice Black's and White's dissents in *Logan Valley*. They quoted Black's dissenting opinion that company-owned towns and shopping centers were not functional equivalents, and White's conclusions that shopping centers extended a limited invitation to the public to "come in and shop."[34]

In a dissent joined by Justices Douglas, Brennan, and Stewart, Justice Marshall criticized the new majority for its refusal to admit that Lloyd Center was dedicated to public use and that government was involved in that dedication. To support his claim, Marshall pointed out that mall security "guards wore uniforms that were virtually identical to those worn by regular Portland police" and had been "given full police power by the city of Portland, even though they are hired, fired, controlled, and paid by the owners of the Center." Marshall also observed that the city vacated about eight acres of public streets, allowing the Center to be built, and that the city made it clear that the streets were vacated for "the development of a general retail business district." From this, Marshall concluded that "it is plain, therefore, that Lloyd Center is the equivalent of a public 'business district' within the meaning of *Marsh* and *Logan Valley*."[35]

Justice Marshall admonished the new majority for not realizing that cities encouraged mall development and other forms of privatization:

> It would not be surprising in the future to see cities rely more and more on private businesses to perform functions once performed by governmental agencies . . . . As governments rely on private enterprise, public property decreases in favor of privately owned property. It becomes harder and harder for citizens to find effective means to communicate with other citizens. Only the wealthy may find effective communication possible unless we adhere to [Marsh] and continue to hold that "[t]he more an owner, for his advantage, opens up his property for use by the public in general, the more do his rights become circumscribed by the statutory and constitutional rights of those who use it."[36]

Marshall's conclusions were prophetic: Many cities and municipalities have turned to private entities to perform functions once performed by government agencies. In Milwaukee County, for example, private companies oversee welfare-to-work programs, operate museums, and build and operate centers in public parks. In the city of Milwaukee, private schools receive taxpayer dollars for educating children. This privatization of the public sphere has substantially reduced the space available for public speech.

Based on the U.S. Supreme Court's decision in *Lloyd Corp. v. Tanner*, the California Supreme Court reversed its original ruling in *Diamond v. Bland*. The California court concluded that "Lloyd's rationale is controlling here," so that property rights of mall owners "outweigh" the First Amendment rights of ordinary citizens.[37]

Four years after the *Lloyd* decision, the Supreme Court overruled *Logan Valley* in *Hudgens v. National Labor Relations Board*, concluding that "the reasoning of the Court's opinion in *Lloyd* cannot be squared with the reasoning of the Court's opinion in *Logan Valley*."[38] The *Hudgens* case arose when striking Butler Shoe warehouse employees in Atlanta decided to picket Butler retail stores, including one located at the North DeKalb Shopping Center, an enclosed mall housing sixty retail shops. When the striking warehouse employees entered the North DeKalb Shopping Center in suburban Atlanta, they were threatened with arrest.

The strikers' union filed an unfair labor practice complaint with National Labor Relations Board (NLRB) against Scott Hudgens, owner of the shopping center, for threatening the picketers with arrest. Basing their decision in part on *Logan Valley*, the NLRB found that Hudgens had indeed committed an unfair labor practice. However, by a 6–3 vote, the Supreme Court overturned the NLRB's order.

Justice Stewart, who was aligned with Justice Marshall in *Lloyd* and *Logan Valley*, joined the Nixon appointees, and wrote the majority opinion. The majority opinion admitted that *Lloyd Corp. v. Tanner* had not expressly overruled *Logan Valley*, but made it clear that was happening here. The majority opinion stated that "we make it clear now, if it was not clear before, that the rationale for Logan Valley did not survive the Court's decision in the Lloyd case."[39] Having overruled *Logan Valley*, the Court thereby held that there was no First Amendment right of free speech in private shopping centers.[40] The decision showed how important political ideology, rather than legal precedent, is in Supreme Court decisions.

Beyond the Federal Morass

Because the First Amendment is negatively expressed, stating that "Congress shall make no law . . . abridging the freedom of speech," the Supreme Court intrepreted it to ban governmental, but not private, restrictions on speech, allowing malls and shopping centers to develop their own policies on public speech. By contrast, the free speech provisions of most state constitutions are positively expressed, leaving some hope after the Supreme Court's ruling in *Hudgen* that state constitutions might extend free speech to privately owned shopping centers and malls. For example, the Washington State constitution declares that "every person may freely speak, write and publish on all subjects, being responsible for the abuses of that right."[41] A bit more expansive, the California constitution declares that "[e]very person may freely speak, write, and publish his or her sentiments on all subjects, being responsible for the abuse of this right. A law may not restrain or abridge liberty of speech or press."[42] Overall, 43 states have positively worded constitutional speech guarantees that are linguistically similar to those of Washington and California.[43]

Despite the positive wordings of these state constitutions, the highest courts in most states have failed to interpret them more broadly than the U.S. Constitution. The high courts of just three states have interpreted their constitutions as protecting speech in privately owned shopping centers, whereas the courts of 13 states have concluded that their constitutions provide protections against state action only. Massachusetts, Oregon, and Washington have concluded that parts of their state constitutions allow signature gathering on petitions at shopping centers, but not other expressive activities. The variation in interpretations of similarly worded state constitutions shows the latitude that courts have in fashioning policy—and the degree to which ideology determines fashion.

The California Decision. California, famous for being an early adopter, permissive and fashionably chic, was the first state to examine the extent to which their state constitution guarantees speech rights in malls. The California Supreme Court was given the opportunity to examine the boundaries of the state's constitutional speech guarantees in 1979, after a group of high school students set up a table in the Pruneyard Shopping Center, a sixteen-acre enclosed mall, and began to solicit signatures on a petition opposing a United Nations resolution against "Zionism." As often occurs, the signature gatherers were ordered to leave. Like most activists, they complied. However, unlike most activists, they sued the mall, claiming the ban on petitioning violated the state constitution's free speech guarantees.

In *Robins v. Pruneyard Shopping Center,* the California Supreme Court by a 4–3 vote concluded that the students had a right under the California constitution to solicit signatures in the mall.[44] Writing for the majority, Justice Frank Newman rejected the mall's claim that the U.S. Supreme Court's *Lloyd* decision gave shopping center owners federally protected property rights. Newman observed that, to the contrary, the Supreme Court had clearly stated in *Hudgens* that "statutory or common law may in some situations extend protection or provide redress against a private corporation or person who seeks to abridge the free expression of others." He also observed that if property rights were federally protected, this "would flout the whole development of law regarding states' power to regulate uses of property . . . . All private property is held subject to the power of the government to regulate its use for the public welfare."[45]

Newman admitted that the court, four years earlier in *Diamond v. Bland II*, had declined to recognize free speech rights in private shopping centers, but noted that the *Diamond* decision had not considered the California constitution's free speech clause.

In upholding the students' right to collect signatures, the California Supreme Court stressed that a ban on expressive activity in malls would not only abridge speech but the right to "petition government for the redress of grievances" through "initiative, referendum, and recall," all of which require large numbers of signatures.[46] (The Massachusetts Supreme Court also decided in favor of petitioning in malls for the same reason.)

Pruneyard Shopping Center, hoping to reverse the California Supreme Court's decision, appealed to the U.S. Supreme Court, believing that the more conservative U.S. Supreme Court justices would rule in their behalf. The owners of Pruneyard—and may other Court observers—were surprised by the decision. By a 9–0 vote, the U.S. Supreme Court upheld the California decision. Writing for the majority, Justice Rehnquist rejected the mall's claim that *Lloyd* barred the California Supreme Court from recognizing a right of free speech in private shopping centers. Rehnquist also rejected Pruneyard Shopping Center's claim that the California Supreme Court unconstitutionally infringed on its property rights, concluding that there was nothing to suggest that signature gathering from a table in the mall courtyard diminished the value of the property. Finally, he rejected Pruneyard Shopping Center's claim that the California Supreme Court unconstitutionally infringed on its First Amendment right not to be forced to use its property as a forum for speech with which it might not agree.[47]

Not only has California been an innovator in interpreting its constitution's free speech guarantees, but the state has been an innovator in other free speech areas as well. In 1975, four years before *Robins v. Pruneyard,* the California state legislature adopted the Moscone Act, which prohibits courts from interfering with organized labor's attempts to communicate legally with the public.[48] The act essentially bars employers from seeking injunctions, restraining orders, or other court orders limiting lawful picketing, leafleting, and other expressive activities.

The implications of the Moscone Act for free speech in malls and shopping centers was demonstrated in 1979, when a Sears, Roebuck & Co. store in Chula Vista sought and obtained a court injunction against the carpenters' union, which was picketing on a Sears-owned sidewalk in front of the store. The union was protesting Sears' refusal to use union carpenters in the store.

Sears charged that the union picketers were trespassing and obtained the injunction, ordering the picketing carpenters to move to the public sidewalk between 220 and 490 feet from the store. The California Supreme Court reversed the injunction, concluding that the Moscone Act was adopted to insulate union picketing from courts' injunctive powers. As a result, the union was permitted to picket on the retail store's sidewalk.[49]

The Colorado Decision. The Supreme Court decision in *Pruneyard v. Robins* invited other state high courts to more broadly interpret their own state constitutions, since most are semantically similar to California's. So far, all but two states have declined the offer.

One that took up the U.S. Supreme Court offer in 1991 was Colorado, where the state supreme court in *Bock v. Westminster Mall* decided by a 4–3 vote that the Pledge of Resistance, a group opposed to the President George H. Bush's Central American policies, had a right under the free speech clause of the Colorado Constitution to distribute literature in Westminster Mall near Denver.[50] Rather than basing its decision solely on the state's constitution, the Colorado court conducted two other evaluations before reaching its decision: It evaluated the mall's restrictions on speech to determine whether they were content-neutral and evaluated government involvement with the mall.

First, the court examined the degree to which the mall's policy of prohibiting the expression of political issues was content-neutral. The court found that the mall permitted religious expression; allowed salutes to the armed forces; undoubtedly permitted the exhibition of politically controversial films; allowed the artistic expressions of dancers and painters; and permitted a market research firm to use common areas of the mall to conduct surveys of consumer attitudes. After examining these activities, the court expressed doubts about whether the mall's policies were actually content-neutral.

Next, the court examined and found substantial "links between the [mall] Company and several government entities and public monies." The court noted that the city paid the mall $2 million for street and drainage improvements that it made, and that numerous government agencies were present in the mall. Based on this, the court concluded:

> Where governmental entities or public monies are shown by the facts to subsidize, approve of, or encourage private interests and such private interests also happen to restrict the liberty to speak and to dissent, this court may find that such private restrictions run afoul of the protective scope of [the state constitution]. It is possible for interests, otherwise private, to bear such a close relationship with governmental entities or public monies that such interests are affected with a public interest.[51]

Although the court decided that the links between the Westminster Mall and government were substantial enough for it to decide in favor of the Pledge of Resistance, it left open the possibility that lesser levels of government involvement might lead the court to reach a different decision.

The New Jersey Decision. Citing the state constitution and several state supreme court cases, the New Jersey Supreme Court in 1994 extended free speech rights to regional malls and one community shopping center. *New Jersey Coalition Against the War in the Middle East v. J.M.B. Realty Corp.*, which established the new free speech right, begun during the 1990 Gulf War, when a coalition comprised of several dozen community organizations, religious groups, and individuals, sought permission from ten regional malls and a community shopping center, the Mall at Mill Creek, to distribute antiwar leaflets. Six of the malls denied the Coalition permission to leaflet, while the remaining malls gave permission but imposed conditions that made it impossible to enter the mall, such as requiring expensive insurance coverage. As a result of these actions, the Coalition sued the malls, and the case finally reached the state supreme court in 1994.[52]

In arriving at its decision that malls could not limit speech, the New Jersey Supreme Court examined the way that malls had replaced—or displaced—traditional public forums such as downtown shopping districts; the meaning of the state constitution's free speech provision; the standards enunciated in *State v. Schmid*, where the state supreme court earlier ruled that leafletteers were not trespassing when they entered and passed out leaflets at Princeton University; and the precedent established by the U.S. Supreme Court's *Pruneyard* decision. First, the court majority concluded that shopping malls so dominate retail sales and pedestrian activity that they "are the functional equivalent of yesterday's business district." To support their conclusion, the court majority noted that 70 percent of the U.S. adult population shops at regional malls an average of once each week, and that malls and shopping centers accounted for over 56 percent of U.S. retail sales.

Second, the court concluded that the state constitution, unlike the U.S. Constitution, protects citizens "not only from State interference but—under certain conditions—from the interference of an owner of private property even when exercised on private property." The conclusion was based on the positive wording of the constitution's free speech clause.

Third, the court then examined and applied the three-prong standard devised in *Schmid*, which was:

(1) the nature, purposes, and primary use of such private property, generally its "normal" use, (2) the extent and nature of the public's invitation to use that property, and (3) the purpose of the expressional activity undertaken upon such property in relation to both the private and public use of the property.[53]

In applying these standards to malls, the court found that malls had a multiplicity of functions and were not dedicated solely to commercial transactions. The malls provided parklike settings where people and even political candidates could stroll, sit on benches, and converse, and offered a variety of activities, including Halloween trick-or-treating, crime prevention exhibits, exercise programs, and voter registration, conducted by political parties and candidate organizations. Several have meeting rooms used by community groups, one housed a police substation, and nearly all were policed by on- or off-duty police. Based on these factors, the court concluded that the purpose of malls was "all-inclusive." Because the malls "encourage[d] a variety of non-shopping activities on [their] premises," the court concluded that the invitation extended by malls to the public was far broader than just shopping. In fact, the court noted, some even promoted themselves as community centers. Consequently, the court concluded that the "first two elements of the [*Schmid*] standard—the normal use of the property, and the nature and extent of the public's invitation to use it—point strongly in the direction of a constitutional right of speech."

As for the third standard, the court found that "more than two hundred years of compatibility between free speech and the downtown shopping district is proof enough of its compatibility with these shopping centers."[54] Overall, leafleting in malls met the three-pronged standard established by *Schmid*, leading the court to conclude that the state constitution's free speech provision protected speakers in shopping malls.

Finally, citing *Pruneyard*, the court dismissed the argument that letting leafletteers into malls violated mall owners' free speech and property rights. Paraphrasing Justice Powell's concurring opinion in *Pruneyard*, the court concluded

> that private property owners who have so transformed the life of soci-
> et for their profit (and in the process, so diminished free speech) must
> be held to have relinquished a part of their right to free speech. They
> have relinquished that part which they now use to defeat the real and
> substantial need of society for free speech at their centers; they should
> not be permitted to claim a theoretically important right of silence
> from the multitudes they have invited.[55]

The justices therefore ordered the owners to open their malls to public speech, but with several constraints. The court limited the right "to leafleting and associated speech in support of, or in opposition to, causes, candidates and parties," but this "d[id] not include bullhorns, megaphones, or even a soapbox; it d[id] not include placards, pickets, parades, or demonstrations; it d[id] not include anything other than normal speech." The court expressly extended these rights to the regional malls and the Mall at Mill Creek, which were involved in the *New Jersey Coalition* case, but not to other shopping centers. Finally, the court stated that the mall owners had "extremely broad" powers to establish time, place, and manner restraints.[56]

Using its broad powers for establishing time, place, and manner restraints, the Mall at Mill Creek adopted several policies that essentially undermined the supreme court ruling: The mall required every leafleting group to obtain $1 million insurance coverage; limited each group's leafleting to one day per year between January 1 and October 31; and made each group agree to sign a license agreement that would "protect, indemnify, save, and keep harmless" the mall from all incidents arising from the leafleting, and require leafletteers to pay the mall's attorneys fees if litigation occurred.[57] The Green Party, as part of its effort to put Ralph Nader and other candidates on the New Jersey ballot, challenged these regulations in state superior court.[58]

The superior court struck down all three, concluding that they effectively barred activists from the mall. The court found the $1 million insurance requirement and its estimated premium of $500 to be cost-prohibitive and unnecessary because under New Jersey law the mall would not be liable for the Green Party's conduct. The appeals court reversed the superior court, upholding all three restrictions, because they represented a "good faith exercise of [the mall's] reasonable business judgment."[59]

However, the New Jersey Supreme Court reversed the appeals court, finding that there was no bases supporting the mall's judgment that a $1 million insurance policy was necessary. Although it overturned the Mall's indemnification and insurance requirements, the court did not address whether the mall could restrict groups of leafleting per year because the parties were at the time negotiating a settlement of that issue.[60]

Other States: "Malled" Speech

While the highest courts of just three states recognize speech rights in shopping centers under their state constitutions' free speech provisions, three state high courts have concluded that other state constitutional provisions protect some petitioning activities in malls. The high court of Massachussetts concluded that the state constitution's free elections provision, declaring that "all elections ought to be free; and all the inhabitants of this Commonwealth . . . have an equal right to elect officers, and be elected, for public employments," protects the collecting of ballot petitioning in malls.[61] The same court, however, refused to extend this right to leaflet distribution unrelated to an election.[62] The supreme court of Oregon and the Oregon appellate court concluded that the Oregon constitution's initiative and referendum provisions, not free speech provisions, entitle citizens to collect signatures on initiative petitions in malls.[63] The Washington Supreme Court also approved the collecting of signatures in malls, but refused to extend the protection to speech.[64] In 1999, the Washington court even backtracked some on the right to collect signatures, ruling that signature gathering in strip malls was not constitutionally protected.[65]

Pennsylvania backtracked even further than Washington. Pennsylvania's high court originally decided that the state constitution provided some protection for speech on private property, but later reversed itself.[66]

The high courts of thirteen states—Arizona, Connecticut, Georgia, Hawaii, Iowa, Michigan, Minnesota, New York, North Carolina, Ohio, South Carolina, Texas, and Wisconsin—have refused to recognize any state constitutional protections for speech in malls.[67] The courts in North Carolina and Georgia did not even ponder the meaning of their state constitutions, relying instead on the U.S. Supreme Court declarations.

North Carolina became the first state in 1981 to declare that the state constitution did not protect speech at shopping centers. The case involved signature gathering on a petition rather than leaflet distribution. The North Carolina Supreme Court accorded the case about as much thought as Senator Jesse Helms does an art exhibit. First, based almost exclusively on the testimony of the mall's security director, the court reported that the defendant was "accosting" people in the mall's shopping lot by asking them to sign a petition. Next, the court concluded that the U.S. Supreme Court held in *Lloyd* that speech in private shopping centers was not protected. Finally, the court said that it "was not so disposed" to interpret the state constitution differently than the U.S. Constitition, even though it is affirmatively worded.[68] That was all it wrote.

The Connecticut high court decided the issue in 1984. There, the state supreme court in *Cologne v. Westfarms Associates* concluded that neither signature gathering nor speech were protected in malls by the state constitution. Because the Connecticut court actually considered the issue, unlike the North Carolina court, the decision has been cited by other state high courts, including the one in Georgia.[69] The case arose when the Connecticut National Organization for Women (NOW) sought permission from Westfarms Mall to gather signatures on petitions supporting the Equal Rights Amendment. When the mall denied permission, NOW member Christine Cologne filed suit. The judge granted Cologne and NOW an injunction requiring the mall to allow NOW volunteers to collect signatures in the mall's central courtyard.[70]

By a 3–2 vote, the Connecticut Supreme Court reversed, holding that under the Connecticut constitution, citizens had no right of free speech in private shopping centers . The court majority rejected NOW's argument that the affirmatively worded state constitution prohibited private infringements of free speech.[71] The court expressed its concern that if it were to rule in NOW's favor, the right of free speech would extend to other places where large numbers of people congregate. The court wrote that it was "unable . . . to discern any legal basis distinguishing this commercial complex from other places where large numbers of people congregate, affording superior opportunities for political solic- itations, such as sports stadiums, convention halls, theaters, country fairs, large office or apartment buildings, factories, supermarkets, or department stores."[72]

Unlike in North Carolina, Georgia, and Connecticut, the free speech- in-malls case in Wisconsin arose from expressive speech rather than sig- nature gathering on petitions. In *Jacobs v. Major* the state supreme court concluded that Nu Parable, a dance troupe, had no constutitional right to publicly perform a choreographed depiction of the horrors of nuclear war in East Town or West Town malls. Although concluding that the state con- stitution did not protect speech in malls, the court left open the possibil- ity that the state legislature could adopt a statute permitting speech on publicly used private property, writing:

> It is not the role of this court to set exact balances between . . . con- flicting private groups which then become inflexible as chiseled in the marble tablets of constitutional adjudication. Balancing between com- peting or conflicting interests is better conducted by the legislature, as long as within the constitutional limitations against governmental interference with property rights.

Despite the court's invitation to the Wisconsin legislature to pass a bill addressing free speech in malls, no bill ever passed. However, bills to pro- tect speech in malls were introduced in nine states, but none have become law, thanks to the lobbying of the retail and real estate industries.[73] In New York, a bill protecting speech in malls passed the Democratic-controlled assembly several times, but was killed by the Republican-controlled sen- ate. In 2001, another bill was introduced to the assembly by Democrat Steve Englebright. The bill (A.B. 4085) amends the state civil rights law to require malls of at least twenty stores to permit some form of public expression in common areas.

The most recent case where a supreme court decided that speech was not protected in malls was in 1999 in Minnesota.[74] The decision arose from leafleting by the Animal Rights League at the Mall of America in Bloomington, Minnesota.

Promoting itself as a "city within a city," the Mall of America offers virtually all of the amenities of a real city: a wedding chapel, a post office, a police station, an amusement park, a miniature golf course, a spa, restaurants, and 30,000 live plants and 400 live trees.[75] Despite its claims to being a city, the mall's rules of conduct sharply limit speech. Groups seeking to disseminate information must first obtain approval, which includes allowing the mall to review the materials that will be distributed. If the mall determines that the materials or the group will "unreasonably violate" its First Amendment and property rights, the mall will withhold approval. If the mall approves, up to two members of the group may hand out their materials from a "community booth" in the mall.[76]

On May 19, 1996, ten members of the Animal Rights League entered the mall, holding placards and handing out literature on the cruelty of killing animals for their fur. They quietly engaged shoppers in conversations and urged them to boycott Macy's because it sold fur products. The group did not obstruct Macy's entrance, but mall security officers nevertheless told the group to leave because their actions violated mall rules. Most of the group left, but four who did not were arrested and charged with trespassing.[77]

The presiding judge in the trespassing case, Judge Jack Nordby, declined to dismiss the trespassing charges, but did issue a 62-page decision ruling that citizens had a right under the Minnesota Constitution to engage in peaceful protests in the mall. Because the mall had received nearly $200 million in public funding, Nordby concluded that the mall was not "in any real sense—logical or etymological or legal or Constitutional—'private.'" Norby wrote:

> The entrepreneur may, on his own land, build and sell what he likes.
> . . . But he may not come to the public, with hat and pocketbook in
> hand, enter into a compact with the public to use the public resources,
> and then close to any members of that public the doors of the structure

he erects with the public's help, or prescribe rules within that structure that diminish, to any degree at all, the Constitutional rights and privileges of anyone.[78]

Nordby's decision was praised by civil libertarians and several newspapers. The *Minneapolis Star Tribune*, the more liberal of the two Twin Cities newspapers, published an editorial praising the decision as "a lasting victory for free speech." The editorial called the decision "a compendium of scholarship that can be used by free speech partisans in balancing acts for years to come—not merely to maintain this essential freedom but to expand it."[79]

As it turned out, Nordby's ruling was not "a lasting decision for free speech." His ruling was overturned on appeal. The Minnesota Supreme Court concluded that public subsidies for the mall had not transformed it into a state actor. Then, endorsing the Connecticut Supreme Court's decision in *Cologne*, not Judge Nordby's, the court decided that the state consitution, like the U.S. Constitution, protected freedom of speech from infringement by governments, not private entities.[80]

Civil libertarians criticized the ruling. One citizen suggested that the mall be forced to guarantee free speech within its walls before getting any more public support, such as a light rail link between the mall and the city.[81] A *Minneapolis Star Tribune* editorial reported that the supreme court decision was a "significant" loss for "free speech advocates," but that a positive outcome of the case was that the Mall of America had developed a more "enlightened" attitude toward free speech, having made booths available to all organizations "that pledge to follow certain behavior rules."[82] However, the mall is under no legal obligation to provide the booths and can withdraw the priviledge of using them at any time.

On remand, Judge Nordby dismissed the charges against the four defendants. In dismissing the charges, Judge Nordby vehemently criticized the Minnesota Supreme Court for failing to recognize a right of free speech in shopping centers under the Minnesota Constitution, stating that the decision "betrays a lack of interest in, knowledge of and respect for the Minnesota Constitution."[83] Judge's Nordby's near-unprecedented criticism of the supreme court, and his dismissal of the charges against the activists, made headlines in Minnesota newspapers.[84]

Lower courts in another dozen states have also refused to recognize free speech rights in shopping malls under their state constitutions, even though their high courts have not ruled on the issue. One of these states was New Hampshire, where Manchester District Court Judge William Lyons rejected the Foot Locker Eight's claim that their leafleting in the Mall of New Hampshire was protected free speech under the state constitution, convicting them instead of trespassing. The New Hampshire Supreme Court subsequently dismissed the Foot Locker Eight's appeal on procedural grounds, and therefore never addressed the issue.[85]

The Footlocker Eight have threatened to challenge Judge Lyons's decision by protesting in the mall, again. If the Footlocker Eight do not stage another protest, others will. It is virtually impossible to forever close off malls to public speech.

7
Private Communities:
Real Property, Real Restrictions[1]

The majority of housing units built in the United States since 1995 have been in "planned unit developments" (PUDs) and condominiums. PUDs are neighborhoods of detached, single-family dwellings that are built by large developers, usually in outlying suburbs or on former farmlands, with attached common areas, such as private parks and golf courses. Condominiums are commonly thought of as, and usually are, attached single-family dwellings but are legally defined as developments where an owner "has individual ownership of a unit and [is] a tenant in common" with other owners of the common elements.[2] Together, these forms of home ownership are commonly referred to as "common interest developments" (CIDs).

(A third form of CID, found mostly in New York City, is the cooperative apartment or co-op. With the co-op, a corporation holds title to the apartment building, and shareholders in the corporation receive a "proprietary lease" granting them the exclusive right to occupy a unit.)

In the Washington, D.C., area, Florida, Arizona, and California, the vast majority of new housing units are CIDs. They have names such as Fox Run, Oak Grove, and Deer Creek Estates that conjure up images of idyllic settings and rural bliss rather than suburban tract housing, or names such as Society Hill, Boston Branch, and Rancho del Oro that suggest exclusivity and wealth. Most provide services for residents, such as garbage collection and snow removal, that in cities are provided by municipal government.

Since the early-1990s, about 80 percent of new homes built in the Washington, D.C., area have been CIDs. In Maryland, nearly one-third of all existing homes are now in these planned developments, and in the San

Francisco Bay Area, 500,000 housing units—where 1.2 million people live—are CIDs.[3]

As of 1999, 42 million Americans—about one in seven—were living in CIDs governed by 205,000 associations. In 1965, there were only 500 such associations.[4] Just over half of the 42 million live in PUDs; slightly more than 40 percent live in condominium developments. Some nine million of the 42 million live in gated communities, the most exclusive form of planned development.[5]

What differentiates planned developments from other housing tracts is that individuals purchase individual dwellings, but housing associations created by the developers have title to or manage the common areas, such as pools, recreation centers, golf courses, and other green space. These housing associations are private—albeit often nonprofit—corporations. Residents pay maintenance and assessment fees to the association to support these common areas, which are open to members but not the public. In most cities and suburbs, these common areas are public rather than private property, allowing citizens to freely recreate, speak, and assemble there.

Corporate developers, typically large conglomerates such as the American Nevada Corp. (ANC), Mobil Oil, and Disney, create the housing associations that govern the CIDs and often retain control over them even after families begin populating the development. The developers sometimes retain ownership of property that appears to be association-owned. For example, in Celebration, Florida, the sprawling PUD planned and developed by the Disney Corporation, Disney owns most of the downtown buildings, including the "Town Hall," which sounds like a public building but is not.[6]

At Green Valley, a PUD built in the midst of desert sand near Las Vegas rather than in a clover-covered valley, the housing association is a nonprofit corporation "designed on paper to represent residents' interests but is without any political or decision-making power; instead, it offers recommendations and suggestions to city and county officials." The real power rests with the ANC and committees that it controls, such as the Architectural Control Committee composed of unelected ANC officials.

As writer David Guterson observed, the "ANC is the homeowners' association; the corporation's owners—the Greenspun family—also own Green Valley's only bookstore, cable-television company, and newspaper," assuring that the conglomerate's views are what residents hear.[7]

Developer control of homeowners' associations in new PUDs is very common. Most developers grant themselves the power to appoint or remove board members, allowing them to remove those who are independent or troublesome; other developers simply write association rules granting them "the right to control the association until the last lot is sold."[8] Because of developers' unwillingness to hand control over to homeowners, some states, including California, have passed laws requiring developers to cede control of the homeowners' association to residents once half the units have been sold.

Although they might control new homeowners associations, developers often avoid paying full homeowners association dues on their unsold homes and lots, which allows them to shift maintenance costs from themselves to homeowners by raising association dues or passing special assessments to pay for upgrades of association-owned property.[9] Some developers do the opposite: They intentionally maintain artificially low assessments to help sell homes, and after they pull out, assessments can double or triple.[10]

At Continental Ranch near Tucson, builders receive three votes for association board members for every lot they will develop, but homeowners receive just one vote for the home they own. In a March 1995 board vote, builders cast 13,000 votes compared to 340 votes for homeowners, allowing the builders to thoroughly control the vote and the board. Although the builders were scheduled to turn control of the association over to homeowners in 1995, they rescheduled the date of homeowner control to 2009, sparking unrest among some Continental Ranch residents. The disgruntled residents picketed outside the development with signs reading, "Don't Buy in Continental Ranch." One picketer, a retired electrician, claimed that the association endlessly raised homeowners' dues and was "a police state." "My wife and I have been to Yugoslavia,

Romania, Bulgaria, and Hungary and I swear they've got more freedom than we have here," he commented.[11]

Until homeowners actually take control, California law allows developers to legally claim three votes on housing associations' governing boards for every unoccupied unit in a new development, whereas homeowners receive one vote per home, regardless of the number of people residing in the homes.[12] As a result, homeowners have relatively little power until the developer withdraws. At Corona Ranch, a PUD in California's Moreno Valley, only one homeowner was elected to the five-member association board, compared to the developers' four board seats. "It's really the board of developers," said Gregg Thatch, the lone elected homeowner on Corona Ranch's board in 1998. "They're the board of developers, not directors, until the majority of homeowners have moved in, until the developers leave."[13]

The control of homeowners associations by developers sometimes has political or social implications for people living outside CIDs, as a conflict between a developer and a homeowner in Crowley, Texas, shows. There, the developer used the homeowners association to hinder the campaign of a political opponent.

In Crowley, an additional city council seat was created that included Deer Creek Estates, whose three-member board of directors was headed by developer Alton Isbell. Among candidates for the seat were Deer Creek Estates residents Kevin Carey and Thomas Hasenbeck. Isbell supported Hasenbeck and volunteered to work on the latter's campaign.[14]

After Carey and his supporters in Deer Creek Estates put up 14- by11-inch yard signs, Isbell had his employees go through the CID pulling out the signs, saying they violated the association's rule against displaying signs. The employees left other signs, including one proclaiming "This house protected by fire ants" and another promoting a children's football team. One Deer Creek Estates resident reported that other signs had been allowed during previous political campaigns. Isbell said that he was unaware of these signs but would have removed them had they been brought to his attention.

Carey called the police to halt the removal of his signs, but the police refused to act, seeing it as a civil rather than criminal matter. Consequently, Carey filed suit against Isbell and the association, claiming that the sign removal violated his and other residents' First Amendment rights. Responding to the suit, state district court judge Jon Barton issued a temporary restraining order against the developer-controlled homeowners association, prohibiting it from assessing fines against those who displayed signs and from removing other signs. The board responded by issuing a letter permitting signs to be posted for thirty days before an election, but refused to completely lift the ban on signs, saying that homeowners needed to vote on that question—even though they never voted for a ban on signs in the first place.[15]

The case was eventually settled out of court, allowing Deer Creek Estates homeowners to display their signs for the duration of the city council election, but putting the sign-posting restriction to a vote of homeowners afterward.[16] In the city council election, neither Deer County Estates resident won. Kevin Carey came close to winning, polling 235 votes to 254 for the winning candidate, whereas Hasenbeck received a mere 32 votes.[17]

Regulating Paradise

Even where homeowners constitute a majority on association boards, developers often retain power behind the scenes. At Celebration, Florida, where homeowners elect the association board, Disney and its subsidiary companies still exercise control. The homeowners association, although touted as an example of participatory democracy by Disney, cannot change any rules "without prior notice to and the written approval of the Celebration Company." The rules, written by Disney, give the corporation a veto over homeowners indefinitely. A Disney spokesperson refers to this corporate veto power as "a system of checks and balances. This is not a dictatorial Disney. This is a participatory Disney."[18]

Even where homeowners actually elect the association's board, there may be little true democracy. Voting is usually on the basis of one-home-owned one-vote, rather than one-resident one-vote, which disenfranchises nearly half of all adults and virtually all renters, and the covenants written into deeds by developers are often difficult, if not impossible, to change. Many covenants require a two-thirds favorable vote from all homeowners, not just those voting, to change covenants.

The homeowners associations in CIDs, unlike neighborhood associations in "unplanned" cities and suburbs, function as quasi-governments that wield substantial power over residents. Because these homeowners associations are private corporations, even though they function like governments, they can adopt and enforce rules that would be unconstitutional if adopted by a government. For example, the housing association of Brandermill in Chesterfield County, Virginia has a rule banning signs, except personal and "For Sale" signs. The association also has rules allowing it to fine residents who violate the rules and to seek liens to collect the fines.

Jerry Warsing, a Brandermill resident, posted a sign reading, "Public notice. This is a shrink-well soil damaged home. Our family wishes to thank Chesterfield County and the Commonwealth of Virginia for their concern. All realtor, contractor and private citizens' inquiries welcome." The sign was meant to protest the use of shrink-well soil, which Warsing believed caused $28,000 to $32,000 damage to his home. The homeowners association decided the sign was improper and ordered him to remove it. After he refused, the association fined him $820 and threatened to place a lien against the home if he did not pay. Warsing did pay, but later moved from Brandermill.

A former chair of the Chesterfield Housing Panel, which studied the problems created by shoddy construction and shrink-well soils in the county, says that the housing association's pursuit of Warsing was an attempt to make the shrink-well controversy disappear. "Warsing and other homeowners . . . are the forgotten victims and they will not be silenced."[19]

If the Brandermill housing association were a municipality rather than a private corporation, it could not legally silence Warsing.

The rules governing life in these CIDs are called covenants, conditions, and restrictions, referred to as "CC&Rs" by the real estate industry. CC&Rs are of two types: deed restrictions or conditions in place when the association is established and rules adopted by the governing association's board, sometimes referred to as "category one" and "category two" restrictions.[20] Category one restrictions are written by the developer before any units are sold and are recorded on the deed, binding first-time buyers and subsequent buyers to their terms. These usually define the structure and composition of the housing association, require home buyers to join and abide by the regulations of the association, compel owners to pay monthly and special assessments, and impose penalties on members who violate the regulations. These are essentially the functions of municipalities—assessing taxes and adopting and enforcing ordinances—except that they are performed by private entities.

Category one restrictions usually describe the rules for selecting association boards of directors, including the procedures for casting proxy votes. Because category one regulations often permit the incumbent board president to be designated as a proxy holder, incumbent boards are difficult to unseat, because they cast more than their own votes.[21] Moreover, some covenants permit cumulative voting, where residents have votes equal to the number of association offices, allowing minority slates to get elected and to dominate the board.

Also included in category one are restrictions on making architectural changes to homes, such as room and garage additions, without approval of the association or developer. These restrictions, which are imbedded in deeds, are very difficult to change.

In many states, many category one–type restrictions have been formalized as civil codes, passed by legislators who were lobbied by homeowners associations and developers. California adopted the Davis-Sterling Common Interest Development Act (Civil Code Section 1350-1376) in 1985 at the urging of the CID industry, which also helped draft the act.[22] The act allows homeowners associations to assess fines, charge interest on delinquent payments, and recover attorney fees. It also frees homeowner association board members from being held personally liable for their actions if their actions were "not willful, wanton, or grossly negligent," even when the homeowners association remains liable.[23] This gives homeowners association board members broad immunity from actions that they take as board members. (This immunity extended to Leisure World board members, who were sued for contributing over a half-million to an anti-airport referendum campaign. Because the board members investigated the issue and decided that the contribution was in the best interests of the gated community, they could not be held liable for spending the money, even if residents opposed the spending.[24]) Virginia law allows homeowners associations to assess fines of $10 per day plus interest against homeowners who violate CC&Rs.[25] Florida statutes establish fines for CC&R violations at $50.[26]

Category two restrictions are those adopted and enforced by housing associations and comprise a list of "do's and don'ts" for residents of the CIDs. These restrictions are more easily changed than category one restrictions. They can include limits on the colors of exterior paint that can be used on dwellings, the types of grass that can be planted, the building of fences, the installation of storm doors, solar panels, and satellite dishes, the use of awnings and shutters, and the placement of air conditioners.[27] Oftentimes, restrictions extend far beyond these long-term changes to property. Housing associations have adopted rules on the types of mailboxes that can be used, the color of drapes, the sizes of house addresses, the types and heights of shrubs that can be planted, the number, the size, and types of pets that can be owned, and even the brands of paint that can be used on exteriors. Some housing associations ban or restrict the use of clotheslines, birdbaths, basketball hoops on garages, and sheds. Many prohibit parking pickup trucks, boats, trailers, and campers within the development, making car repairs, or parking on streets overnight. Others require that guests staying in the development for more than a few days be screened.

Others have restricted the planting of vegetables, the flying of flags, the height of flagpoles, the display of religious symbols, the posting of signs, and door-to-door distribution, including the distribution of political campaign literature.[28] (Celebration, apparently anticipating the negative publicity that could result from a complete ban on political signs, allows homeowners to post a single, 1 1/2- by 2-foot sign for forty-five days prior to an election.) The Estrella housing development in Phoenix, built by convicted Savings and Loan embezzler Charles Keating, Jr., banned pornographic videos and magazines from the community —even from homeowners' bedrooms.[29]

There have been conflicts between homeowners and housing associations over nearly all of these restrictions. Two days after he purchased a residence in Carrollwood Village in Florida, the homeowners association ordered resident Mark Gardiner not to park his Ford F-150 pickup in his driveway overnight. The association rules prohibits "downscale" pickup trucks, even though it allows sports utility vehicles and minivans. In California, the Promontory Point Homeowners Association refused to allow resident James Thomson to install a window air conditioner, which Thomson says he needed because of allergies and sleep apnea. In California's Walnut Creek, a couple moved out of their CID after battling with the homeowners association about their satellite dish. In Florida, the Hunter's Green Community Association fined resident Robert Henning and ordered him to change the color of his front door, which Henning had painted in an unapproved color, and in California's Gold Creek development, the homeowners association ordered resident Lola Hutchinson to uproot two rose bushes she had planted and to remove a Valentine's Day banner she had on her front door.[30]

Similar actions of the Superstition Springs homeowners association in Arizona led retired military veteran Jerry Murphy to comment, "After 23 years in the military, I feel like a prisoner in my own neighborhood. . . . And, of course, after voicing my free speech rights, I now have to wonder how much retribution I will encounter from the 'Association.'"[31]

The restrictions imposed on individual homes and homeowners also extend to common areas, so that clubhouses, parks, golf courses, and picnic areas that can be used for social and recreational purposes cannot be used for potentially controversial purposes, such as political campaigning. At Columbia, Maryland, at a sprawling CID built by the Rouse Company with financing from the Connecticut General Life Insurance Company, leafleting near the village center or holding a political rally in a park is prohibited. Even relatively innocuous activities, such as collecting signatures on political petitions, are prohibited. Green Party activist Scott Tippets asked the Columbia association permission to gather signatures on a petition to place Ralph Nader on the 2000 presidential ballot during a waterfront arts festival at Lake Kittamauandi on Columbia property, but was refused after the association's vice president for community services checked with the association's attorney. "It's private property and we determine the usages that take place," explained association vice president Maggie Brown of the decision to bar Tippets's signature gathering.[32]

Similarly, after opponents of a new property tax in Calvert County, Maryland, were stopped by Chesapeake Ranch Estates board members from passing out leaflets door-to-door at the 10,000 resident CID, they assembled near the entrance gate, where they again attempted to pass out leaflets. Because they were still on private property, the leafleteers were told to stop or face arrest for trespassing. The group then moved to the street outside the CID, but the police, apparently called to the scene by some board members, told the group they couldn't be in the street leafleting, either.[33] Distributing leaflets from streets is prohibited in nearly every municipality.

The restrictions on signature gathering at Columbia and leafleting at Chesapeake Ranch Estates suggest that CC&Rs can restrict the speech and expression of nonmembers—citizens who have never joined the homeowners association or accepted the restrictive covenants in deeds.

Ironically, many people move into CIDs because of the restrictions on personal behavior. A director of the community association at the Klahanie CID near Seattle, Washington, explained that "for 99 percent of the people, the reason they're in Klahanie is because of the restrictions. . . . The whole idea of a self-sufficient community, with regulations for color of house and standard of lawn care and protecting the environment, that's what's driving this."[34] A resident at Celebration explained that the "rules are there to make sure your neighbor's front yard doesn't turn into 'Sanford and Son.'"[35]

Part of the CID sales pitch is the protection that restrictions provide—protection from neighbors, protection for the investment in the home, and protection from outsiders. Wedgewood, a CID near the Twin Cities, informs potential buyers that Wedgewood is "governed by a set of design standards and land use restrictions which provide the community with stability, control and predictability."[36] The Preserve in Panther Ridge, a Florida CID, puts it more euphemistically, promoting its restrictions as "additional safeguards designed to help maintain each owner's property and investment [and]. . . a community of compatible homes and lifestyles."[37] Green Valley near Las Vegas reports that "the lots within have been established with certain beneficial restrictions."[38]

With a bit of Orwellian logic, promoters of CIDs describe these restrictions as freedom. Of his CID's restrictions, Celebration master planner Robert Stern stated, "In a freewheeling capitalist society, you need controls. . . . In the absence of an aristocratic hierarchy, you need firm rules to maintain decorum. I'm convinced these controls are actually liberating to people. It makes them feel safe. Regimentation can release you."[39] David Guy, president of Arvida Company's central Florida division, says that "covenants are a way for homeowners to protect their rights."[40] Stern's and Guy's beliefs are summed up by the advertising slogan of another CID, which touts its community as a "heritage of freedom in a free land."

Although developers, realtors, and housing associations contend that CC&Rs safeguard property values by regulating behavior, there is very little empirical evidence supporting this contention. By analyzing selling price information, data on each unit's size, and covenants on pet ownership, University of Illinois professor Roger Cannaday found that condominiums in north Chicago that barred pets actually sold for less than condominiums that allowed cats. However, condos that allowed dogs, particularly large dogs, did sell for less than those barring pets or those allowing cats.[41] Another analysis found nearly the opposite. Louisiana State University professors William Hughes, Jr., and Geoffrey Turnball analyzed the covenants and selling prices of houses in Baton Rouge between 1985 and 1992 and found that bans on pets reduced housing prices, as did requirements that lawns be mowed. They also found that bans on the use of storage sheds reduced prices, but that bans on signs increased prices. Overall, they found that multiple restrictions increased housing prices, but only temporarily. As the housing ages, multiple restrictions actually lower prices.[42] The evidence on the financial advantages of CC&Rs is weak and contradictory at best.

What the CC&Rs appear to do best is to assure that people with different cultural outlooks cannot express themselves. For example, allowing sports utility vehicles but not pickup trucks in housing developments curtails the expression of blue-collar preferences, not white-collar preferences. Banning automotive repairs rather than woodworking and pottery-making serves the same end. In practice, the rules restrain the activities of "Sanford and Son" and "the Dukes of Hazard," not the J.R. Ewings.

One of the supreme ironies of CIDs is that they are populated by Republican voters, who like the cultural uniformity of CIDs but ideologically oppose the principles underlying them. For example, homeowners associations are responsible for maintaining conformity and uniformity within the CID, whereas Republicans speak out for individualism, which they assert is suppressed by government. Homeowners associations have the power to, and often, prohibit the ownership of handguns, another position typically opposed by Republicans. Finally, homeowners associations maintain commonly held property, which Republicans typically denounce as a form of socialism.[43]

Because CIDs are heavily Republican, many of the conflicts that arise are between conservative homeowners and their associations over issues such as American flags and crosses. In California, a homeowners association told a resident to take down Old Glory because the CC&Rs prohibited flags. The resident defiantly refused.[44] In Boca Raton and West Palm Beach, Florida, CID residents were also told to take down flags, as was a

Henrico County, Virginia, veteran, who adorned his house with three patriotic flags.[45]

In Arizona, the Terravita homeowners association ordered elderly war veteran Doc Wussow to take down a twenty-foot flagpole, which violated the association's rules. Wussow refused, claiming that the rule was adopted after he moved into the CID, and that it was his patriotic duty to fly the flag. In this case, the homeowners association tried to negotiate a compromise, rather than strictly enforce the covenants, apparently out of fear of appearing unpatriotic. It suggested that Wussow use a removable flagpole, put up on national holidays.[46]

The publicity given Wussow's case stirred several "patriotic" state legislators in Arizona to sponsor a bill that "would have prevented associations from regulating the display of the flag."[47] After homeowners associations lobbied against the bill, it was killed. In Virginia, Republican state senator Bill Bolling, after hearing about the plight of the Henrico County veteran, introduced legislation prohibiting homeowners associations from barring flag displays. Apparently oblivious to the constitutional concerns raised by the ban on flag waving, Bolling said, "I certainly understand their goal behind enforcing reasonable covenants, but that has to be balanced against fundamental property rights and the right to express one's patriotism."[48]

As a result of incidents like this, Florida legalized flag flying in condominiums in 1989. The Condominium Act amendment reads: "Any unit owner may display one portable, removable United States flag in a respectful way regardless of any rules or requirements dealing with flags or decorations."[49] California law also permits flag displays in CIDs.

In Palm Beach, Florida, a condominium association barred a resident from using the clubhouse for a prayer and meditation group.[50] In Orange County, California, the homeowners association at Springs Condominium ordered Jean Amato to remove a five-foot cross from a planter on her front patio that was visible to other residents. "If someone put a refrigerator out there, we would have reacted the same way," the association's president said about the order.

Amato refused, saying that the CC&Rs were being selectively enforced. She claimed that other residents were allowed to display nonreligious signs such as "Pet Heaven." Amato obtained legal assistance from the Pacific Justice Institute, which specializes in religious freedom cases, and filed a countersuit against the homeowners association. An out-of-court settlement was eventually reached, whereby Amato agreed to remove the cross from the planter, the homeowners association would pay her $10,000, and Amato's insurance company would reimburse the association $5,000 toward its legal fees.[51]

Regulating the Regulators

Although homeowners associations claim that conflicts between boards and homeowners are rare, Arizona state senator Tom Freestone, a Republican, says they are not. "I've had 400 complaints," says Freestone, who conducted hearings about homeowners association abuses in 2000.[52]

Florida held similar hearings in 1990, interviewing 1,200 condominium owners around the state. Based on the interviews, the Condominium Study Commission recommended changes in the state's condominium laws, including a ban on the use of proxy votes in board elections, requiring boards to make financial statements available to homeowners, levying fines against boards that violate these laws, and creating an arbitration board to resolve conflicts between associations and condominium owners.[53]

Even before the law was signed by the governor, condominium boards started protesting its provisions. Faced with these protests, legislators suspended the law and then removed some its most controversial provisions before it became law.[54]

Other residents of abusive homeowners associations have banned together to create "Homeowners Supporting Homeowners in Associations," an organization that began in Arizona but now has national membership. The group was formed to combat associations levying fines on members for such things as flying flags.[55]

One reason why some Republican politicians are angered by home-owners associations is out of self-interest: CIDs are heavily Republican, but Republican homeowners cannot campaign or post signs of support in their neighborhoods. For example, Cynthia Crowe, a former Republican state committeewoman in Florida, was stopped by her housing association from posting signs for the Republican candidate for Sarasota sheriff. According to association president Dick Ozimek, the CC&Rs of the association pro-hibit all except "For Sale" signs from being posted.[56] In largely Republican Arizona, housing associations have also stopped the posting of, and even removed, political campaign signs from front yards in CIDs, saying that the signs violated CC&Rs.[57]

By contrast, Democratic candidates, whose constituents are more like-ly to reside in urban areas, have few impediments to campaigning, because the Supreme Court ruled in *City of Ladue et al. v. Gilleo* that cities cannot restrict political signs in residential yards.[58]

While the Supreme Court overturned bans on signs imposed by municipalities, courts have consistently found that bans on signs imposed by homeowners associations are constitutional.[59] In *Murphy v. Timber Trace Association Linn*, two homeowners displayed a "For Sale" sign out-side their home twenty-four hours a day, despite CC&Rs prohibiting this. When the homeowners failed to remove the signs, the homeowners asso-ciation removed the signs. Missouri courts upheld the restrictive covenant and the right of the homeowners' association to remove the signs, even though a state statute specifically forbids any "political subdivisions" from "enact[ing] or enforc[ing] any ordinance which forbids or restricts the right of any owner . . . from displaying on the property a sign of reason-able dimensions."[60]

In *Linn Valley Lakes Property Owners Association v. Brockway*, home-owners also posted a sign in violation of a restrictive covenant. The court observed that "the covenant in question places a limitation on the use of property by the landowners. There is nothing constitutionally impermis-sible per se in a private agreement restricting signs in a residential neigh-borhood, and enforcement thereof does not constitute improper state action."[61] And in Pennsylvania, a restrictive covenant requiring home-owners to obtain prior written permission from the association before posting signs was upheld. The court in *Midlake on Big Lake Boulder Condominium Association v. Cappuccio* concluded that the precepts of freedom allowed citizens "to contractually restrict, or even give up those rights. The Cappuccios contractually agreed to abide" by the restrictive covenants, "thereby relinquishing their freedom of speech concerns regarding placing signs on [their] property."[62]

Courts have consistently upheld CC&Rs and association rules, providing they are reasonable and not enforced arbitrarily.[63] In New York, courts upheld a rule banning motorcycles from a condominium, adopted after a motorcyclist purchased his residence. The motorcyclist argued that he purchased his unit specifically because it did not bar motorcycles. The court nevertheless ordered the resident to get rid of the motorcycle.[64] In Florida, the courts upheld a regulation banning the installation of satellite dishes, and in California, courts upheld a ban on pets that included indoor cats, even when the pets never left the unit or bothered other residents.[65]

In Iowa, the State Supreme Court upheld a ban on a flagpole that served as a symbolic protest against homeowners association rules.[66] In Indiana, the Supreme Court even concluded that a restrictive covenant specifying that the development consisted of single-family homes trumped a state law, subsequently withdrawn, that invalidated deed restrictions prohibiting the use of residential properties as group homes for the disabled and mentally ill. The court concluded "restrictive covenants permit property owners to collectively provide or obtain protections significantly contributing to the peace, safety, and well-being of themselves and their families," and that a state law undermining the covenants exceeded the permissible police powers of the state.[67]

Court decisions upholding CC&Rs are based on the assumption that CIDs are voluntary associations, and that home buyers contractually agree to their restrictions when they purchase homes. The problem with the assumption, like many assumptions about economic behavior, is that it bears little relationship to reality. Most of the CC&Rs are too long and complicated to read, and most home buyers move in without knowing all of the restrictions on the property. A survey of home buyers found fewer than half of home buyers are even given copies of the association rules before closing. The survey also found that there was "considerable confusion in homeowners' minds pertaining to the legal powers of the association, their relationship to the local municipality, and their power over residents. Half of the respondents considered the association simply a group of friends and neighbors formed to help one another with mutual problems."[68]

Also, many home buyers looking to buy a new house eventually buy in planned developments simply because the majority of new houses built today are in these developments, not because they prefer CID housing to other housing. More than likely, homeowners move into a CID because it lies within a given municipality that has good schools or other services sought by the owner. Lastly, the associations are also rarely voluntary: Most home buyers in CIDs are compelled to join.

Because courts have generally upheld restrictive covenants, disgruntled home owners and affected industries, such as the solar power industry, have found that it is more effective to lobby legislators to enact laws limiting the power of housing associations than to go to court to change covenants. In Arizona, the solar power industry has been lobbying to prevent associations from regulating the use of solar panels. Arizona law currently allows associations to regulate, but not ban, solar panels.[69]

In Maryland, politicians became upset about the bans on political signs imposed by homeowners associations and passed a law allowing residents to post signs. The law castigated homeowners associations, describing their bans as "contrary to the principles of free speech," and prohibited them from banning signs for candidates and ballot measures for thirty days before, and seven days after, an election.[70] In Illinois, legislators passed the Condominium Property Act that prohibits condominium associations from adopting rules that "impair any rights guaranteed by the First Amendment to the Constitution."[71]

On the federal level, Congress was lobbied heavily by satellite dish manufacturers and direct broadcasting corporations to stop municipalities and homeowners associations from banning the installation of satellite dishes. Section 207 of the Telecommunication Act of 1995 directed the Federal Communications Commission (FCC) to develop regulations making it easier for homeowners to install satellite dishes and other antennas.

In 1996 the FCC adopted regulations, revised in 1998, that prohibit homeowners associations and governments from banning satellite dishes on balconies, patios, and other non-common property.[72] Despite the FCC rule, many homeowners associations continued to prohibit residents from installing dishes. The Satellite Broadcasting and Communications Association, a trade group for the satellite industry, reported that it received nearly 300 calls a day reporting homeowners association's obstructions to dish installation, which finally prompted the FCC to act. After several homeowners associations steadfastly prohibited residents from installing dishes and other antennas, the FCC invalidated their covenants.[73]

A few courts have also invalidated covenants. In 1949, in a landmark case that preceded *Brown v. Board of Education*, the Supreme Court in *Shelley v. Kraemer* ruled that a racially restrictive covenant limiting the sale of homes to whites was unenforceable. Because the covenant was a private agreement, the court did not declare it unconstitutional, but instead declared that any attempt by a court to enforce the covenant would constitute state action that violated the Fourteenth Amendment.[74]

Since then, most courts have interpreted *Shelley* to be a straightforward race discrimination case, but have never explained why the logic of *Shelley* should not apply to other covenants that infringe on constitutional rights. In *Linn Valley Lakes Property Owners Association v. Brockway*, the Supreme Court of Kansas simply declared that the issues raised by *Shelley* were "easily distinguished" from the constitutional issues raised by a sign-posting case, but never enunciated the differences, and the Supreme Court of Pennsylvania ruled that a lower court decision, citing *Shelley* as precedent, that refused to uphold an anti-sign covenant "was an error of law."[75]

By contrast, a U.S. District Court in Florida, using *Shelley* as precedent, struck down a restrictive covenant restricting flag displays to designated days. The court concluded that "applying the principles of *Shelley* to the situation . . . this court finds that judicial enforcement of private agreements contained in a declaration of condominium constitute state action and bring the heretofore private conduct within the ken of the Fourteenth Amendment, through which the First Amendment guarantee of free speech is made applicable to the states."[76]

Because of the different interpretations of the applicability of *Shelley* to restrictive covenants that are not concerned with race discrimination, Rutgers University law professor Frank Askin concluded that *Shelley* "sits around as a sort of wild card that may be used by some courts to trump private property claims when they come into conflict with individual rights."[77]

Another legal approach to challenging restrictive covenants has been under the public function doctrine enunciated in *Marsh v. Alabama,* where the Supreme Court ruled that a company town was the functional equivalent of a municipality.[78] A California court in *Laguna Publishing Co. v. Golden Rain Foundation* drew heavily on *Marsh* when concluding that a housing association decision to ban the distribution of a giveaway newspaper amounted to discrimination against the newspaper, because the association allowed another, competing newspaper to enter the housing development and pass out newspapers.[79] In *Laguna Publishing Co.*, the court concluded that the analogy between a company town and Leisure World, a gated housing development, was not entirely appropriate because "there are no retail businesses or commercial establishments in Leisure World. It is solely a concentration of private residences, together with supporting recreational facilities, from which the public is rigidly barred." The court nevertheless concluded that the "attributes of Leisure World which in many ways approximate a municipality bring it conceptually close to a company town, and such attributes do weigh in our decision."[80] However, the court's final decision was based largely on the state rather than federal constitution, concluding that "the discriminatory exclusion of one such newspaper represents an abridgment of the free speech, free press rights of the excluded newspaper under our state Constitution."[81]

In New Jersey, a court also relied on the state constitution to order access to the Galaxy Tower Condominiums, drawing similar conclusions to the court in *Laguna Publishing Co.* In that case, the Galaxy Towers Condominium Association barred a political organization from entering the condominium to distribute leaflets, even though the association endorsed candidates and passed out leaflets within the condominium supporting its candidates. An analysis of past voting showed that association-endorsed candidates consistently won in the condominium's district, where condominium residents were the majority of voters, but consistently lost in other districts. The court concluded that this voting pattern was attributable to the association's being "the only game in town."

The court ruled that the association's activities at election time resulted in a "significant dedication of this property from private to political and thus public use," creating an "implied invitation" to other political groups to respond. Consequently, the court ordered the condominium association to allow other political organizations to distribute literature "in essentially the same manner as in which the association's literature is distributed."[82]

The court's conclusion in *Laguna Publishing Co.* that company towns and private housing developments are different was repeated in *Midlake on Big Boulder Condominium Association*, where the court concluded that there is "no correlation between Midlake [housing development] and a company town or municipality. Midlake's facilities are entirely privately run. While there is a sewer service, private streets, and private maintenance, Midlake provides no facilities for community public use that are typically found in a municipality, such as schools, libraries, and other public functions."[83] In *Brock v. Watergate Mobile Home Park Association*, a Florida court concluded that "a homeowners association lacks the municipal character of a company town. . . . the services provided by a homeowners association, unlike those provided by a company town, are merely a supplement to, rather than a replacement for, those provided by local government."[84]

Although it may be true, as the court said, that smaller private housing developments such as Midlake on Big Boulder lack public facilities, distinguishing them from company towns, the statement is not true for large developments such as Columbia, Maryland, and Celebration, Florida. Columbia consists of 13,690 acres with a population exceeding 80,000—far larger than any company town. "Columbia has gas stations, supermarkets, specialty stores, and convenience shops. It also boasts several swimming pools, tennis courts, parks, and various sized ponds."[85] The homeowners association there assesses annual fees on the basis of property values, just as municipalities do, and Columbia streets are patrolled by Howard County police officers, just as Chickasaw, Alabama's streets were once patrolled by deputies. Applying the reasoning employed in previous court decisions, it would seem that large private developments such as Columbia are the functional equivalents of municipalities and therefore must accord citizens First Amendment rights under the *Marsh* decision.

Some private developments are not just the functional equivalent of municipalities, they have become municipalities in order to obtain tax dollars to reduce their assessments and maintenance fees. While becoming municipalities for taxation purposes, they have nevertheless tried to maintain their private nature.

In North Carolina, a 1,650-resident, gated development called Bermuda Run applied for and received municipal status from the state legislature in 1999. The legislation was introduced by Senator Betsy Cochrane, a longtime resident of the development, and it passed the legislature by a 110–0 vote, making it the second gated municipality in the state. The first, Grandfather Village, was incorporated in 1998.[86]

Bermuda Run residents voted to apply for municipal status because of the high costs associated with maintaining common areas, which were built in the 1960s. By incorporating, the development is able to levy a property tax and receive a portion of the Davie County sales tax, but is not eligible for state road maintenance funds because its roads are not open to the public. By placing its town hall outside its gates, the development apparently hopes that it will be able to maintain its gated status, claiming that the "public facilities"—the town hall—are open to all citizens, while keeping the actual development closed to the public.

North Carolina isn't the only state with gated communities that double as municipalities. California also has a handful, including Rolling Hills near Palos Verdes, Hidden Hills near Calabasas, Canyon Lake in Riverside County, and Laguna Woods in Orange County. Laguna Woods is the most recent to incorporate, and essentially consists of Leisure World, a convalescent home, and a few businesses outside of Leisure World's gates. By and large, the residents of Laguna Lake live in Leisure World, even though the city offices will be outside, as at Bermuda Run.[87]

Given Supreme Court rulings, such as *Dunn v. Blumstein*, which declared that "the right to travel is an 'unconditional personal right,' a right whose exercise may not be conditioned,"[88] it seems highly unlikely that federal courts can uphold the legal fiction that a gated development such as Bermuda Run is distinguishable from the Bermuda Run municipality, merely because the town hall is outside the development's gates. Public monies are being used to subsidize the development, so the public should have a right to engage in constitutionally protected activities such as leafleting within the development.

While not trying to become municipalities, other CID residents claim that being taxed by municipalities for services provided by their associations constitutes a form of double taxation. The argument is that residents of CIDs should be reimbursed by municipalities for the services that their associations provide, such as garbage collection and street cleaning, even though developers and homeowners contractually agreed to forgo these services in order to build and maintain these private enclaves. Despite its inherent illogic—arguing on the one hand that association fees are private payments used to maintain private areas, and arguing on the other that association fees are a form of taxes—the argument has caught the ear and votes of some politicians.

Responding to lobbying by homeowners associations, which represent nearly one million people in New Jersey, the state legislature passed the Municipal Services Act in 1990, which requires municipalities to provide equal services to CIDs or reimburse them for their costs. Similar bills have been introduced in other states.

Before the New Jersey law could take effect, the League of Municipalities filed suit, claiming that the law was unconstitutional because it discriminated against apartment owners. A state court upheld the league, but an appeals court reversed that decision. The league asked the state supreme court to review the case, but before a decision was handed down, struck a deal with the Community Associations Institute's New Jersey affiliate, agreeing to a scaled-down version of the bill.[89]

The municipal funding of services in these private enclaves raises the issue of whether CIDs in New Jersey and other states that invite in public garbage trucks, street sweepers, and snowplows can then bar the public from exercising their free speech rights in these municipally-supported areas. The answer is, "Hopefully not." If citizens pay for the removal of snow on CID-owned sidewalks, they should be allowed to exercise their rights on these sidewalks.

CIDs that are tax-supported yet private, whether they are gated communities like Bermuda Run or simply conventional CIDs with open gates but severe restrictions on the exercise of free speech rights, have ominous implications for freedom: The United States could conceivably become a conglomeration of publicly subsidized, but nevertheless private fiefdoms. With citizens recreating in private rather than public parks, retreating into private developments that bar door-to-door leafleting, and shopping at malls that bar speech, the concept of free speech, when applied solely to public spaces, becomes completely meaningless.

PART IV
THE MUTED MEDIA

In *Four Theories of the Press*, a book written nearly a half-century ago, professors Fred Siebert, Theodore Peterson, and Wilbur Schramm presented four topologies describing how the world's mass media were controlled and organized: the authoritarian, Soviet Communist, libertarian, and social responsibility systems. The authoritarian system was organized to support and advance the interests of the governing elite through tight controls over the press. By contrast, the Soviet system promoted Communist Party political orthodoxy with party members originating, and party leaders censoring, media content.

These press systems differ from the libertarian press system operating in the United States. The libertarian system is characterized by freedom from governmental control, based on "a negative concept of liberty, which [is] loosely define[d] as freedom from government."[1] The assumption of the libertarian system is that government rather than the private sector is the major source of censorship, and that the private sector is a better guarantor of freedom than government. Consequently, media corporations, not government agencies, determine nearly all media content in the United States.

In contrast with the libertarian system, the social responsibility system rests on a positive assumption about freedom—that freedom is "a necessary implement for the attainment of a desired goal," such as more robust debate or a wider diversity of expressed views. For that reason, media operating under this system are far more likely to serve the public interest than media operating under a libertarian system.

According to *Four Theories of the Press*, the social responsibility system is characterized by the principles that "freedom carries concomitant obligations," and that the press "is obligated to be responsible to society." These obligations include enlightening the public about governmental affairs, serving as a forum for debate about public issues, and "maintaining its own financial self-sufficiency so as to be free from the pressures of special interests."[2]

The British Broadcasting Corporation (BBC) represents an example of a medium of "social responsibility." The BBC is funded by receiver license fees, so that it is dependent on its audience, not advertisers; has been designed to be politically fair, giving candidates free time and equal access to its stations; and develops programs to educate as well as entertain audiences.[3]

According to Siebert, Peterson, and Schramm, the Communication Act of 1934 contained elements of the social responsibility system, requiring broadcasters to operate in the "public interest, convenience, and necessity." To ensure that radio and television stations operated in the public interest, the Federal Communications Commission (FCC) required broadcasters to address significant social issues in their communities and provide the public with a diversity of opinions on social issues. Although the FCC rarely enforced its regulations, never policed the airwaves, and seldom penalized broadcasters for sub-par performance, the rules did assure some compliance, even if limited.

Championing the cause of "deregulation," Congress and the FCC repealed these social responsibility requirements during the last decade and a half. Congress and the FCC deregulated telecommunications after repeated lobbying by the media industry, which also lavishly contributed to congressional candidates' campaign committees. An example of the media's influence peddling is provided by the News Corp., headed by Rupert Murdoch. Murdoch's group had a lobbying budget of $800,000 for the first half of 1997, and he gave nearly $1 million in "soft money" to political campaigns between 1991 and 1997.[4]

Not only has deregulation eliminated the few social responsibility requirements imposed on U.S. media owners, but it has opened the door to a succession of media mergers that have placed the mass media in fewer and fewer corporate hands. Nearly all of the major electronic news outlets have become units of ever-larger corporations, whose stocks are traded on Wall Street. Because they are expected to meet earnings forecasts, the MBAs who now run these news outlets prefer advertising dollars over accuracy and profits over Pulitzer Prizes.[5] This emphasis on revenues makes news media more deferential to their primary revenue sources—advertisers. Chapter 8, "Advertisers: Muscling the Media," examines the influence that advertisers have on the news media.

In addition to making the news media more deferential to advertisers, the deregulation and mergers have also turned the news media into small cogs in huge self-promoting profit machines, such as AOL Time Warner. CNN, *Time,* and AOL are parts of the vast AOL Time Warner entertainment empire, a profit engine that also produces comic books, operates theme parks, publishes magazines, and produces movies and popular music recordings. When CNN or AOL review feature films such as *See Spot Run* and *3,000 Miles to Graceland,* it often amounts to self-promotion: These films are produced and released by Warner Brothers, part of the AOL Time Warner conglomerate. When CNN or AOL feature stories about Madonna, the Red Hot Chili Peppers, or Matchbox Twenty, this is also self-promotion: These "artists" record for Warner record labels. And when AOL features a Web page, People.com, this is also self-promoting hype: *People* is one of AOL Time Warner's many magazines. Within the integrated marketing vision of a conglomerate such as AOL Time Warner, news is both a revenue source and a promotional vehicle for the company's many products.

As one component of the corporate media conglomerate, news must positively enhance and promote the other components. Negative news about the conglomerate's theme parks, films, recordings, and professional sports teams is avoided, allowing the news unit to coexist with, and promote, the conglomerate's other parts. In effect, news within the modern-day libertarian system promotes private gain rather than the public interest. Chapter 9, "Muzzling David: Corporate Media Goliaths," presents many examples of the news media protecting their corporate owners and CEOs.

Given the profit-making rationale of this system, the First Amendment is also reduced to a mechanism for enhancing corporations' profits. Consistent with this view of the First Amendment, AOL Time Warner and AT&T, the nation's two largest cable company owners, filed suit against FCC-imposed limits on the number of cable subscribers that the companies could enroll and limits on the number of channels that their cable systems could fill with their own programs. The limits were imposed to assure a modicum of diversity in cable. In court, the conglomerates argued that the FCC restrictions violated their First Amendment rights because the restrictions limited the number of people to whom they could sell their services, thus limiting their speech, and limited the number of programs they could disseminate. Unfortunately, a federal appeals court in March 2001 agreed with AOL Time Warner and AT&T and threw out the limits, allowing these large conglomerates to perhaps grow even larger.[6]

8

Advertisers: Muscling the Media

In *Freedom of the Press* (1935), reporter and press critic George Seldes charged that advertisers, not government, were the principal news censors in the United States. Seldes reported that advertisers often pressured newspapers to kill or alter stories about their businesses or personnel, but newspapers also censored stories out of deference "toward the sources of their money" without being pressured. According to Seldes, the "suppression of news by department stores [the largest advertisers at the time] is the most frequent and flagrant story."[1]

Newspapers and other media edit or kill stories offensive to advertisers because media profits come from the sale of advertising, not sales of the medium to consumers. With newspapers and magazines, subscription and single-copy sales typically account for less than 25 percent of gross revenues; profit comes from advertising.[2] With electronic media—except for noncommercial and pay cable services such as Showtime that do not carry advertising— almost all of the revenues and profits are derived from advertising.

Seldes recounts numerous instances where advertisers succeeded in suppressing news during the 1930s. For example, news about a rape case in which the son of a Philadelphia department store owner was the defendant was suppressed in every newspaper in that city, apparently at the request of the father. Seldes reports that in July 1932, Procter & Gamble cancelled its advertising in newspapers that carried a syndicated article telling readers how to make soap at home. These are examples of direct censorship, where advertisers pressure media to change or kill stories or punish media for their reporting by withdrawing advertising.

Direct advertiser pressure still exists. The *Duluth News Tribune*, the only daily newspaper in the city of Duluth, Minnesota, responded to threats from real estate advertisers by firing a columnist who wrote a "Smart Shopper" column claiming that homeowners could sell their homes themselves. The newspaper also gave the executive vice president of the Minnesota Association of Realtors, whose members purchase a large percentage of the newspaper's advertising, space to reply to the column, and the newspaper's editor wrote an editorial criticizing the columnist for being "contradictory. . . incomplete. . . and unfair." In response, the columnist filed a libel suit against the newspaper.[3]

However, advertising censorship is usually not as direct or heavy-handed as this. As Seldes pointed out, media often kill stories out of deference "toward the sources of their money" without being asked. For example, the *New York World*, one of the most prestigious newspapers of the 1930s, refused to publish an O. Henry story about an underpaid department store employee who was willing to sacrifice "her virtue." The *World* refused the story out of fear that it would "harm its relations with all department stores."[4] This is an example of self-censorship, which also still occurs. A more recent example is the killing of a story about an airplane crash that was "uncomfortably close" to an airline advertisement at the *Wisconsin State Journal*.[5]

Media can also bury a story to appease advertisers. Burying a story means that the story is run, but is given less prominence than it deserves. A buried story can be moved from the front page to the business section, reduced to a paragraph or two, or edited so that potentially offensive content appears at the end of the article, where few readers will see it. For example, a *New York Times* story by reporter Blake Fleetwood examined how the Tiffany jewelry store on Fifth Avenue, one of the *Times*'s most consistent advertisers, received a $4.5 million tax break from a state program designed to keep businesses from moving out of state. Although the story appeared on page one of the newspaper, it was rewritten with the discussion of Tiffany in the nineteenth paragraph.[6]

During the decades following the publication of *Freedom of the Press*, numerous examples of how advertisers have influenced the content of news and entertainment shows surfaced. For example, when *Playhouse 90* staged a docudrama on the Nuremburg trials in the 1950s, CBS prohibited use of the words *gas chamber* because the show's sponsor was a gas company. In 1954, General Motors withdrew its advertising from the *Wall Street Journal* because the newspaper refused to accept the release dates set by GM on stories about new models.[7]

Albert N. Halverstadt, the advertising manager for Procter & Gamble, the country's largest advertiser, testified in 1965 that his company had policies prohibiting its advertisements from appearing in programs that did not "minimize the 'horror' aspects" of war, depicted men in uniform as villains, or cast businessmen "as cold, ruthless and lacking all sentiment or spiritual motivation." Without advertising from large firms such as Procter & Gamble, programs with this content were never produced.[8]

There are numerous examples of advertisers pressuring mass media to kill or alter stories during the 1970s and 1980s. The New York Times Company was forced to sell *Modern Medicine* magazine to Harcourt Brace Jovanovich in 1976 after pharmaceutical firms threatened to withdraw their advertising. The threat was made because the *New York Times* newspaper published articles on medical malpractice that angered the pharmaceutical industry. Since these firms didn't advertise in, and therefore couldn't punish the newspaper, they threatened the Times-owned magazine.[9] During the same period, Braniff Airways, First National Bank of Chicago, Westinghouse, and other corporations cancelled their advertising in *Business Week* after the magazine upset the companies by its reporting.[10]

Similar pressures are exerted on weekly newspapers, which are far more dependent on advertising revenues from a small group of businesses than daily newspapers. In Iowa, Pottsville State Bank withdrew its advertising from the *Pottsville Herald* after the weekly carried an Associated Press report stating that the bank had one of Iowa's lowest ratios of loans to assets. The bank never advertised in the paper again, and even helped form a "community improvement committee" that drove the *Herald* out of business.[11]

The biweekly *Valley Star* in Velva, North Dakota, faced a similar boycott in 1999. Alarmed by the paper's investigative stories, such as one about the city auditor using her public office to run a real estate business, members of Velva Association of Commerce launched an advertising boycott of the paper. The city bank, the local electric utility, and other businesses boycotted the paper, hoping to shut it down.[12]

Advertising pressure is even exerted on alternative media, which pride themselves as modern-day muckrakers. Nemer, Fieger, and Associates, Inc., which buys three-fourths of the motion picture advertising in the Twin Cities, withdrew its ads from the *Twin Cities Reader* because it was angered by a column describing that year's crop of movies as bores.[13] In Detroit, the *Metro Times* conducted an investigation of the strong-arm methods used by record chains against small retailers selling used CDs. After receiving ad boycott threats from record companies, the paper dropped the story.[14]

Publisher Gloria Steinem described some of the advertiser pressures on *Ms.* magazine before it went adless in 1990. Clairol withdrew its advertising from *Ms.* after the magazine briefly mentioned a congressional inquiry into the possibility that hair-dying chemicals were carcinogenic. Procter & Gamble, which has repeatedly influenced media content, attempted to restrict reportage by writing into advertising contracts stipulations about editorial content. According to Steinem, Procter & Gamble prohibits its products from being advertised "in any issue that included any material on gun control, abortion, the occult, cults, or the disparagement of religion." Another example of how advertisers pressured *Ms.* occurred when the magazine pictured dissident Soviet women without makeup on its cover: Revlon decided not to advertise in the magazine.

Print media—newspapers and magazines—are not the only media pressured by advertisers. Many television and radio stations have also been pressured by advertisers to kill or alter news stories. In Los Angeles, veteran consumer reporter David Horowitz was let go in 1996 from

KCBS-TV, a CBS owned and operated station, after automobile advertisers repeatedly complained to management about his stories on car safety.[15] As this example illustrates, working for a large corporation like CBS doesn't mean that reporters will be protected from advertising censorship.

Some defenders of advertising—mostly professors who teach advertising and marketing—deny that advertisers pressure the news media, despite the ample anecdotal evidence. For example, *Advertising, Its Role in Modern Marketing*, a college text written by four advertising professors, reports that "some reason exists to believe that small, financially insecure newspapers or broadcast stations are more likely to be influenced by outside pressure than the large, financially stable ones. There is little reason to believe that large, prestigious papers, magazines, or television networks cater particularly to advertisers, as charged by critics. . . . We suspect that the media are probably much less 'kept' than most people think. He who pays the piper does not necessarily call the tune," the text concludes.[16]

Not only does evidence contradict this assertion, but there is also evidence that the mass media provide positive coverage for advertisers, and this practice is quite old. In her memoir, *The Girls in the Balcony*, former *New York Times* reporter Nan Robertson revealed that writers for the women's page were required to do positive stories about *Times* advertisers in the 1950s. She wrote that "every fashion writer was assigned a group of department and specialty stores. We were required to come up every month with articles whose column-inches reflected the relative advertising strength of every store. . . . The monitor of all this was Monroe Green, the advertising director of the *New York Times*, who had been a powerful executive for many years at Macy's. There was hell to pay from Green every time an advertiser was not adequately represented in the 'news' columns of the women's page."[17]

This practice hasn't stopped. The *Greensboro News & Record* devoted half its November 30, 1997, front page and an additional forty-eight column inches on page four to a story about holiday shopping. The article mentioned the newly opened Target department store fourteen times and an additional three times in captions under photos taken at Target.[18] The *Detroit News* and the *Detroit Free Press* published numerous stories, photos, and sidebars about the Somerset North shopping mall that opened in 1997, including two full-color sections with copy written by the news staffs, not the advertising department.[19]

Some newspaper executives openly admit that newspaper stories promote advertisers. *Chicago Sun Times* executive editor Larry Green said this about plugging advertisers: "We have to take care of our customers."[20]

Advertising Pressures on Newspapers

Of the major media, daily newspapers should be the least susceptible to advertiser pressures because most dailies are monopolies. In the vast majority of U.S. cities, there is only one daily newspaper. In just a few dozen of the largest cities, such as New York, Boston, and Chicago, are there competing newspapers. In most cities with two dailies, such as San Francisco, Seattle, and Detroit, the dailies do not compete directly for advertising because they are either owned by one publisher or are published under the Newspaper Preservation Act. The Newspaper Preservation Act allows "competing" newspapers to share an advertising department and printing plant, but requires the papers to maintain separate news departments. As a consequence, jointly published newspapers do not compete for advertising.[21]

In addition, there has been a consolidation in the newspaper industry, with large chains such as Gannett, Knight Ridder, Ingersoll, Scripps-Howard, and the New York Times Corporation buying up and owning more newspapers today than ever before. These large companies and their newspapers should be less susceptible to advertiser pressure than small, independent newspaper publishers, as the authors of *Advertising, Its Role in Modern Marketing* suggest. Large media corporations are not as dependent on a few advertisers as are small independent newspapers, and the largeness of the companies should insulate their papers from pressure applied by local advertisers.

Despite the theory, there is overwhelming evidence showing that advertisers pressure newspapers to kill or change news stories, and that many large and small newspapers have caved in to the pressure. The most pressure comes from two industries—real estate and automobile— that are heavy advertisers in newspapers. For their money, these advertisers expect to get favorable coverage or will withdraw their advertising from newspapers. As Leon Edward, former president of the National Automobile Dealer Association, said, "Dealers have the right to spend money where they want to spend it. If somebody is giving you a black eye, it is hard to spend money with them."[22]

The pressure from automobile dealers was described in a *Washington Journalism Review* article titled, "Auto Dealers Muscle the Newsroom."[23] The article provides some examples of the types of pressure applied by auto dealers. When the *Daily Spectrum* in St. George, Utah, published a syndicated article telling readers how to bargain for new cars, area auto dealers withdrew their advertising from the paper. Under pressure from the dealers, the paper published a retraction, claiming that the article was run because of an editor's "poor judgment." After the *Manchester Herald* ran the same article, the editor responsible was sacked.

After the *San Jose Mercury News,* the flagship paper of the Knight Ridder Corp., ran an article headlined, "A Car Buyer's Guide to Sanity," which told readers how to negotiate lower prices, area auto dealers became enraged and demanded a meeting with the paper's publisher, Jay T. Harris. Harris met with the dealers, apologized, and offered them a free full page of advertising to make up for the story, but was unable to lessen their anger. After meeting with Harris, the dealers—members of the Santa Clara County Motor Dealers Association—met in a nearby hotel, where they decided to collectively withdraw their advertising from the paper. The action cost the *Mercury News* $1 million in revenue and attracted the attention of the Federal Trade Commission (FTC), which issued a complaint against the association and its members, asserting that the collective action violated federal antitrust laws.[24]

The Santa Clara County Motor Dealers Association settled the FTC complaint in 1995, agreeing to avoid advertising boycotts in the future, amending the association's bylaws to include the federal restriction, and educating member auto dealers about the terms of the settlement. Although settling the suit, the Association maintained that it had done nothing wrong.[25]

Another tactic used by newspapers to appease auto dealers has been to move the automotive section from the news department to the advertising department. *The Birmingham News* created the "Wheels" section to appease advertisers. It was created because "we were losing automotive advertising," reported section manager Dennis Washburn to the *Washington Journalism Review.* "Our editorial people began writing some very critical stories. . . . We lost two major advertisers—$300,000 to $500,000 a year—right here. Then we started the 'Wheels' section," which Washburn says is "designed to sell cars."[26]

The Birmingham News isn't the only newspaper that created an advertorial section to appease auto dealers. *The Milwaukee Journal-Sentinel*, a monopoly newspaper, turned its "Transportation" section over to the Automobile Dealers Association of Mega Milwaukee (ADAMM). ADAMM writes the articles for the section, which has the appearance of being a regular section of the newspaper. However, the section carries advertorials with headlines such as "Cadillac DTS Sedan Debuts as Showcase for High-Tech Hardware" and "Infiniti I30 Sedan Mixes Strong Engine with Plush Comforts."[27]

Real estate brokers and builders also throw their advertising weight around the newsroom, as the "Smart Shopper" columnist for the *Duluth News Tribune* learned. And the pressure is common. In a 1991 survey of real estate editors, 44 percent reported that publishers or senior editors prohibit the real estate section from carrying balanced news for fear of angering advertisers. Instead, the editors produced industry-friendly copy. The publisher and senior editors' fears are not imagined, either: More than 80 percent of the real estate editors said advertisers had threatened to cancel their advertising because of a news story.[28]

One survey respondent reported that nearly every real estate agent in town complained after the newspaper carried a story about selling a home without a broker. "The result is that now we only run fluff." Another reported that a story about slumping condominium sales angered condo brokers, who complained that the coverage was going to make sales worse. Several large advertisers cancelled their advertising in protest.

The experiences of *The Islander*, a small circulation newspaper on Edisto Island, South Carolina, are illustrative of the problems that papers can face when they anger the real estate and building industries. The newspaper ran a front-page story based on a Duke University report commissioned by the Edisto Beach Property Owners Association which concluded that the best method for dealing with beach erosion was to stop rebuilding houses that have been washed away. The story, which was accompanied by a satiric illustration of a postcard reading, "Greetings from Beautiful Erosion City," led to a boycott, which caused advertising to drop by 50 percent. One real estate agent was so angered by the story that he drove around town gathering up the newspaper's orange street boxes, which he dumped on the porch of the newspaper office.[29]

Larger circulation newspapers have also been pressured by realtors. Some, including the Fort Lauderdale *Sun Sentinel* and Boca Raton *News*, have their advertising or marketing departments produce the real estate section, as is done with some automotive sections.[30]

Newspapers are pressured by other large advertisers, not just auto dealers and real estate brokers. Department stores, airlines, and apparel manufacturers are among the advertisers that have applied advertising pressure on newspapers. For example, Northwest Airlines stopped advertising in the *Minneapolis Star Tribune* and *St. Paul Pioneer Press* after the papers carried stories critical of the airline's request for state funding to build maintenance bases.[31] The airline also banished *City Pages*, a free alternative newspaper, from its Twin Cities property after that paper carried a series of stories critical of the airline's lobbying. Since the airline didn't advertise in *City Pages*, it was unable to exert advertising pressure on it.

In an example of self-censorship, the *San Francisco Examiner* killed a column written by *Examiner* columnist Stephanie Salter in 1997, who criticized the "twisted values" of Nike, as exhibited in the "wretched excess" of the Nike Town superstore in San Francisco. Editorial page editor Jim Finefrock chose not to run the column because it could potentially harm the newspaper's planned Nike-sponsored "Bay to the Breakers" race.[32]

Although the anecdotal evidence of advertisers pressuring newspapers to kill or alter new stories is compelling, this is also systematically collected evidence suggesting that ad pressures on newspapers are widespread. A 1992 survey conducted among members of the Society of American Business Editors and Writers, a professional association of reporters and editors in print and broadcast, found that advertising pressures were "getting worse." Of the fifty-five anonymous members who completed questionnaires at the society's 1992 annual conference, more than 80 percent reported that advertiser pressure was a growing problem and 55 percent reported that advertiser pressure had compromised editorial integrity at their medium.[33]

A questionnaire sent to 250 daily newspaper city editor found very similar results: 55.1 percent reported that there had been "pressure from within [their] paper to write or tailor news stories to please advertisers." The survey also found that nearly 90 percent reported that advertisers attempted to influence the content of news stories. More than 70 percent of the editors reported that advertisers "tried to kill" stories at their paper. Overall, the questions indicate that advertiser pressure on newspapers is pervasive.

The editors' comments about the questions are also very informative. While some advertising and marketing professors have downplayed advertiser pressures, several editors who provided open-ended responses on the questionnaires indicated advertiser pressure is common. One editor wrote: "Anyone who worked for a newspaper any length of time would know the answers to these questions." Another wrote, "Of course advertisers have tried to influence the content of stories. Most people do."

Several editors' comments suggest that a few large advertisers—such as auto dealers— may be responsible for much of the pressure. One editor wrote:

> The worst offenders are car dealers. One cancelled $9,000 a month in advertising after the news department wrote a story that was not critical but the headline writer described the car as a "funny-looking car."

The biggest problem, yet the one most difficult to quantify, was summarized by one editor, who wrote:

> The real problem is much more subtle and, I suspect, far more widespread. . . . In 13 years, at three newspapers, I have never had a publisher who wasn't a member of the Chamber of Commerce, never had a publisher who didn't at least attend Rotary if he wasn't actually a member, have never seen a newspaper official who wasn't in some way tied into the local power structure. The danger is not an overt threat. I haven't seen a publisher come back from a Chamber meeting and say, "Hey, Al at the [auto] dealer said we have to have a story about xxx." But there is a similar worldview, a similar feeling about what is important and what isn't, a likeness of mind about what the newspaper should be covering. They don't need to be told by an advertiser that something is important or that a news story should focus in a particular direction. Editors and publishers probably don't think about advertisers when they make those decisions. They don't need to. They already share the same attitudes, convictions and worldviews.

Bullying Broadcasters

The anecdotal evidence suggests that advertisers also pressure television station, even those owned by large media corporations like ABC. For example, when a segment of ABC's *20/20* news magazine examined some of the pitfalls of buying a car from dealers, auto dealers pulled their advertising from several ABC affiliates.[34]

This type of pressure has had enduring effects. In Chicago, ABC-owned station WLS-TV killed an *Inside Edition* story several years later about fire hazards in Ford vehicles because it "didn't want to risk offending auto dealers who advertise heavily on the station." The episode was scheduled the week that the station was sponsoring Chicago's biggest auto show.[35]

In 1995, when a segment of ABC's *Primetime Live* carried a story about the hidden costs of car leasing that bent over backward to be balanced, the affiliate in Buffalo, New York, decided against carrying the program, and WXYZ-TV, the ABC affiliate in Detroit, carried a follow-up discussion about leasing during its news programs in an effort to appease automobile advertisers.[36]

Detroit's WXYZ-TV has had other problems with automobile dealers. In 1999, reporter Shellee Smith did a story on auto dealer Mel Farr, a former Detroit Lions football player, whose dealership was accused of charging illegally high interest rates and of repossessing cars from buyers when Farr failed to find financing for them. Farr refused to grant Smith an interview about the accusations, but news director Dave Roberts convinced him to tell his side of the story to anchor Guy Gordon, which he did. Farr refused to respond directly to Gordon's questions about the allegations. Instead, the football player-turned-auto dealer stated that it "seems to me the bigger story should be that Mel Farr, an African-American, ex-Detroit Lions football player, took a bankrupt dealership to $596 million in sales in 1999." After the interview, Farr cancelled his six-figure advertising contract with the station.[37]

Some station have gone even further than killing stories and sacking reporters to appease advertisers. Cincinnati station WLWT-TV reportedly allowed auto dealers to prescreen a story by consumer affairs reporter Noel Morgan about rental cars being sold as factory official cars, and then allowed the dealers to prepare a response to the story. The dealers were allowed to practice "their responses on cue cards," reported Morgan, whose contract with the station was not renewed.[38]

Stories about automobile dealers pressuring television news rooms are not the only stories about advertiser pressures to surface. Other large advertisers, such as airlines, department stores, and drug stores, have also pressured newsrooms into killing stories about their sales practices.[39] Stations in both large and small cities have been pressured. For example, WHDH-TV of Boston axed a story critical of American Airlines, apparently because of advertiser pressure.[40]

A survey of members of Investigative Reporters and Editors (IRE) working in television suggests that advertiser pressures on television newsrooms is common.[41] Nearly three-quarters of the reporters and editors (74.2 percent) reported that advertisers had "tried to influence the content" of news at their stations. The majority also reported that advertisers had attempted to kill stories.

Moreover, the responses show that advertisers use monetary leverage as part of their pressure. More than two-thirds reported that advertisers threatened to withdraw their advertising because of the content of news stories. Forty-four percent of the reporters said that advertisers had "actually withdrawn advertising because of the content of a news report."

Comments made by the reporters and editors suggest that automobile dealers are a major source of censorial pressure. One wrote, "It would be interesting for you to take a look at the role car dealers play in governing what's said about them by local television. They are practically untouchable."

Citing another censorious industry, one reporter noted, "We are currently battling with the local restaurant association and the members who advertise on our station whether we should air the city's weekly restaurant inspection ratings." The reporter added, "In this instance, my bosses are backing me." Grocery stores and "lawyers who advertise on television" were also mentioned as sources of pressure.

When asked whether advertisers "succeeded in influencing a news report at your station," nearly as many said their stations had capitulated (40 percent) as had withstood the pressure (43 percent). Seventeen percent reported that they "don't know" whether their stations capitulated.

Several provided in-depth descriptions of the internal pressures at their stations. One reporter wrote, "I've found that many general managers at TV stations (including my own) are former TV salespeople and therefore know the advertisers very well. It is common for advertisers to call a station and express their concerns about a story. While I have never been asked to lie or mislead viewers, I have been asked to soften a story an advertiser might find objectionable."

While other groups try to influence or suppress coverage, advertisers wield a unique economic club over television stations by withdrawing or threatening to withdraw advertising. However, advertisers do not exert the pressure by themselves. As one respondent wrote,

> The pressure comes from outside the station and within the station and often the two sides are working together to either kill stories or alter them. I know of an instance where a sales executive actually met with the focus of an investigative report over lunch and told him what the story would be about. How did the sales executive know the content of an investigative report before it aired? A news executive told him.

Not all news executives have sold out, of course. But with pressures for greater profits, the incentive to produce news stories that will either please or not offend advertisers is great. The problem was summarized by an investigative reporter, who wrote:

> The pressure from outside influences doesn't bother me; it's always been there and I suspect it always will be. However, there seems to be a frightening trend for the powers that be at corporate [headquarters] to give in to that pressure and pretend everything will go on as before, business as usual.
>
> Unfortunately, in many cases, that's all it is, Business. A gold-card advertiser can keep the dirty secrets secret and in some cases keep their victims in the dark. Those victims are our viewers who expect more and many times rely too much on the so-called power of the press. What they don't know is power has a price, and it's for sale.

Muscling Magazines

Although magazines are usually described as a single medium, advertisers and publishers classify magazines by their audiences, circulation type, and purpose. There are farm, consumer, and business magazines, which are distributed differently. Farm publications such as *Southeastern Peanut Farmer* and *North Dakota Stockman* are a distinctive class of magazines that are often distributed regionally. Most are "controlled circulation," meaning that they are sent for free to specific farmers. Consumer magazines are sold by subscriptions or single copies, which are available through retailers and newsstands. These publications are available to the general public. Business or trade publications are sometimes sold, but are most often distributed through the mail for free to employees within an industry or to members of professional associations.

There is substantial evidence that advertisers influence the content of all three classes of magazines, but that the influence differs by magazine class. Advertisers have much more influence over farm magazines than consumer or business magazines, according to a study conducted by University of Illinois professors Robert Hays and Ann Reisner, who surveyed farm magazine writers. Their survey found that 47 percent of writers believed that farm magazines' efforts to please advertisers made it difficult to work "at arm's length, without any kind of vested interest." Over one-third of farm writers (37 percent) reported that advertisers' attempts to influence editorial material was harming agricultural journalism, and an additional 50 percent reported that the practice was a "problem in some cases."[42]

Based on these responses, professors Hays and Reisner concluded that "advertiser-related pressure on farm magazine writers and editors is a serious problem." The problem exits because farm magazines "have a somewhat narrow advertising base. The inherent danger of losing a single advertiser that might be displeased by unfavorable editorial content necessarily weighs more heavily on the minds of farm magazine editors and publishers" than editors and publishers of consumer or business magazines.

A survey of consumer and business magazine editors conducted by *Folio* magazine, a trade publication for magazine managers, found that 41.2 percent of consumer magazine editors and 40.2 percent of business publication editors had "been told by the ad director or the publisher to do something that seriously compromised editorial" integrity. Of the business publications editors who were pressured, 40 percent said they protested but did what the ad director or publisher requested. Fewer than half said that they would "just say no" to the request. Consumer magazine editors were much more likely to turn down requests to please advertisers.[43]

In the past few years, the editorial integrity of consumer magazines has been severely compromised, as the industry has been forced to compete with the Internet for advertising dollars. Even the largest, most prestigious publications have knuckled under to advertising pressures. According to G. Bruce Knecht of the *Wall Street Journal*, many large advertisers, including Chrysler Corp., Ford Motor Co., Ameritech, and Bell South, now demand that magazine publishers provide them with prior notice when an issue in which they are advertising contains "controversial" stories.

To assure that publishers comply with advertisers' demands concerning story content, the companies' advertising agencies send notices to publishers telling them about their rules concerning content. If a magazine violates the rules, the advertising gets yanked. This can be costly to a magazine like *Esquire*, which gets about $56,500 for a one-page, four-color advertisement.[44]

A letter sent to publishers by PentaCom, Chrysler's advertising agency, stated, "In an effort to avoid potential conflicts, it is required that Chrysler Corporation be alerted in advance of any and all editorial content that encompasses sexual, political, social issues or any editorial that might be construed as provocative or offensive." The Young & Rubicam advertising agency also admitted that it has warned publishers about producing stories it "considers antisocial or in bad taste," while an Ameritech spokesperson said the company steered clear of "anything controversial."

Advertisers were not bluffing about pulling their advertising. *Sports Illustrated* lost more than $1 million in golf ads after doing a story on lesbian golf fans at the Dinah Shore tournament in Palm Springs. IBM and its software subsidiary Lotus withdrew its advertising from *Fortune* after the magazine carried a less-than-flattering profile of IBM's chief executive, Louis Gerstner, Jr. Ford pulled six months' worth of car ads from *The New Yorker* after a full-page pitch for Mercury ran next to a story that quoted Nine Inch Nails' explicit rock lyrics.[45]

Some publishers have apparently become very cautious about what they print as a result of the letters and ad cancellations. *Esquire* cancelled a story containing a few explicit words about a gay man who writes college term papers in exchange for sex. The story was killed out of fear that it would violate Chrysler's rules about controversial content.

(In response to widespread publicity about Chrysler's advertising policies, and assertions that it amounted to censorship, the corporation announced that it would no longer prescreen magazines because magazine editors know "what our advertising guidelines are. There is no need for prenotification anymore." Despite the announced change in policy, the corporation hinted that it would nonetheless withdraw its advertising from magazines with controversial content. The spokesperson said that the company is "less likely to take a chance on publications with an editorial edge in the future."[46])

Advertisers are not the only businesses that pressure magazine publishers about content. Retail chains are also a source of pressure and wield considerable influence because they control large percentages of consumer magazine single-copy sales. Supermarkets and discount stores such as Wal-Mart control 55 percent of single-copy sales; Wal-Mart alone controls 9 percent. The Winn-Dixie supermarket chain with 1,186 stores, Wal-Mart with 2,700 stores, Walgreen's drug store chain with 2,363 stores, and the Kroger supermarket chain with 1,300 stores are among the retailers that prescreen magazines or request that publishers provide them with an advance warning that controversial material will be carried in the magazine. The retailers then decide whether they will sell the magazine.

The retailers report that they screen magazines to avoid getting complaints from customers, but the retailers do not have clear policies about what is and isn't acceptable. As Walgreen's spokesperson Michael Polzin said, "We don't have written guidelines that we send to distributors, but they know what we're concerned about."[47] Winn-Dixie refused to carry an issue of *Cosmopolitan*, the largest-selling magazine in single-copy sales, when a cover headline read, "His & Her Orgasms," and Wal-Mart refused to carry an issue of *Vibe*, an urban culture magazine, because of a risqué photo of singer Toni Braxton on the cover. While most of the retail censorship concerns sexual material, the absence of clear policies allows retailers to refuse magazines with "articles on controversial subjects such as abortion, homosexuality, and religion."[48]

Magazines are not alone in having their content censored or shaped by retailers. Manufacturers of compact discs and motion picture videotapes have also been pressured to change content or be banished from the shelves of Wal-Mart, Kmart, Blockbuster, and other large retailers.[49] Wal-Mart, which sells nearly 10 percent of the compact discs in the United States, has refused to carry recordings that carry "parental advisory" stickers. The Arkansas-based retailer demands that recording companies produce tamer versions of their recordings to stock in Wal-Mart stores, with controversial or objectionable lyrics edited out and risqué portions of photos airbrushed out. Record companies and recording artists usually acquiesce to Wal-Mart's request for a different version of a recording because of the retailer's huge sales. Even superstars like John Mellencamp acquiesce to these demands, even if the demand doesn't concern sexual or violent content. Wal-Mart requested that images of Jesus and the devil be airbrushed off the cover of the Mellencamp album, *Mr. Happy Go-Lucky*, and Mellencamp complied.[50]

One artist who wouldn't comply was Sheryl Crow, whose song "Love Is a Good Thing" contained the lyrics, "Watch our children while they kill each other with a gun they bought at the Wal-Mart discount stores." Wal-Mart demanded that Crow delete the lyrics or be banished from their stores. The chain claimed that the lyrics were irresponsible and unfair, even though Wal-Mart has been sued twice by relatives of victims killed by Wal-Mart -purchased guns. Crow refused. The ban cost Crow an estimated half a million in sales.[51]

Trouble Brewing

Advertiser pressures and media self-censorship are serious issues, not just because they deprive citizens of information, but because they place impediments in the way of others' speech. Citizens' groups that advocate policies opposed by large advertisers are not just banished from news stories, they even find it difficult to buy advertising time. Major media are not willing to sell advertising time or space to advocacy groups that might offend large advertisers with their messages. As a consequence, these opposition views are rarely heard.

Under current law, the commercial media determine the advertisers to which they are willing to sell time or space. A television station or newspaper can refuse to sell advertising for any reason—not just because the ad is offensive, although "offensiveness" and "distastefulness" are frequently used excuses for refusing to carry issue ads. When a peace group, Neighbor to Neighbor, tried to buy television commercials calling for a boycott of Folgers coffee in 1990, a brand marketed by Procter & Gamble, the country's largest advertiser, Boston stations WBZ-TV and WCVB-TV refused to sell it time. The commercial, which suggested that money from coffee sales helped prolong the Salvadorean civil war, ended with blood dripping from a coffee cup. Anthony Vinciquerra, the general sales manager of WBZ-TV, called the commercial "terribly distasteful," adding that the claims made in the commercial lacked substantiation. WCVB-TV public relations director Burt Peretsky said his station normally did not accept issue advertising except during elections, but had rejected the commercial because it called "for damage to a particular product."[52]

Although WBZ-TV and WCVB-TV rejected the commercial, WHDH-TV aired it twice, causing Procter & Gamble to cancel $1 million in advertising on the station. Procter & Gamble cancelled its advertising for all brands—Pampers, Tide, Crest, Oil of Olay, and Charmin—not just Folgers. When cancelling the ads, Procter & Gamble warned that it would cancel advertising on any station that aired the "distasteful" commercial.[53] Stations apparently heeded Procter & Gamble's warning.

Boston television stations also refused to sell Neighbor to Neighbor advertising for a 1993 ad campaign that called for a "single payer" national health plan, similar to the one in Canada. Using a General Accounting Office report as its source, the commercial stated that "if we get rid of health insurance companies, we can have complete coverage for everyone for the same money."

Although the commercial was not offensive, it was nevertheless rejected by WHDH-TV and three other Boston television stations. Apparently fearful that it would lose health insurance advertising, as it had Procter & Gamble advertising, WHDH-TV announced that it would not air the commercial because "the issue is not addressed in a comprehensive manner in a 30-second format and [the station] will address it itself in a longer form sometime in the future."[54]

Boston isn't the only market where advocates of a single-payer national health plan have had difficulty buying time. Washington, D.C., stations refused to sell commercials to an advocacy group, the Campaign for Health Security, which asked, "Why don't we get rid of health insurance companies?" WRC-TV, owned and operated by NBC, said in rejecting the commercials that statements in the ad weren't supported by facts. "Statements which are presented as facts have to be substantiated," a station spokesperson explained, even though the station had been given an article from the prestigious *New England Journal of Medicine* that reached the same conclusion as commercials, and the *New England Journal* findings were publicized by a page three story in the *Washington Post* a few weeks earlier.[55]

Although they refused to sell commercial time to the consumer group, the stations ran numerous commercials unsupported by facts for health insurance companies and the Health Insurance Associations of America, which backed a mixture of public and private insurance.[56]

Washington, D.C., stations also refused to sell commercial time to another consumer group, the Health Care Reform Project, whose commercials criticized Pizza Hut for not providing health insurance for newly hired workers. Pizza Hut, a large television advertiser, warned the stations in a letter not to run the commercials, and none did. One station said that it wasn't influenced by the letter; it rejected the commmmercial because the appeal was "purely emotional."[57]

In the Twin Cities, television stations refused to sell commercial time to the Prairie Island Sioux community, who produced a commercial critical of Northern States Power Company's plan to store spent nuclear fuel rods on the island. When rejecting the Sioux community's request to buy advertising time, the television stations claimed that the commercials, which were professionally produced by an advertising agency, didn't meet their standards of professionalism. Northern States Power, the local utility monopoly, was a large advertiser on the television stations.[58]

In Detroit, radio stations refused to sell advertising time to the United Auto Workers, which was calling for a boycott of Hudson department stores following the corporation's intimidation of union organizers. Hudson was a large advertiser on the stations.[59]

During the 1997 test marketing in Cedar Rapids and Waterloo, Iowa, of Frito-Lay potato chips made with olestra, KCRG-TV and KWWL-TV refused to sell commercial time to the Center for Science in the Public Interest. The Center's television commercials described some of the health problems posed by olestra. In New Jersey, the *Asbury Park Press* refused to run an advertisement produced by local community groups that criticized several beer companies' "marketing beer to children" during the Halloween holiday season.[60]

"Offensive" was the excuse given by billboard companies, which refused to sell space for a 1999 anti-meat campaign sponsored by People for the Ethical Treatment of Animals (PETA). Billboard advertising is used extensively by the dairy and beef industries to promote consumption. The U.S. Dairy Producers, the seventy-second largest advertiser in the country, relies extensively on billboards, as does McDonald's, the largest seller of beef in the world. McDonald's was the fourteenth largest advertiser in the U.S. in 1998.[61]

The banished PETA billboard showed a bikini-clad model holding a string of sausages with the headline, "I Threw a Party But the Cattlemen Couldn't Come." Underneath was the line, "Eating Meat Can Cause Impotence." The purpose of the billboard was to promote vegetarianism by linking meat eating and impotence, for which there is some medical evidence. The evidence suggests that arteriosclerosis, which restricts blood flow, is higher for individuals who have high levels of saturated fats in their diets, and restricted blood flow can lead to impotence. Meat and dairy products are major sources of saturated fats.

Billboard companies in Wisconsin, Minnesota, Texas, Kansas, Nebraska, Oklahoma, and Colorado refused PETA's campaign, citing "offensiveness" as the reason. Michael Aloia, general manager of Chancellor Outdoor Advertising, which rejected the campaign for its billboards in Wisconsin and Minnesota, said, "What we like to do with any political advertising is, we prefer to have positive messages about the cause. We also have policies with regard to sexual orientation or sexual connotations," which the PETA campaign failed to meet.[62]

Of course, PETA is not the only group or advertiser that has been banished from billboards. In Utah, Wasatch Beer attempted to advertise, without success, Polygamy Porter, a beer that satirizes the Mormon practice of polygamy. The beer's billboard poster, which shows a scantily clad man, cherubs, and a six-pack of wives, advised drinkers to "take some home for the wives." Because it had received complaints about previous billboards used by Wasatch, which contained phrases such as "Baptize your taste buds" and "serving the local faithful," Reagan Outdoor Advertising Co., along with the Young Republic Sign Co., refused to carry the advertisements for Polygamy Porter.[63]

Even messages that are unoffensive, unemotional, and do not target a specific product have been rejected by mass media. The Media Foundation, which publishes *Adbusters* magazine and opposes the overcommercialization of society, has had difficulty finding media that will accept commercials for its annual "Buy Nothing Day." These "un-commercials" urge people to boycott businesses one day a year to protest crass consumerism. *Adbusters* editor Kalle Lasn reports that the un-commercials are routinesly rejected by station managers with comments such as, "Well, why should we shoot outselves in the foot by running your ads. We don't have to work against our legitimate business interests."[64]

Although the media frequently refuse to sell activist groups advertising time, the media apparently have no scruples when it comes to business-sponsored groups such as the Coalition for Health Insurance Choices, a front for the Health Insurance Associations of America; the National Smokers Alliance, an organization created and funded by the tobacco industry; the Partnership for a Competitive Texas, a front for AT&T; and Wisconsin Manufacturing and Commerce, an ostensibly nonpartisan organization that spends hundreds of thousands of dollars on issue ads attacking Democrats and liberals. These business front groups are well funded and buy huge amounts of advertising. Their advertisements are never rejected, even when emotional, unfair, and clearly deceptive.

The Coalition for Health Insurance Choices ran a multimillion-dollar advertising campaign featuring fictitious characters named "Harry" and "Louise" that opposed President Clinton's health care proposals. Although the group was not a coalition as claimed—it had no membership or funding except from the health insurance company trade association, the Health Insurance Associations of America (HIAA)—it had no difficulty buying advertising time on radio and television stations, including some that refused to carry commercials favoring a "single payer" plan. The HIAA campaign became the focus of many media stories, and the trade group "considered the bulk of this coverage to be very positive."[65]

In California, the National Smokers Alliance ran a newspaper advertising campaign against California's smoking restrictions, claiming that they hurt business and were "discriminatory." The Alliance, which existed only on paper, was the creation of the Philip Morris tobacco company and was industry-funded.[66] In Texas, a television advertising campaign was waged by the Partnership for a Competitive Texas that featured a fictitious character, "Carolyn," who claimed that Southwestern "Bell and GTE are fighting so hard to stop competition." The campaign suggested that the Partnership was a grassroots group that advocated telecommunication deregulation. In reality, the Partnership and the advertising campaign were created and funded by AT&T, a Bell and GTE competitor.[67]

In Wisconsin, Wisconsin Manufacturers & Commerce, a business-funded group that refuses to reveal the sources of its funding, and Americans for Job Security, a Washington, D.C.–based organization funded by insurance and paper companies, purchased numerous "issue ads" supporting Republican candidates and attacking Democrats in the 1998 elections, despite a state ban on business involvement in elections and a state law requiring the disclosure of campaign contributors. The groups claimed that they was running issue ads, not campaign ads, because the commercials did not explicitly recommend voting for Republican candidates. Television stations accepted these groups' deceptions and a half-million dollars from their advertising. Business front groups such as these exist for nearly every industry and in every state, giving corporations an incomparably large voice in policy debates.

The acceptance and rejection practices of commercial media suggest that they have two standards for accepting ads. One is for well-heeled advertisers like Calvin Klein, Wisconsin Manufacturers & Commerce, and the Coalition for Health Insurance Choices, which are free to create and air offensive, emotional, or deceptive ads. The other is for community and activist organizations, whose advertisements are rejected whenever they jeopardize an advertising account, even when the assertions can be documented. Facts are apparently irrelevant when they go against the interest of a large advertiser.[68]

9

Muzzling David: Corporate Media Goliaths

onoma State University's "Project Censored," which has examined national news coverage every year for over two decades, selected the Telecommunication Act of 1995 as the most underreported story of the year.[1] Although the mass media extensively covered federal legislation addressing media obscenity and the cutthroat competition between local and long distance telephone companies that year, coverage of the Telecommunication Act before its passage was virtually nonexistent, thereby eliminating public discussion about the content and wisdom of the act.[2]

The Telecommunication Act, passed by Congress and signed into law by President Bill Clinton in February 1996, eliminated the limits on media ownership that had been the foundation of U.S. telecommunications policy for decades. The ownership limits were developed to create a diversity of owners and voices among media owners, assuring that no corporation or small group of corporations would monopolize mediated discourse.

The Telecommunication Act of 1995 eliminated many of the Federal Communication Commission's (FCC) rules that limited the number of AM and FM radio stations that a corporation could own; abolished the FCC ban on the cross ownership of radio stations, television stations, and newspapers in the same market; eliminated numeric restrictions on television station ownership; and allowed telephone companies to own television stations and operate cable systems.

The mass media were publicly silent about the deregulation bill, even as the media industry lobbied intensively in Washington—behind the scenes—to assure the bill's passage. Media lobbyists argued the act would increase media competition, reduce prices to consumers, and make American media products more competitive in the global market.[3]

Rather than increasing competition in the mass media industry, as the media corporations argued during their Washington lobbying sessions, the Telecommunication Act stimulated a wave of mergers that reduced competition, decreased diversity, and increased prices. As it turned out, the only beneficiaries of the act were media owners, who saw the value of their radio stations, television stations, cable systems, and newspapers soar, as large media corporations sucked up smaller media companies in a tsunami of consolidation unmatched since the days of the robber barons.

An example of this consolidation is provided by the Westinghouse Corp., a large media, electronics and energy production company, which bought CBS at the end of 1995 for $5.4 billion from real estate magnate Laurence Tisch. Anticipating passage of the Telecommunication Act, Westinghouse paid nearly three times what Tisch had paid for his CBS stock ten years earlier.[4]

Westinghouse then acquired another radio network and station owner, Infinity Broadcasting, in a $4.7 billion deal that made Infinity CEO Mel Karmazin Westinghouse's biggest stockholder and one of America's most influential people. Karmazin was best known for putting shock jock Howard Stern on Infinity in 1985 and giving him the freedom to say almost anything—except about Karmazin.[5] The Infinity CEO ordered Stern to keep his name out of broadcasts. In 1998, Karmazin became CBS's president and chief operating officer.[6]

Next, Westinghouse gobbled up two cable networks, the Nashville Network and Country Music Television, in a $1.55 billion deal, and then bought American Radio Systems for $2.6 billion.[7] Within three years of the passage of the Telecommunication Act, Westinghouse owned 175 radio stations, the Westwood One radio network, fourteen television stations, and three television and cable networks. These acquisitions transformed Westinghouse from an electronics and power conglomerate into a media empire, dominating the electronic media in many large U.S. cities. In New

York City, Westinghouse wound up owning WCBS-TV and seven radio stations, capturing over 20 percent of the listening audience and 37 percent of radio advertising dollars. It owned ten stations in Chicago capturing 20 percent of the audience, and ten stations in Dallas/Fort Worth that captured 25 percent of the audience.[8] Westinghouse also owned at least four stations in Los Angeles, San Francisco, Philadelphia, Detroit, Houston, Boston, and Baltimore, where it dominated broadcasting.

In 2000, the CBS-Westinghouse giant was purchased for $34.9 billion by Viacom, Inc., the owner of the Nickelodeon, Showtime, and MTV cable channels, the Paramount studio, Simon & Schuster publishing, Blockbuster video stores, and UPN television network.[9] The merger produced the second largest U.S. media corporation.[10]

In 1997, Cumulus Media Corp. entered the feeding frenzy, gobbling up 304 radio stations in medium-sized cities such as Dubuque, Toledo, Green Bay, and Savannah in just three years. In many markets, Cumulus has become the dominant radio voice. For example, Cumulus owns seven stations in Savannah that program news-talk, classic rock, country, contemporary hits, urban music, gospel, and rhythm and blues, and seven stations programming a variety of formats in Montgomery, Toledo, and Youngstown.[11]

In cities where Cumulus is not dominant, another media company usually is. For example, the dominant radio broadcaster in Cincinnati is Jacor Communications, which owns four FM and two AM stations that control 30 percent of the listening audience and about 60 percent of radio advertising dollars.[12] Jacor acquired 131 stations nationwide within two years of the passage of the Telecommunication Act.

Even smaller media companies, such as the Belo Corp. of Dallas, owner of the *Dallas Morning News* and seven television stations in 1994, became involved in the frenzy of consolidations triggered by the Telecommunication Act. At the end of 1995, Belo bought the *Bryan-College Station Eagle* and in 1996 bought the *Messenger Eagle* in Owensboro, Kentucky. In 1997, it bought the Providence Journal Company, publisher of the *Providence Journal-Bulletin* and owner of eight television stations and

Northwest Cable News; the Riverside, California, *Press-Enterprise*; and Gleaner and Journal Publishing Company, owner of a daily newspaper, seven weekly newspapers, and an AM radio station. As a result of these acquisitions, Belo has become the dominant media voice in Texas, reaching over 60 percent of households with its television stations.[13]

The Telecommunication Act opened the door to even larger mergers that make the Cumulus, Jacor, and Belo consolidations look small. For example, the act allowed the merger of Time Warner, Turner Broadcasting, and America Online, producing a television-film production company, magazine publisher, cable operating system, cable network owner, theme park operator, and Internet giant unrivaled in size. This conglomerate owns cable networks, including CNN, HBO, Cinemax, TNT, and the Cartoon Network; 32 magazines, including *Time*, *Money*, *Sports Illustrated*, and *People*; Warner Music, which includes the Warner Brothers, Atlantic, and Electra labels; the WB television network; sports entertainments, including the Atlanta Braves and World Championship Wrestling; book publishing ventures including the Book-of-the-Month Club, Time-Life Books, and Little, Brown & Co.; DC Comics; Warner retail outlets; Great America theme parks; and the second-largest cable company in the U.S.

Corporate Ownership, Corporate Censorship

Given the benefits that the Telecommunication Act conferred on media corporations and their CEOs, there was a strong incentive for their keeping the public ignorant about the act until it was enacted. The media's silence about the Telecommunication Act is an example of media censorship, where newspapers, magazines, broadcasting stations, cable services, and Internet providers restrain coverage or provide one-sided coverage of issues for economic, personal, or ideological reasons. The lack of coverage of the Telecommunication Act is an example of censorship for economic reasons: The mass media, aware that the act would benefit them financially, avoided covering it, even though the legislation was the most significant telecommunication legislation adopted since 1934.

Media censorship is distinguishable from traditional "gatekeeping," where stories are selected by editors for inclusion in news reports based on importance and timeliness. Gatekeeping is influenced by many factors, such as reporting routines, time and space constraints in the media, the worldview and news standards of journalists, the availability of information, or pressures and complaints from powerful groups and readers.[14] Media censorship, by contrast, is a willful attempt to keep information from the public, and it occurs when the mass media censor or distort news stories to further their own institutional interests.

Although the Telecommunication Act is a dramatic recent example of the mass media censoring news, history suggests that the media have consistently censored or distorted news to protect their economic interests. When FM radio emerged, AM broadcasters like RCA, owner of the NBC network, sought to halt the development of FM, which was capable of providing listeners with higher-quality signals than AM. RCA falsely claimed that FM would make exisiting radio receivers obsolete, forcing listeners to needlessly buy new receivers.[15] And when subscription television emerged in the early 1960s, motion picture exhibitors and television broadcasters united to oppose the new pay-per-view medium, and conducted an alarmist campaign claiming that the new technology meant the end of "free" television.[16] In California, the established media industries sponsored and then campaigned for a ballot initiative, the Free Television Act, that banned subscription television. Although the industry-sponsored propaganda campaign convinced the California electorate to vote for the initiative, the California Supreme Court voided the law, saying that it violated free speech.[17]

More recently, newspapers in Michigan overwhelmingly opposed a state telecommunication bill that allowed telephone companies to become advertising and information-delivery providers competing directly with newspapers. A systematic study of the coverage of the Michigan telecommunication bill conducted in 1993 by Marquette journalism professor August Gribbin, a former *Detroit News* executive, found that the reportage was "lopsided" and "distorted." Of 3,560 paragraphs about the bill in news articles, features, editorials, and letters to the editor, there were nearly twice as many unfavorable as favorable statements about the bill, even though many specialists and public interest groups favored it. Almost two-thirds of the editorials failed to mention that newspapers had a vested interest in the legislation, and nearly a third engaged in name-calling, such as describing the local telephone company as "greedy" or a "monopolistic monster."[18]

Another recent example is provided by the *San Francisco Examiner*, where Hearst Corp. news executives in New York ordered *Examiner* publisher Timothy O. White to kill a story about the *San Francisco Chronicle*, which the Hearst Corp. was trying to buy. Fearing that the story could jeopardize Hearst's bid for the paper, Hearst newspaper chief George Irish ordered White to make sure "that there is no chance it would reach publication."[19]

In court testimony arising from a lawsuit over Hearst's bid to buy the *Chronicle*, White testified that he had also promised favorable editorial coverage of Mayor Willie Brown in exchange for Brown's support for the Hearst takeover plan. The positive coverage would appear in the editorial, not news, section of the paper. Despite White's testimony and the disclosures that Hearst had axed the story about the *Chronicle*, the Hearst Corp. issued a hypocritical statement saying that the *Examiner*'s "news and editorial coverage may not be . . . compromised in any way."[20]

The mass media also function as censors by refusing to carry advertisements that challenge the financial, ideological, or personal views of media owners. Ironically, media owners claim that they are exercising their First Amendment rights when they reject advertising with which they disagree, even when it is for entirely selfish motives. An example of this censorship is provided by the *Los Angeles Times*, which refused to publish advertisements for Pacific Bell's At Hand website, which competes with the *Times*'s website. Both carry news, information, and advertising.[21]

Another example is provided by K-III Publishing's *Spy* magazine, a shopworn version of the *National Lampoon*. The magazine accepted and then rejected an advertisement by Local One of the Amalgamated

Lithographers of America, which had been harassed by HLH/Panoramic, a lithography firm that prints *Spy*, *Soap Opera Digest*, *Seventeen*, and other K-III owned magazines. HLH/Panoramic repeatedly threatened union organizers, and the National Labor Relations Board found that the firm engaged in unfair labor practices.

To pressure HLH/Panoramic, the union purchased a full-page advertisement in *Spy* for $10,000 that described HLH's anti-union policies. The ad listed the magazine publishers that used HLH and urged readers to express their support for the union. When *Spy*'s publisher saw the union advertisement, he stopped its publication.

The union and its advertising agency, Lopez Communications, then decided to publicize *Spy*'s censorship by buying an advertisement in *Adweek*, a publication read by workers in the advertising industry. *Adweek* accepted the ad, but two days later decided not to publish it, fearing that the ad might anger K-III executives.[22]

An example of the mass media censoring a story—rather than censoring advertising—for personal reasons is provided by the largest tax fraud case in U.S. history, brought by the Internal Revenue Service against the owners of Newhouse media, who control Advance Corp., the parent company of Condé Nast, publisher of *Vanity Fair*, *Vogue*, *Glamour*, *Mademoiselle*, *GQ*, and *Brides*, and fifty newspapers, including the *Cleveland Plain Dealer*, *Newark Star-Ledger*, and the *New Orleans Times-Picayune*, and Newhouse Broadcasting, owner of five television stations and a cable operator with 1.2 million subscribers. When the Internal Revenue Service brought the tax evasion charges, Newhouse-owned media ignored the story, even though the IRS claimed that the Newhouses owed a record $609.5 million in estate taxes, which they refused to pay.[23]

Only when the Newhouses won their case against the IRS in 1990 did the story garner significant coverage, and then only in non-Newhouse publications.[24] Thereafter, the Newhouse News Service and Newhouse-owned newspapers carried numerous articles ridiculing the IRS. The articles bore headlines such as "Death Called No Excuse for Not Paying

Taxes," "IRS: Taxes Due on Loan State Forgave," "IRS Conflicts Charged," and "Boy's Estate Taxed for Uncollected Damages."[25]

This is not the only example of Newhouse censorship. Si Newhouse, the son of S. I. Newhouse who oversees the family's publishing empire, has a history of complaining about the stories published in their magazines and firing magazine and book editors. For example, Newhouse sacked Pantheon Books head Andre Schiffrin in 1990 for being fiscally irresponsible and publishing too many books, particularly left-wing ones. Schiffrin's severance agreement, like the agreements used by tobacco companies, prohibits him from talking about his dismissal.[26]

Gag clauses in employment and severance agreements have been used with other Newhouse executives, making it difficult to research and write about the Newhouse media corporation. When *Newsday* reporter Thomas Maier was writing *Newhouse*, a book about Si Newhouse, he discovered that current and former executives couldn't talk with him about the eccentric publishing magnate because of gag agreements they had signed; others wouldn't talk out of fear.[27]

The Newhouses also refuse to grant interviews about their family, empire, or finances; the corporation is privately owned and financial data about the corporation are not disclosed; and Newhouse publications and stations do not discuss their owners.[28] After Maier published *Newhouse*, *Vanity Fair* refused to run an advertisement for the book, and Newhouse-owned newspapers would not review it. When syndicated columnist Liz Smith mentioned the book in her column, Newhouse newspapers axed the column.[29]

Carol Felsenthal, who also wrote a book about the quirky Si Newhouse, encountered even more problems than Maier: Viking Press, which became a subsidiary of Penguin Putnam, Inc., after Felsenthal signed her book contract, took the unusual step of cancelling the book after it was finished. According to Felsenthal's agent, the presidents of Viking and Penguin Putnam said that they could not publish the biography because too many people mentioned in the book were their friends. Al Silverman, Felsenthal's editor at Viking before the Penguin Putnam takeover, said the book "was dropped because of the relationship between Newhouse and the top people at Viking Penguin."[30] Both reasons—to protect friends or powerful people—are examples of censorship exercised for personal reasons.

Felsenthal was paid by Viking and got back the rights to her book, but no large book company was willing to publish it, apparently out of fear that it would upset their relationship with Newhouse-owned Advance publications, whose magazines and newspapers are important publishers of book excerpts and reviews upon which large book publishers depend. In 1998, tiny Seven Stories Press eventually published the book, which was ignored by Newhouse magazines and newspapers. Daniel Simon, the founder of Seven Stories, said that "I was as scared of Newhouse as the next guy, but if a small, independent press like Seven Stories doesn't do this, then, well, we ought to just hang out our hats."

This was not Felsenthal's first run-in with powerful media moguls. In 1993, she published *Power, Privilege and the Post*, a biography of Katharine Graham, the influential owner of the *Washington Post*. Graham protested the book's characterizations in a 15-page letter sent by her attorney to the publisher, G. P. Putnam's Sons, forcing Felsenthal to spend an additional two months documenting the disputed parts. During those months, the publisher's support for the book waned. It was never brought out in paperback, and Ted Turner's contract to transform the book into a made-for-cable movie was cancelled.[31]

Other books about media executives and their friends have also been axed. Marc Eliot contracted to write a book about Walt Disney with Bantam Books, publisher of the highly successful "Walt Disney Fun-to-Learn" book series distributed through supermarkets and the "Disney Choose Your Own Adventure" library. After learning that Eliot's book would reveal Walt Disney's shady side, such as serving as an F. B. I. informant for twenty-five years, Disney public relations executive Robyn Tynan contacted Eliot, saying that the company was not happy about the book's portrayal of their patron. Bantam could not explain to Eliot how the Disney Corp. obtained a copy of his book proposal.

After Eliot shook off these comments, the Disney Corp. offered to "license the book and make it a Walt Disney product," even allowing Eliot to reproduce Disney archival materials and photographs in it. Eliot refused the offer because it would give Disney editorial control of the book. When Eliot went to the Disney Corp. offices in Burbank to do research, he was escorted from the premises by a security guard. Not long afterward, Bantam decided not to publish the book, saying that it was not of publishable quality.[32] Like Felsenthal's *Citizen Newhouse*, Eliot's *Hollywood's Dark Prince* was picked up by a small independent publisher, which brought out the book in 1993. It received rave reviews.

This isn't the only example of a Disney company censoring a story for personal reasons. ABC News, run by corporate attorney David Westin and owned by the Disney Corp., spiked a story about foreign sweatshops manufacturing ABC talk show host Kathie Lee Gifford's clothing line. Not only was Kathie Lee an ABC employee, but she and her husband were friends of Westin's. About axing the story, Westin says, "We did think of doing a piece, then concluded we shouldn't."[33]

Skin Tight by Christopher Byron had its promotion budget and press run slashed after editors at Simon and Schuster learned that the book contained many references to Paramount Communications president Stanley Jaffe's wife. At the time, Paramount owned Simon and Schuster. The press run was cut from 35,000–40,000 to 11,000; Simon and Schuster never sold the paperback rights; and Byron's publicity appearances were cancelled, effectively burying the book.[34]

A well-publicized example of ideological censorship, as opposed to personal censorship, where media owners prohibit a particular political or cultural view from being expressed, is provided by country singer k.d. lang, who appeared in a television commercial promoting vegetarianism produced by People for the Ethical Treatment of Animals (PETA). The commercial was part of PETA's "Meat Stinks" campaign. As a result of lang's antimeat advocacy, radio station KRVN in Nebraska banned her songs from the air. LS Radio, Inc., owner of eight radio stations in Kansas and Nebraska, and the Shepherd Group, the owner of radio stations in

Missouri and Montana, joined the boycott, as did other country stations in Montana. Hugh James, program director for KBOW in Butte, Montana, declared that "if she's going to boycott one of our state's major industries, we're going to boycott her."[35]

Although the lang boycott is a striking example, ideological censorship occurs daily in the form of *screening,* one of the best kept secrets in radio broadcasting. Screening is asking callers to radio programs what they intend to say before allowing them on the air. Although representatives of talk radio claim that the callers are screened to weed out "kooks and nuts," screening is often used as an ideological litmus test. As the *San Diego Union* noted, Rush Limbaugh "carefully screens his [calls] so that only those who avidly agree with him get through."[36] Some dissident callers do get through, but they are dismissed and ridiculed, making true debates on the program quite rare.

Mogul vs. M.B.A. Censorship

During the past decade, several writers have attributed media censorship to the increasing corporatization of the media and the conflicts of interest this creates. For example, Jim Naureckas, editor of *Extra!,* publication of the liberal media watchdog group, Fairness and Accuracy in Media, writes that "a corporate owner is fundamentally different from an individual or family owner. An individually owned news outlet may be good or bad, but if the owners want to, they can pursue quality journalism even if such decisions hurt their bottom line. The management of a corporate news outlet does not have that luxury. By law, management must not allow other considerations (like journalistic ethics or the public interest) to stand in the way of corporate profits—otherwise it would be abandoning its fiduciary responsibility to its stockholders and would be subject to a lawsuit."[37]

Naureckas attributes censorship at the NBC television network to General Electric's ownership of the network. GE is also a major defense contractor, nuclear power plant builder, and consumer electronics manufacturer, producing conflicts of interest for NBC when it reports on these issues. Although GE executives have not specifically directed NBC news executives to tailor news to serve GE's corporate interests, corporate executives made it clear that they owned NBC, and that they did not want NBC news to "bend over backwards to go after us just because we own you."[38]

GE's attitude encouraged NBC executives to champion the corporate, rather than public, interest, quickly undermining the network's credibility. A year after GE's 1986 takeover of NBC and the Chernobyl disaster, NBC aired a documentary, "Nuclear Power: In France It Works," extolling the virtues and safety of nuclear power. The documentary announced that "looking at a foreign country where nuclear power is a fact of life may restore some reason to the debate at home [where] emotions drive the nuclear debate."[39]

During 1987–1992, NBC, aware that the nuclear power program was a sensitive topic with top GE executives, covered the issue less than ABC or CBS. Of twenty-eight network evening news stories addressing U.S. nuclear power safety and nuclear plant closings, eleven were carried by ABC, eleven by CBS, and seven by NBC.[40] NBC also failed to cover as a breaking story disclosures in the Reed Report, a secret study produced by GE showing that its nuclear power plants had not been adequately tested. The report, which GE hid from the public, utility companies, and even federal regulators for a decade, was accidently discovered by a reporter for the *Cleveland Press*, which broke the story on June 2, 1987. The Associated Press and United Press International picked up the story that day. The *New York Times* ran a story on June 3, 1987, and followed up with another report on June 9. ABC covered the story twice—on July 24, 1987, and revisited it again on November 3, 1987—pointing out that GE was being sued by Ohio utility companies, which alleged that cost over runs and failures at the Zimmer nuclear power plant were due to fraud on the part of GE. NBC covered the story in just one newscast on August 7, two months after the story broke.

In a 1987 appearance on NBC's *Late Night with David Letterman*, cartoonist and social critic Harvey Pekar brought up GE's long list of criminal convictions and the conflicts of interest posed by GE's ownership of NBC. As Pekar put it, Letterman made wisecracks about GE-installed NBC president Robert Wright, so he thought Letterman would "dig it if I joined the fun. Boy was I wrong." When Pekar mentioned GE's criminal record, Letterman went to a commercial, then brought on another guest. On another show, Pekar again raised the issue of GE's ownership of NBC, and it prompted an on-air argument between him and Letterman.[41]

In a news report by award-winning investigative reporter Peter Karl about defective bolts used for building planes and nuclear-power plants, *Today* show executive producer Marty Ryan deleted mentions of GE. After being lambasted for a week about the edits, *Today* show did a follow-up report that mentioned GE by name. Although Ryan denied that GE's ownership of NBC affected his original decision to edit out the references to GE, Karl attributed the editing to "the chilling effect [of GE ownership] that everyone feared would occur at NBC."[42]

A year after pulling the plug on the GE references, *Today* producers decided to do a segment on consumer boycotts, so they called Todd Putnam, editor of *National Boycott News*. *Today*'s Amy Rosenberg asked Putnam about the "biggest boycott going on right now," so Putnam explained that it was the INFACT boycott of GE. Rosenberg replied, "We can't do that one. . . . Well, we could, but we won't." *Today* cancelled its segment on boycotts. When *Today* eventually did a segment on boycotts, the INFACT boycott was never mentioned.[43]

In 1992, *Today* abruptly cancelled a scheduled appearance by author and anti-nuclear activist Helen Caldicott, who was promoting her book, *If You Love This Planet: A Plan to Heal the Earth*. After learning that the book criticized GE, NBC decided that Caldicott lacked credibility and called off her interview.[44]

Such episodes help explain the public's cynicism toward the mass media, which is often exhibited in public opinion polls. For example, about two-thirds of the respondents to a 1993 *Los Angeles Times* poll thought that "the press looks out mainly for powerful people," and nearly 70 percent agreed that "the news media give more coverage to stories that support their own point of view than to those that don't,"[45] as NBC had done in its coverage of GE.

NBC is not the only television network that has engaged in censorship to further the interests of a conglomerate owner. ABC has also censored stories. ABC News killed a story about Disney, ABC's owner, which reported that weak screening procedures had led the company to hire pedophiles at its theme parks. ABC news chief David Westin allegedly screamed at investigative reporter Brian Ross for doing the story, asking him, "Are you crazy?"[46] A story about corporate CEO salaries was dropped by *20/20* because of fear that it would draw attention to Disney CEO Michael Eisner's immense salary, and ABC killed a story about a cruise ship because Disney operates a competing cruise line. ABC even killed another story about a feature film, *Chicken Run,* because it was produced by Disney rival DreamWorks.[47]

James D. Squires, a former editor of the *Chicago Tribune* and *Orlando Sentinel,* described in his autobiographical book, *Read All About It! The Corporate Takeover of America's Newspapers,* the attempts of Tribune Company executives to influence news and editorial content at their papers. According to Squires, after the Tribune Company purchased the Chicago Cubs, executives wanted the paper to function as a Cubs booster, providing the team with positive rather than critical stories. Tribune executives lobbied the editorial page editor about political endorsements and local issues that would benefit the company, and when legislation was pending that affected the company's interests, they demanded that the paper speak in the company's behalf.

Like Naureckas, Squires asserts that these actions were the result of corporate ownership. Squires says that when newspapers were run by publishing moguls like the *Tribune*'s Colonel Robert McCormick, rather than by M.B.A.s, they were more likely to serve the public interest.

Despite Squires's admiration for McCormick, he describes several instances of the newspaper mogul's censoring stories for personal, political, or ideological reasons. Squires reports that after the Rhode Island legislature passed horse-racing legislation that Colonel McCormick opposed, the newspaper mogul banned the name of the state from the newspaper and ordered *Tribune* maps to delete Rhode Island.[48]

There are many other examples of McCormick censoring the news. McCormick, a conservative and arch anti-communist, used his newspaper to attack President Franklin D. Roosevelt during the 1930s and 1940s. McCormick made sure his newspaper printed every scurrilous, and often-times meritless, attack on the president and withheld important positive reports. Because of its distorted coverage, the *Tribune* came in second for "least fair and reliable" newspaper in a 1936 poll of Washington correspondents.[49]

The *Tribune*'s coverage of Soviet Russia was no better. To assure that only negative stories about the Russians appeared in his newspaper, the Colonel hired Donald Day as his Baltic correspondent. Day was an anti-communist, pro-Nazi, propagandist who defected to Germany near the end of the Second World War and became a "radio traitor," broadcasting pro-Axis radio shows to the United States.[50] According to George Seldes, Day "faked the news [while working for the *Tribune*] for more than twenty years and that Colonel McCormick knew that Day lied and printed his lies because he liked those lies."[51]

The *Chicago Tribune* was not the only mogul-run newspaper that presented unreliable news to readers. William Randolph Hearst's newspapers, which accounted for 13.6 percent of U.S. daily and 24.2 percent of Sunday circulation in 1935, were worse, having been voted the "least fair and reliable" newspapers in the 1936 Washington correspondents' poll. Hearst often engaged in censorship. After learning that Orson Welles's 1941 RKO movie *Citizen Kane* was loosely based on his life, Hearst ordered his newspapers to eliminate every mention of RKO films, not just *Citizen Kane*, from film reviews, articles, and even gossip columns to bring pressure upon the studio. Hearst then enlisted Hearst columnist Louella Parsons in his campaign against the film. Parsons threatened every power broker in Hollywood, saying that their unsavory private lives would be bared in Hearst newspapers if *Citizen Kane* were released. Members of RKO's board of directors were also threatened and the manager of RKO-owned Radio

City Music Hall in New York City was told that Hearst papers would not review or accept advertising for films playing at the Music Hall if *Citizen Kane* played there.

After RKO hesitatingly released *Citizen Kane*, some national theater chains refused to show the film out of deference to, or fear of, Hearst. Although considered the one of the best motion pictures ever made, *Citizen Kane* wound up a box-office casualty.[52]

Although claiming to be a champion of labor, Hearst's newspapers assailed unions and the National Labor Relations Act, which granted employees protection against employers' anti-labor abuses, calling it "one of the most vicious pieces of class legislation that could ever be conceived."[53] Hearst even instructed his editors on the content and spin of anti-labor news stories. For example, during a 1934 general strike in San Francisco, Hearst instructed his editors to carry stories on how a general strike in England was crushed by the government in 1926, hoping that the stories would inspire government intervention to end the San Francisco strike.

In an effort to turn the public against the strikers, Hearst papers—and almost all other Northern California newspapers—described the strike as a "revolution" led by "radicals" and "anarchists." In its report on coverage of the strike, the *New Republic* said that the newpapers "lied ruthlessly and repeatedly in the endeavor to fan the flames of hostile public opinion. . . . By suppressing the facts about what has happened and by continued false statements about the extent of radicalism and pretended 'revolutionary purposes' of the strike leaders," the newspapers managed to shift public opinion against the strikers.[54]

The same year, Hearst and other newspapers engaged in a systematic campaign of lies and distortions against California gubernatorial candidate Upton Sinclair, whom they feared would encourage the unionization of all California workers if elected. In an effort to defeat Sinclair, newspapers reported that hobos were pouring into California to illegally vote for Sinclair, since they would be the primary beneficiaries of his policies. Hearst's *Herald-Express* and other papers, including the *Los*

Angeles Times, published a still from the Warner Bothers movie, *Wild Boys of the Road*, claiming that it was an actual photo of hobos arriving in California.[55]

Movie moguls Irving Thalberg and Louis B. Mayer even produced faked newsreels that were distributed free to theaters in their effort to defeat Sinclair. One newsreel contained nice-looking, well-dressed, articulate people speaking in favor of Republican candidate Frank Merriam "and criminal-looking types with Russian accents" speaking in favor of Sinclair.[56] Another newsreel, apparently constructed using outtakes from *Wild Boys of the Road*, showed hobos streaming into California. On- and off-camera figures asserted that hundred of these hobos, mostly criminals and Communists, were entering California on every freight train to vote for Sinclair.[57]

Framing Labor

The reason why the new media present anti-labor stories is not just ideological, but also economic: Media owners have consistently opposed unions because they organize newspaper employees, who then get a slice of the newspaper's profits.

Systematic studies have shown that representatives of labor are either portrayed negatively during labor strikes or blacked out from news reports during other periods. Two studies conducted during the early 1980s by the International Association of Machinists and Aerospace Workers found that labor was neglected in news reports except during strikes, that the reasons why workers struck were rarely explained, and that dramatic programs "depicted unions as violent, degrading, and obstructive."[58] A study published during 1989 of sources in network television news stories found that government officials, business spokespersons, and professionals, such as attorneys, professors, and physicians, often appear as news sources, but not representatives of labor.[59]

A study of newspapers in Illinois found that strikes were the most frequently covered labor action, but that employers' actions affecting employees were infrequently covered.[60] The news media's silence about employers' attacks on labor, which occur on a continuing basis, is perhaps the most blatant and shameful form of media censorship.

The mass media are most likely to frame stories from an anti-union perspective when a union takes on a medium. A study of elite newspaper and magazine coverage of the 1975 *Washington Post* pressmen's strike found that most news stories contained "unjustified biases."[61] In adddition to portraying the strikers negatively, the press never explained the reasons for the strike.

As in the pressmen's strike, the *Detroit Free Press*'s coverage of the more recent Newspaper Guild strike against it and the jointly published *Detroit News* has been consistently slanted. After a federal judge ordered the newspaper to hire back striking employees, the newspaper on June 21, 1997, ran the following headline: "Strike Ruled Unfair; Appeal Planned." In contrast, the *New York Times* headline reported, "Judge Orders Detroit Newspapers to Rehire Strikers"; the *Los Angeles Times* headline reported, "Detroit Told to Rehire Striking Workers"; and the *Boston Globe* headline reported, "Detroit Papers Ordered to Rehire Workers."[62]

And it isn't just newspapers or for-profit media that engage in anti-union censorship. Pacifica Radio, a nonprofit "alternative" to commercial radio, confronted a strike by freelance reporters at KPFA by prohibiting all on-air mentions of the strike. In 1999, Pacifica management not only locked out strikers and banned on-air discussions of discord at their stations, but even used hired security personnel to drag a commentator away from the microphone as he was talking about the job actions.[63] And when a California legislative auditing committee attempted to examine Pacifica expenditures for fighting the strike, Pacifica acted like the tobacco companies, attempting to keep the documents from becoming public. Pacifica turned the documents over only after being threatened with a subpoena.[64]

These examples suggest that corporate ownership by itself is not responsible for media censorship, but that corporate ownership can increase the effectiveness of censorship and the conflicts of interest that often result in news censorship. The reason why corporate ownership can increase the effectiveness of censorship is that corporations tend to own far more media outlets in a single city, state, or region than individual owners, making it easier to suppress news. Oftentimes, one corporation dominates a city's or a state's media, as Journal-Communications, Inc., does in Milwaukee. Journal-Communications owns the only daily newspaper in Milwaukee, the *Journal Sentinel*, the suburban weekly newspaper chain, NBC-affiliate WTMJ-TV, WTMJ-AM, the city's top-rated radio station, and WKTI-FM. Given this dominance, the corporation easily controls the public's access to local news information.[65]

An example of how Journal-Communications, Inc., used this control to suppress or distort information is provided by its campaign to obtain taxpayer funding for a baseball stadium for the Milwaukee Brewers. The corporation was a registered lobbyist for the stadium campaign, something Milwaukeeans were not told, and its media consistently provided one-sided coverage of the issue.[66] Corporate executives even axed a story on the way that state legislators intended to vote on the issue. The newspaper executives feared that the article would publicly commit legislators to vote against the bill, and this would give Journal Communications and other lobbyists a more difficult time convincing them to change their vote.[67]

Conglomerates like Time Warner and GE, which are in many businesses in addition to news production, have many more financial incentives for censoring news than do owners of a single news medium. Time Warner needs to protect its investments in the Internet, television and cable networks, cable systems, professional sports, theme parks, motion pictures, and retailing, and GE needs to protects its investments in consumer electronics, defense, television, radio, and power production. As *Extra!* editor Jim Naureckas observed, these corporations have a fiduciary responsibility to stockholders to protect their other businesses, even if means resorting to censorship.

Time Warner's cable blackout of ABC network programming, including *ABC World News Tonight* and *Nightline,* shows how conglomeration can lead to censorship. During July 2000, Time Warner and ABC's owner, the Disney Corp., were unable to reach an agreement on the amount of money that Time Warner should pay for carrying on its cable systems the Toon, Soap, and Disney cable channels and retransmitting the programming of eleven Disney-owned ABC stations in New York, Los Angeles, and other major cities. When Disney refused Time Warner's offer, Time Warner deleted ABC network shows from cable systems in seven regions during July 2000, depriving eight million viewers access to the highest-rated television network. When viewers turned their television sets to ABC, they discovered a message from Time Warner explaining that the programs were not available. The FCC declared Time Warner's blackout a violation of FCC rules, so the media giant backed down, and put ABC back on.[68]

Although the Disney blackout was ostensibly about cable payments, financial analysts and former FCC chair Reed Hundt said that the real conflict concerned two other issues: Disney's agreement with satellite dish company DirectTV and Time Warner's merger with Internet service provider AOL. In several markets, Disney was reimbursing DirectTV customers for the price of satellite dishes and installation, allowing customers to receive the Disney Channel without subscribing to cable. Time Warner executives branded the DirectTV offer a "nakedly hostile act" aimed at undermining its cable business. It was apparently a factor in Time Warner's decision to black out ABC programming.[69]

Disney opposed the AOL-Time Warner merger because it would give AOL Time Warner too much control over programming delivered over the internet, where Disney has few holdings. "That's the big fight here," says former FCC chair Hundt. "Disney is gearing up for its survival on the Internet."[70] If the former FCC chair is correct, Time Warner deleted ABC from its cable system to punish Disney for its opposition to the proposed AOL-Time Warner merger.

Disney feared that Time Warner could demand part ownership of the company in return for delivering Disney programs over the Internet, make it difficult for computer users to find Disney programming on the

Web, or even delete Disney's signal entirely. Time Warner has a long history of refusing to carry competing cable networks on its systems and shamelessly demands part ownership of the cable programming that it carries. Long ago, Time Warner cable systems refused to carry Showtime, which competes directly with Time Warner's HBO pay cable network. After acquiring part ownership of CNN, the media goliath refused to carry the NBC cable news network and Rupert Murdoch's Fox News Channel, but eventually gave in under government pressure. In Manhattan, Time Warner has part or complete ownership of 40 percent of the cable networks that it carries.[71] Time Warner could be even more predatory on Internet program delivery, which is largely unregulated by government.

Disney's fear was not just that AOL Time Warner could demand a piece of Disney, but that the multimedia giant could easily shut Disney out of the Internet. Internet service providers (ISPs) often engage in censorship and justify it by claiming that their systems are "private property." In 1994, America Online shut down a feminist discussion forum, justifying the action by saying that young girls might be exposed to adult discussions; CompuServe threatened a subscriber with termination if he discussed his lawsuit against the company online; and Prodigy censored anti-Semitic remarks on its online forums.[72]

In 1997, AOL intercepted and deleted unsolicited e-mail messages sent to AOL subscribers by Cyber Promotions, Inc. Cyber Promotions was a "spammer," sending bulk e-mails filled with get-rich-schemes, flim flams, and even pornography. In the court case arising from AOL's action, AOL argued that it was the electronic equivalent of a mall, not a common carrier or a company town, and that it had the right to bar speech within its cyberspace. "The First Amendment simply does not apply to private entities like AOL," its lawyers argued. "[W]hen a nonmember, such as Cyber, intrudes into the service. . . AOL has the right to restrict nonmember's access to AOL's private property."[73]

Cyber's attorneys argued that AOL had opened its system to the Internet and therefore was serving as a public forum. "AOL could have tried to survive as a closed service, providing its members with access only to AOL's content. Instead, AOL chose to connect its subscribers to the Internet." Nobody owns the Internet, Cyber's attorneys argued, and therefore AOL cannot claim that its service is the equivalent of private space.[74]

AOL's arguments won out in federal court. Judge Charles Weiner reached the right decision for the wrong reason, concluding that "AOL's e-mail servers are certainly not a traditional public forum. . . . AOL's e-mail servers are privately owned and are only available to the subscribers of AOL who pay a fee for their usage." As a result, the judge concluded, AOL can bar e-mails sent by non-AOL subscribers."[75] Had Weiner concluded that "spamming" was a form of commercial speech that does not deserve the same protection as social speech, or that Cyber's messages were deceptive, the public would have been better protected against censorship.

The court decision allows AOL to censor incoming messages. Among other messages that AOL has censored are email sent by Harvard University to applicants, informing the applicants of their acceptance to the ivy league school. AOL spokesperson Nicholas Graham says that "it's hard to say what would have caused the system to filter email from Harvard."[76] However, there is an explanation: AOL aggressively censors incoming messages.

AOL is not the only ISP censoring email. Many ISPs, including CompuServe and Earthlink, have also banned "unsolicited" emails.[77]

The court decisions suggest that if ISPs can stop e-mails sent to their subscribers, they are also free to pick and choose the programs that their systems will deliver to subscribers, allowing AOL Time Warner to virtually shut competitors such as Disney out of their systems. At the least, AOL could make it difficult for subscribers to access the Web pages of rivals, as AOL did with Yahoo during the 1990s. Subscribers wanting to use Yahoo had to click through an extra page asking them if they wanted to return to AOL.com instead.[78]

Prodigy, a joint venture of IBM, Inc., and Sears, Roebuck & Company, went even further, punishing subscribers from sending e-mail messages that the company didn't like. In 1990, after Prodigy started charging subscribers who sent more than thirty e-mail messages a month a 25 cents per message surcharge, subscriber Henry Niman rebelled. Niman opposed the surcharge and compiled the names of like-minded Prodigy subscribers, to whom he sent an online newsletter. Niman also complained to Prodigy advertisers. To punish Niman and twelve other protesters, Prodigy terminated their service. Prodigy justi-fied its decision, saying that "they violated the member agreement by using harassment and by using the system for purposes for which it was-n't designed." Prodigy also rewrote its rules a few weeks later, prohibit-ing users from sending e-mails to advertisers except to place orders or inquire about products.[79]

And it isn't just ISPs among high-tech businesses that have engaged in censorship. Many parts of the computer industry, as well as companies with websites, also have. As an example, software manufacturers have increasingly placed nondisclosure clauses in licenses that ban negative reviews of their software.[80] Software licenses containing these speech restrictions constitute civil contracts with terms that users unknowingly accept when they load the software onto their computers.

Another example is provided by Microsoft, Inc., which threatened Slashdot.org, an online news site for computer nerds, with violating the Digital Millennium Copyright Act for including portions of Microsoft's version of Kerberos in a discussion of the program. Kerberos is actually a shareware program Microsoft adopted to run on Windows 2000. Kerberos was discussed in the Justice Department's anticompetitive practices com-plaint against Microsoft because the software giant made their version less "interoperable" with other versions. Slashdot.com publicly characterized Microsoft's threat as an attempt to stifle public criticism of its programs and practices.[81]

A more comic example of e-speech suppression is provided by Bank of America, which was upset that users could parody its website, using Internet site "Dialectizer." Dialectizer was a program developed by soft-ware engineer Samuel Stoddard that allowed users to convert standard

English texts into several humorous "dialects," such as Redneck, Swedish chef, Pig Latin, and Jive at Rinkworks.com. Using Dialectizer, "I know my legal rights" becomes "Ah knows mah legal rights" in Redneck. The Dialectizer site was visited about 7,000–8,000 times a day by Internet surfers. After a Dialectizer user converted the text of Bank of America's website into a "dialect," the bank moved against Stoddard, threatening him for copyright infringement. Fearing that a court fight would bankrupt him, Stoddard shut down Dialectizer.[82]

After Slashdot.com alerted Internet users about Bank of America's threats, Stoddard and Bank of America received thousands of e-mails criticizing the "corporate bullies." Emboldened by the outpouring of support, Stoddard reactivated Dialectizer, but this time placed a link allowing companies to block access to their websites. Bank of America announced that it was satisfied that the site would now end the parodies of its Web page, so it withdrew its threats.

Rather than increasing free speech, new computer technologies and the laws that they have spawned have actually made it easier for companies to stifle speech. ISPs assert that their networks are the equivalent of malls rather than company towns or common carriers, allowing them to curtail speech within their networks, and software manufacturers claim far more rights to their product than do publishers of other media products, allowing them to severely curtail what consumers can say about, or do, with their software purchases.

High-tech corporations have also lobbied vigorously for legislation benefitting their industries, as the broadcasting industry has, and have threatened that if states do not adopt the legislation, they will move their businesses to those states adopting business-friendly laws. One of the most restrictive bills that the industry has been pushing is the Uniform Computer Information Act (UCIA). Versions of the statute were brought before the Maryland, Virginia, and Illinois state legislatures in early 2000. Some versions legalize the speech restrictive clauses in licenses; almost all would allow software manufacturers to forbid the subsequent sale or transfer of their software programs.

Most require users to delete the software on hard drives before selling their computers.[83]

Putting the Mass in the Media

Clearly, passing industry-serving legislation such as the UCIA is a step in the wrong direction. What is needed are laws that protect consumers from corporations; not laws that allow corporations to exercise even more power over citizens. Any law or court decision that limits rather than expands public discourse needs to be reversed.

An example of a court decision in need of reversal is *Cyber Promotions, Inc. v. America Online, Inc.*, which ruled that ISPs operate within private cyberspace. The conclusions of Judge Weiner in this case were ill-informed and illogical compared to the arguments of Cyber's attorneys. The attorneys were correct when they stated that subscribers pay AOL for the Internet access that it provides, and that the other services, such as games and movie reviews, that AOL provides, are secondary. If the other services were primary, AOL would operate as a closed network, which it does not.

If subscribers do go to a private ISP to obtain access to the government-created Internet, then it follows that ISPs are common carriers, whose function is to link citizens with an electronic public forum. As common carriers, ISPs should have no rights to censor materials or engage in actions that make access to some information more difficult than access to other information.

Clearly, Congress has the power to make ISPs function as nonexclusionary common carriers. If ISPs want to maintain the fiction that they are electronic malls, not common carriers, they should sever their Internet links and operate as truly private networks.

The same is true of cable television systems. In the past, cable systems were regulated as though they were common carriers. Local and federal regulations determined what broadcast signals cable stations could carry, required cable systems to provide and subsidize public access channels, required cable operators to operate educational and government access channels, and even determined the rates that cable systems could charge. Unfortunately, cable has been deregulated, giving large corporations like Time Warner rather than public officials the power to determine the programs to which viewers will be exposed. It is time to rethink deregulation, which has ultimately increased the power of media corporations—and their ability to control the flow of information.

Until the 1980s, when Reagan administration appointees to the FCC began deregulating the broadcasting industry, there were many regulations, albeit weak ones, that required broadcasters to address public issues in an evenhanded manner. One rule, called "ascertainment," required broadcasters to determine the "problems, needs, and interests" of the community through surveys of citizens and opinion leaders, and then address these issues in their programming.[84] Under this rule, broadcasters could not ignore particular public issues; they were required to address them in public service announcements, public affairs programming, or newscasts. Failure to abide by ascertainment could result in license revocation. Unfortunately for the public, the FCC ended ascertainment in the 1980s, allowing broadcasting corporations, not the public, to determine what issues would be addressed or ignored by the broadcast media.[85]

Another regulation, called the Fairness Doctrine, required broadcasting stations to provide the public with "a reasonable opportunity to hear different opposing positions on the public issues of interest and importance to the community."[86] Although the doctrine did not require broadcasters to be fair in their presentation of news, it required broadcasting stations to provide listeners with points of view that contrasted with the stations' editorial positions. The doctrine actually promoted a variety of viewpoints in talk radio, a very different situation from today, where conservative commentators like Rush Limbaugh, G. Gordon Liddy, Michael Reagan, and Ken Hamblin dominate discourse. For a while in the 1960s, the FCC even applied the Fairness Doctrine to the advertising of controversial products such as cigarettes.[87]

The revocation of the Fairness Doctrine in 1987 stripped broadcasters of their fairness requirement, allowing broadcasting corporations to present highly biased, one-sided presentations of issues, if they so chose.[88] Not surprisingly, the public's confidence in news dropped precipitously following the revocation of the Fairness Doctrine and other deregulatory acts. A Yankelovich poll found that public confidence in the news was at 55 percent in 1988; by 1993, it was down to 20 percent.[89]

The rationale for revoking the Fairness Doctrine was that there were many different broadcasters in communities, assuring that a diversity of views would be presented. Although the rationale for revoking the Fairness Doctrine in 1987 was weak to begin with, because most stations even then were owned by corporate entities, the rationale lacks all merit in the post–Telecommunication Act era, where massive consolidations have drastically limited the number of corporate owners.[90] (This consolidation actually began during the Reagan era, when the FCC changed its longstanding 7-7-7 ownership limit, which prohibited a corporation from owning more than seven AM, seven FM, and seven television stations nationwide. In 1984, Reagan's appointees to the FCC allowed companies to own twelve AM, twelve FM, and twelve television stations. This rule change led to the first wave of consolidations in the broadcasting industry, allowing Capital Cities Communications, Inc. to purchase ABC and GE to purchase NBC. These takeovers were a mere opening act for the massive corporate mating dance that followed passage of the Telecommunication Act.)

Because of the consolidation spawned by the Telecommunication Act, there are fewer media owners in each market today than when the Fairness Doctrine was revoked. As a consequence, there is a pressing need to resurrect the "public interest" doctrine that guided broadcasting and which led to ascertainment and the Fairness Doctrine. The now-forgotten "public interest" doctrine, the basis of U.S. telecommunication policy for a half-century, required broadcasters to operate in the "public interest, convenience, and necessity." Broadcasters who failed to serve the public interest could have their licenses revoked.

The public interest doctrine actually involved citizens in the licensing of stations. Citizens and community groups often challenged the licenses of broadcasters who failed to air public service announcements, ignored the Fairness Doctrine, or refused to address pressing public issues in their programming. Although the FCC rarely revoked licenses, media corporations did face a threat of license revocation if they failed to perform in the "public interest, convenience, and necessity." Because Congress and the FCC have scrapped the regulations underlying the public interest doctrine, broadcasters now operate as if they own the airwaves, which they do not.

In addition to returning to the public interest doctrine, a greater diversity in station ownership is needed. This can come about in just two ways: awarding broadcasting licenses to groups that do not currently own stations and reducing the number of stations that a single licensee owns.

There have been attempts to increase ownership diversity, but every attempt has been countered by media corporation lobbying and propaganda campaigns. In 1993, the FCC opened the upper end of the AM band—1605 to 1705 kHz—to broadcasting. As with the Telecommunication Act, there was virtually no media coverage of the proposed change, although it was covered by magazines targeted to the media industry, such as *Broadcasting & Cablecasting.*[91]

Rather than opening this portion of the spectrum to new voices, the FCC acquiesced to the lobbying of media owners and reserved these frequencies for already-licensed AM broadcasters, who could petition to move their stations from lower to higher frequencies. The FCC and the industry claimed that the decision wasn't a gift to the broadcasting industry; it was needed to alleviate crowding in the AM band.

Similarly, when the FCC adopted rules creating a new class of low-power FM stations that would compete for listeners with existing stations, the industry quietly lobbied Congress to roll back the new rules, falsely arguing that the new stations would create interference problems.[92] At the urging of the National Association of Broadcasters, the main lobby group for the broadcasting industry, the House of Representatives passed the

Radio Broadcasting Preservation Act of 1999 (H.R. 3439), a modern-day version of the Free Television Act, that banned the new low-power stations even before they went on the air. As with the Telecommunication Act, H.R. 3439 was not discussed by the news media, and the bill passed with little public or even congressional debate about its wisdom or truthfulness.

The other alternative, reducing the number of broadcasting stations that a single company can own, reverses the Telecommunication Act. Had the mass media not blacked out discussion of the act, it is doubtful that this self-serving legislation would have passed. Although the large media corporations that benefitted from the act will claim that reversing the act is unfair and would cost them millions—perhaps billions—of dollars, the argument is hypocritical because it was the unfairness of the media's coverage of the act that allowed it to be adopted. Reversing the act merely redresses the media's past unfairness.

The passage of the Telecommunication Act not only demonstrates how media corporations use their media outlets for selfish ends, but also shows how the political system has been thoroughly corrupted by corporate lobbying. Clearly, media corporations, like all other corporations, need to be reigned in.

10

Freeing Speech

In an article in *New Jersey Lawyer*, Rutgers University law school professor Frank Askin observed that there was an "incredibly shrinking public forum," which reduced the number of venues where politically involved citizens can exercise their First Amendment rights. Askin observed that traditional downtowns have been replaced by shopping malls, and that neighborhoods with public streets are being replaced by common interest developments (CIDs) with private roadways.[1] Askin referred to these democracy-threatening developments as the "privatizing" of public forums.

Contrary to the claims of free market advocates, deregulation and "privatization" have produced censorship; they have not reduced censorship. This is clear from examining the privatization of public properties that has occurred in the United States since the 1980s. Public thoroughfares, such as Canby Avenue in Northridge, California, that have been privatized now have gates that restrict access to roads, sidewalks, and homes that were formerly accessible to the public. In Milwaukee, many streets and adjacent sidewalks have been privatized, closing them off to speech and assembly. The city "vacated" public streets to Miller Brewing Co. and Masterlock, Inc., so that North Lite Lane and North Miller Mall now occupy the areas that were formerly 39th St. and 40th St. North Lite Lane and North Miller Mall are private property and off-limits to the public.

In numerous cities and counties around the United States, public facilities and buildings have been privatized in the name of efficiency and the free market. City, county, and university hospitals have been transferred to the private sector; public museums have been turned over to private, albeit nonprofit, corporations; and even traditional public schools have been replaced with charter schools and "choice" schools, where students are permitted to attend private schools that receive tax dollars.[2] Citizens lack the constitutional protections on these properties that they have on public property.

Public lands have also been sold or leased to the private sector, eliminating free speech rights on these properties. For example, Milwaukee County has sold to developers acres of the Milwaukee County Grounds, a large parcel of public land that includes hiking trails, bike paths, and county buildings, such as the sheriff's station. The tracts of land that were sold are now private property, where speech can be restricted.[3]

Governments have also been engaged in numerous private sector–public sector "partnerships," where the private sector's property rights trump the public sector's contributions to the projects. For example, Wisconsin taxpayers, like taxpayers in many states, built a new stadium for the Milwaukee Brewers professional baseball team. Under this "partnership," the sales tax in a five-county area was increased, producing $160 million to build a retractable, dome-covered baseball stadium. Although the Brewers corporation ostensibly contributed $90 million toward the construction of the stadium, $40 million of the $90 million came from the sale of the "naming rights" for the stadium—meaning that the baseball corporation didn't contribute this money at all. (The "naming rights" were sold to Miller Brewing, a subsidiary of the Philip Morris Corp., so that the taxpayer-built stadium is now called "Miller Park.") The remaining $50 million came from city loans, local foundations, and businesses, which the baseball corporation will repay at $3 million per year—about half the salary that San Francisco Giants baseball player Barry Bonds earned annually in 1998 and 1999. The Brewers corporation will also pay a paltry $1.1 million per year to lease the $393 million stadium.[4]

As for the status of the stadium, executive director of the state-created stadium board, Mike Duckett, says, "In all honesty, I can't answer whether we're a public or a private place." Duckett explains that the stadium board has "a 99-year ground lease, and in turn leases [the stadium] to the

Brewers." Neither lease discusses public speech at the park, "but the Brewers might have policies about that," Duckett says.[5]

And the Brewers do have a policy—the Brewers corporation views the stadium as its private property and prohibits the distribution of handbills and other political activities on its premises. Although the Brewers corporation designates an area outside the stadium where people are allowed to hold up placards, "we don't allow them to distribute literature," says Scott Jenkins, the vice president of stadium operations for the Brewers, who says that expression at the taxpayer-funded stadium "is based on our terms."[6]

The baseball corporation also prohibits all political and social expression within the park. "Miller Park is not a facility for airing political messages. If it's a baseball message [on a placard] and is not controversial and doesn't cover up advertising," then it is permitted, Jenkins says. But politically controversial messages are expressly prohibited. For example, the Brewers stopped a spectator from holding up a sign about Cuban child Elian Gonzalez during a game with the Florida Marlins.[7]

Despite banning the political expression of others, the Brewers held a highly charged political rally at the old County Stadium, which they also leased, to pressure the state legislature into financing a new stadium. The corporation passed out "Build It Now!" placards for baseball fans to wave during baseball games, held a political rally before a game, and even had fans fill out cards at the old stadium demanding that a new publicly funded stadium be built. The cards were to be sent to the governor. The rally also criticized political figures who failed to back a new publicly funded stadium for the Brewers.[8] Apparently political expression is tolerated when it promotes the Brewers' interests; otherwise it is banned.

Another example of a private sector–public sector partnership in Milwaukee is provided by the city's convention center, called the Midwest Express Center, built to lure tourists and conventions to Milwaukee. (Like Miller Park, Midwest Express Airlines paid for the "naming rights," not the building's construction costs.) The convention center is managed by a state-created body called the Wisconsin Center

District and is tax-supported, but the district's president, Richard A. Geyer, considers the convention center to be private property.[9] When asked whether citizens are free to set up tables, pass out leaflets, or solicit signatures in the convention center, Geyer said, "We don't allow anybody to just come in and pass out pamphlets. Most facilities in the country do the same." He said that only a sponsor of an event could pass out brochures and leaflets.[10]

This blurring of the distinction between private and public property has created confusion in the minds of the public as to what is private property and what is public property, just as it has confused administrators like the Wisconsin Center District's Geyer. The blurring has also confused citizens as to their constitutional rights, as a survey of residents in Wisconsin, where the state's high court has ruled that the Constitution does not protect free speech on private property, shows.[11] Despite the high court ruling, over 60 percent of the survey respondents believed that the Constitution protects the collecting of "signatures on political petitions in malls and shopping centers."[12] A similar percentage believes that the Constitution protects setting "up tables containing political literature in malls." Just 10 percent more—70.3 percent—responded that the Constitution allows "people to collect signatures on political petitions in public parks." Clearly, the majority of respondents do not distinguish between the constitutional protections citizens have on public property and private property.

Despite this confusion, a majority of respondents (i.e., 56.3 percent) believe "that people should be allowed to collect signatures on political petitions in malls and shopping centers" and an even higher percentage (i.e., 62.5 percent) believe that "people should be allowed to set up tables containing political literature in malls and shopping centers." The responses suggest that a majority of citizens believe that malls should allow free expression, even though mall owners have argued that shoppers do not want their "shopping experience" disturbed by these activities. Mall owners are essentially using the attitudes of a minority of shoppers to rationalize their restrictions on speech.

Restricting Private Sector Speech Restrictions

The private sector has far more methods at its disposal to restrict speech than does government. The methods include restricting speech on private property; threatening to file or actually filing strategic lawsuits against public participation (SLAPPs); requiring employees to sign contracts restricting employees' rights to speak during and even after their employment; banning dissident views from company publications; pressuring the media to kill stories; inserting speech restrictions into legal settlements and contracts; placing restrictive covenants in deeds; and a myriad of other methods. The number of speech restrictions that can be imposed by the private sector is limited only by the imaginations of corporate executives and their attorneys. In contrast, governments are restricted by the First Amendment from placing unreasonable burdens on speech.

Corporations even hide behind the First Amendment to limit others' speech, as a recent case involving American Telephone and Telegraph Corp. (AT&T), the largest cable operator in the United States, shows.[13] AT&T challenged in federal district court the Broward County, Florida, ordinance requiring "broadband" cable television operators—cable television systems whose wires are also capable of simultaneously transmitting telephone and Internet signals—to give competing Internet service providers (ISPs) access to their systems for a fee. The ordinance essentially stopped AT&T and other broadband network operators from banning other ISPs from their wires. The Broward ordinance was designed to keep cable firms from creating an information monopoly, to increase competition among Internet services, and to assure that broadband service subscribers had access to a diversity of Internet providers—and, consequently, a diversity of Internet sources.

Diversity is necessary because ISPs subtly control the websites available to users. For example, AOL uses filters to eliminate sexually explicit sites that doubtlessly filter out medical and artistic websites, while at the same time subjecting subscribers to pop-ups for CNN and other AOL Time Warner sites. Search engines also direct users to particular websites and not others.[14]

Although local telephone lines are regulated by local authorities, AT&T argued in federal court that its wires were a form of a protected speech and that its First Amendment rights were abridged by the ordinance. AT&T argued that the ordinance violated the corporation's constitutional rights because it forced the company to carry the messages of rivals on its system. In November 2000, in a decision that turned the First Amendment upside down, U.S. District Judge Donald Middlebrooks concluded that AT&T and other broadband providers were more similar to newspapers than telephone services—even though AT&T is primarily a telephone service—and that the ordinance deprived AT&T of its free speech rights. Judge Middlebrooks wrote that "the cable operator, unlike a telephone service, does not sell transmission but offers a collection of content. . . . The Broward County ordinance both deprives the cable operator of editorial discretion over its programming and harms its ability to market and finance its services thereby curtailing the flow of information to the public."[15]

AT&T and other corporations in the broadband industry hailed the decision, claiming that Middlebrooks's decision proved that any attempts to open their wires up to other providers, whether ISPs or programmers, were unconstitutional. The companies hailed the decision because it handed them a virtual information monopoly in the areas where they operate.

Despite Judge Middlebrooks's opinion that the Broward County ordinance curtailed "the flow of information to the public," the ordinance would unquestionably increase the flow, because the public would have a wider array of ISPs from which to choose.

Many other corporations, including AOL Time Warner, have also claimed that governmental restrictions on their business prerogatives constitute grave First Amendment violations.[16] Time Warner filed suit against the Federal Communications Commission's limits on horizontal and vertical control of cable television. The horizontal limit, adopted so that no single "cable operator or group of cable operators can unfairly impede. . . the flow of video programming from the video programmer to the consumer," limited to 30 percent the number of subscribers in the United

States that a single company could have. Time Warner convinced the U.S. Court of Appeals for the District of Columbia to strike down the limit on the grounds that it unconstitutionally limited the number of people to whom it could market or "speak."[17]

The vertical limit, which required cable operators to reserve 60 percent of their programming for channels and shows produced by nonaffiliated firms, was also struck down on the grounds that the limit interfered with Time Warner's editorial decision-making.

The decision essentially equated a corporation's desire to increase market share with speech. Unfortunately, market share and speech are not positively related. They are negatively related: Larger market shares allow corporations to place even more limits on others' speech.

Similarly, AT&T's court victory essentially allows it to ban competing ISPs from its broadband network, limiting consumers' and other ISPs' speech.

These court decisions have blurred the distinction between commercial transactions and social and political speech, which the First Amendment was designed to protect. The blurring of the distinction between commercial transactions and expressive speech has allowed corporations to argue that First Amendment affords protection to all instances where data transmission or speech occurs. For example, the telephone giant U.S. West, Inc., successfully argued in federal court that the Federal Communications Commission's rule that it obtain consumers' permission before using proprietary information about consumers for marketing purposes constituted interference with its speech rights, because it limited what U.S. West could say to consumers.[18]

One small step that would limit AOL Time Warner's, U.S. West's, and AT&T's claims that government limits on their marketing practices constitute violations of the First Amendment is to return to the distinction that existed between commercial speech and protected speech prior to 1976, when the Supreme Court decided *Virginia State Board of Pharmacy v. Virginia Citizens Consumer Council.*[19] In that case, the Supreme Court extended First Amendment protection to advertising and other marketing-related speech on the grounds that advertising can provide consumers with important decision-making information.

Since *Virginia State Board of Pharmacy v. Virginia Citizens Consumer Council*, federal courts have shifted from consumer-based assessments—that commercial and corporate speech is protected if it enhances consumer decision-making—to the view that laws and regulations limiting advertising restrict free speech.[20] *Central Hudson Gas & Electric Corp. v. Public Service Commission* extended constitutional protection to commercial speech far beyond that extended in *Virginia State Board of Pharmacy*, and *U.S. West, Inc. v. Federal Communications Commission* extends rights to commercial speech far beyond those in *Hudson Gas & Electric Corp.*

The recent court decisions on commercial speech have allowed corporations to argue that laws, ordinances, and regulations limiting their market shares and marketing practices are unconstitutional restrictions on their speech. Reversing these decisions is a small step in curbing corporate power, and corporations' power to limit others' speech.

Another, much more significant way to curb the power of corporations, and their control over speech, is to declare that corporations are not individuals and therefore should not be accorded the same rights as individuals. AT&T's and AOL Time Warner's suits against the Federal Communications Commission are predicated on the assumption that corporations are individuals with First Amendment rights, and that government regulations violate corporations' constitutional rights. As Andrew Jay Schwartzman of the Media Access Project, a liberal lobby group, stated, "Corporations are artificial entities. Yet they are afforded speech rights as if they were living, breathing, voting citizens."[21] Corporations' constitutional rights are based solely on courts' extending the rights to them.

For example, the Supreme Court in 1978 extended First Amendment protection to corporations' advertising about referenda issues. In *First National Bank of Boston v. Bellotti*, the Court struck down a Massachusetts law designed to stop corporations from dominating the referenda and initiative process by prohibiting corporations from advertising about ballot issues. Rather than ruling that corporations have the same constitutional rights as individuals, the Court focused on the political nature of the speech and citizens' rights to hear these views.[22] Nevertheless, the decision has allowed corporations to get involved in ballot issues, allowing them to spend almost unlimited sums in support of their positions, which are invariably self-serving.

Recognizing that corporations are not individuals is an important step in broadening the free speech rights of individuals. This recognition requires the reversing of a century of court decisions beginning with *Santa Clara County v. Southern Pacific Railroad* that have extended constitutional rights to corporations, falsely equating corporations and their massive power— which they use to censor speech and influence the political system—with that of individuals. Courts and legislatures need to recognize that U.S. constitutional amendments are designed to protect individuals, not "artificial entities."

Reigning in corporate claims to constitutional protection is, of course, nearly impossible, given the political influence that corporations have. At the state and federal levels, corporations contribute lavishly to political candidates through their political action committees (PACs), which gives them substantial lobbying power relative to most individuals. Politicians, many of whom are now dependent on contributions from corporate PACs, are unlikely to vote against the interests whose money keeps them in office.

Consequently, small changes are first necessary to curb corporate power, influence, and censorship. The first change that is needed is campaign finance reform that would curb the influence that corporations have with elected officials. Laws that ban PAC contributions outright are a good start.

The most meaningful campaign finance reform would be public financing of elections, and the requirement that media corporations give free, equal time on their broadcasting stations to candidates running for public office. Public financing would essentially eradicate the influence that corporations and wealthy CEOs have because it would eliminate the private campaign contributions on which elected officials now depend. With politicians freed from their dependence on contributions from deep-pocketed CEOs and PACs, elected officials would be more likely to vote for legislation benefitting the public, rather than private, interest.

Not surprisingly, media corporations oppose giving candidates free time, claiming that giving candidates free advertising time violates their rights However, these corporations do not own the airwaves on which they broadcast, and they don't even pay a fee for occupying the frequencies. The airwaves belong to the public, despite the corporations' assertions to the contrary. Because the airwaves belong to the public, it follows that candidates for public office should have access to them.

In addition to curbing corporations' claims to constitutional protections and campaign finance reform, there are many laws that could be adopted to curtail corporate censorship. Among states, California has been a leader in passing legislation that protects individuals from the corporate gag.

In 1975, California adopted the Moscone Act, which bars employers from going to court to enjoin lawful union organizing. The act was designed to end "judicial interference in labor disputes." It prohibits California courts and judges from issuing a "restraining order or preliminary or permanent injunction" against picketing, rallies, and other forms of speech that communicate information about labor conflicts. For example, the act prohibits judges from restraining such actions as "giving publicity to, and obtaining or communicating information regarding the existence of, or the facts involved in, any labor dispute, whether by advertising, speaking, patrolling any public street or any place where any person or persons may lawfully be, or by any other method not involving fraud, violence, or the breach of peace."[23] The act can serve as a model statute to protect the speech rights of workers in states that currently lack such laws.

In the midst of the debates about "politically correct" speech codes adopted by colleges and universities during the early 1990s, the California legislature modified the state education code, guaranteeing public college and private college students the same rights on campus that they enjoy off campus. The legislation was proposed by conservatives who feared that dogmatic leftists were attempting to stifle debate on college campuses. The legislation assured that campus speech codes would not abridge free speech. Based on this legislation, a court struck down Stanford University's restrictive speech code.

The version of the code applying to public universities, which is similar to the wording for private universities, prohibits "the Regents of the University of California, the Trustees of the California State University, [and] the governing board of any community college district" from making or enforcing "any rule subjecting any student to disciplinary sanction solely on the basis of conduct that is speech or other communication that, when engaged in outside a campus of those institutions, is protected from governmental restriction by the First Amendment to the United States Constitution" or the California Constitution.[24]

Although designed to curb the excesses of a "political correctness," which seems to have vanished nearly as fast as it appeared, the legislation nevertheless protects students from an array of potential abuses. Based on the legislation, students are free to criticize the governing boards of their universities or the increasing ties between universities and corporations without fear of reprisals. The legislation should serve as a model statute for other states, because most private universities have rules that place limits on speech, such as requiring students to have literature approved before its can be distributed on campus.[25] Failure to abide by these rules can result in disciplinary action.

California has also adopted an anti-SLAPP law, limiting the ability of individuals and companies to use the courts to stifle speech. The statute allows defendants to file a "special motion to strike" when they have been sued as a result of petitioning or speaking about a public issue, and courts are required to act on the motion within 30 days of filing. Unless the plaintiff can demonstrate a probability of prevailing on the claim in court, the suit is to be dismissed. If dismissed, the defendant is entitled to "recover his or her attorneys' fees and costs," which serves as a deterrent to the filing of frivolous claims, since it monetarily penalizes SLAPP filers, rather than defendants.[26]

Although other states have passed anti-SLAPP laws, California's is one of the most far-reaching, because it covers SLAPPs filed by private and public sector individuals and institutions; applies to all public issues; and protects statements made in all public forums, not just statements made before legislative, executive, and judicial bodies. For that reason, the California anti-SLAPP law is a better model statute than most others, since it offers defendants the most protection against vexatious law suits.

California is also one of the few states that has extended free speech rights to malls and shopping centers. As a result of *Robins v. Pruneyard*, Californians have greater free speech rights than shoppers, residents, and activists in most states.

Civil libertarians in states where high courts have decided that malls are purely private property need to challenge these decisions using a variety of arguments—that most malls receive direct or indirect public subsidies, have been built on formerly public property, are often patrolled by local police, have community meeting rooms, and usually permit a variety of civic groups to set up tables, advertise themselves as public gathering places, house government offices, and other original arguments.

Short of overturning past decisions or obtaining favorable decisions in states that have not yet ruled on the issue, such as New Hampshire, civil libertarians need to carve out niches where some, even if limited, speech in malls is permitted. For example, courts may be more favorable to extending free speech rights to bus stop areas in mall parking lots than in malls themselves. Courts may also be more open to signature gathering in malls than distributing literature, as the high courts of Massachusetts and Oregon were. There, the high courts concluded that the state constitutions' free elections and referendum provisions trumped malls' property rights claims.

In states where high courts refuse to accord citizens even limited free speech rights in malls, legislation can be passed to override the court decisions. Legislation can require malls, shopping centers, or other private properties receiving public subsidies, tax breaks, or other forms of government assistance to open their properties to free speech. Legislation can also extend state civil rights acts to malls, as New York State Assembly bill 4085 (2001) does. The bill requires shopping centers that allow one group to speak in the mall to open the mall to others, subject to "reasonable time, place, and manner regulations." The bill requires each mall to develop a plan to accommodate free speech in common areas.

Legislatures of other states have also taken steps to protect free speech, particularly in CIDs. For example, the Maryland legislature passed a law that declared CID bans on election signs illegal. The law permits CID residents to post election signs thirty days before an election, despite covenants, conditions, and restrictions (CC&Rs) to the contrary.

One problem with the law is that it is restricted to election-related campaigning. Signs protesting military actions, tax policies, and other political issues are unaffected by the law, allowing the boards of CIDs to infringe on all but election-related speech. By contrast, Illinois's Condominium Property Act provides residents with broader speech rights, prohibiting CC&Rs that "impair" residents' First Amendment rights. The latter law is far broader, and its wording should be incorporated into future statutes protecting CID residents' speech rights.

The statutory approach to protecting free speech from private sector restraints has its limitations, because companies can always find loopholes in any law, and then come up with an unforeseen method to circumvent the law's intent. For example, federal and state laws protect employees' advocacy of unions and political speech , and prohibit employers from hindering this, but new technologies such as e-mail make it easy for employers to monitor, hinder, and intimidate employees' protected communications. According to a survey conducted by the American Management Association, nearly three-fourths of large U.S. companies monitor their employees, oftentimes using new technologies. Some review e-mail, listen into telephone conversations, check up on Internet use, and examine employees' computer files.[27] Monitoring employees—and making employees aware that they are being monitored—can effectively impede employees' protected speech.

Although "yellow dog " contracts—contracts that prohibit employees from joining unions—are illegal, employers can still use a variety of other means to curtail employees' speech. For example, employers can require employees to sign contracts with gag clauses as a condition of employment. Although employers claim that gag clauses are needed to protect companies' proprietary information, the clauses are often used to punish or silence whistle-blowers.

Because of this, an employees' bill of rights is in order, prohibiting companies from using employment agreements to silence current and former employees. Just as yellow dog contracts have been outlawed, so should other employer-employee agreements that restrict speech. When employers assert that proprietary information needs to be protected, the companies should be required to prove that the information is indeed proprietary and that, if disclosed, could be used by a competitor to gain a marketplace advantage.

Toward a New Ethic

AT&T's court argument—that Broward County's ordinance requiring broadband cable systems to open their wires up to other ISPs trampled on AT&T's free speech rights—was developed by Florida attorney Terry Bienstock, who has represented the cable television industry in a number of lawsuits. According to the *Miami Business Review,* Bienstock is currently working with real estate developers such as Arvida to sell the rights for providing cable, telephone, and cable services in CIDs being built in Jacksonville, Orlando, Pensacola, and Tallahassee.[28] If these negotiations pan out, home buyers will not just have a host of restrictive covenants controlling their expressive behavior but will discover they won't even be able to choose their own cable or phone company: The developer will choose, and profit from the selection of, the cable, Internet, and telephone services that will be available in the CID.

These negotiations underscore a problem with legal ethics: that attorneys act in the best interests of their clients, even when the actions might be detrimental to the public. In legal ethics, the client's interest comes before the public interest.[29] Because of this, attorneys are important contributors to private censorship.

To aid their clients, attorneys routinely seek gag orders from judges, write restrictive covenants, place confidentiality clauses in contracts, file SLAPPs, and engage in a host of censorial activities. Because these actions constitute routine civil actions—and are considered ethical—they are not recognized as censorship by attorneys.

Just as it is very difficult for attorneys to recognize that SLAPPs constitute a specific class of lawsuit because they are sometimes filed as intellectual property cases, sometimes as defamation cases, and sometimes as business interference cases, so too is it difficult for attorneys to recognize their role in private censorship. Attorneys view their acts as legal routines and maneuvers, rather than censorship.

Aiding clients by suppressing information and engaging in other forms of censorship usually has negative social costs. For example, attorneys representing some individuals injured when the ATX tires on their Ford Explorers gave out identified over two dozen cases of ATX tire failure on Ford Explorers in 1996, before Firestone and Ford knew of the problems. The attorneys sat on the information rather than submitting it to the National Traffic Safety Administration (NTSA) because the strength of their lawsuits could have been weakened if a NTSA investigation ended "without a finding of defect," one of the attorneys admitted.[30] The attorney said that their duty was to win as much money in the lawsuit as possible, not to protect the public. (After learning about the tire problems, Ford and Firestone also kept information about the dangers from the public.)

As a consequence of their suppressing this information, the NTSA was late in launching their investigation of the ATX-Explorer accidents, and many people probably died as a result. Of the attorneys' actions, Ricardo Martinez, a trauma surgeon and head of the NTSA between 1994 and 1999, said, "It's outrageous; I can't say that enough. If I saw something was killing my patients and I didn't say anything because that would reduce the demand for my services, I would be putting my benefit over the benefit of my patients and the public and that would be clearly unethical."[31] Martinez was indignant because 190 of the 203 ATX-related deaths occurred after 1996, when the attorneys became aware of the problem.

Despite Martinez's declaration, the attorneys' actions are considered ethical within their profession. Geoffrey Hazard, Jr., a professor at the University of Pennsylvania law school, contended that suppressing the accident information was neither unethical nor illegal. "They had a civic responsibility the same as you or I do, but didn't have a legal duty" to reveal the information, Hazard says.

This example suggests a need for changes in the ethics of the law profession, particularly when it comes to civil suits. Putting clients' interests before the public interest can have very negative consequences. Clearly, suppressing information that could have spared nearly 200 peoples' lives should not be considered ethically permissible.

Incorporating a public interest standard into the ethics of civil procedure would be a starting point for reforming the legal profession and, consequently, reducing private censorship. Private censorship would be reduced because the public interest is almost always served by releasing and discussing, rather than suppressing, information.

Endnotes

Notes to Preface

1. For examples, see Thomas L. Tedford, *Freedom of Speech in the United States* (New York: Random House, 1985); Rodney A. Smolla, *Smolla and Nimmer on Freedom of Speech* (New York: Matthew Bender & Company, 1994); Leonard Levy, *Legacy of Suppression* (Cambridge: Belnap Press, 1960); and Zechariah Chafee, Jr., *Free Speech in the United States* (Cambridge: Harvard University Press, 1948). Chafee's book ends with the Alien Registration Act of 1940, whereas Levy's ends with the demise of the Alien and Sedition laws of 1798. In addition to the different periods they cover, Chafee and Levy present vastly different interpretations of the intent of the First Amendment.

2. 268 U.S. 652 (1925); 299 U.S. 353 (1937); 496 U.S. 310 (1990).

3. Tedford, op. cit., 48. In *The Political Economy of Slavery* (Middletown, CT: Wesleyan University Press, 1989), Eugene D. Genovese reports that Southern plantation owners "commanded Southern politics," determining not just the laws that were passed, but virtually all other important facets of Southern existence.

4. Eldridge Foster Dowell in *A History of Criminal Syndicalism Legislation in the United States* (Baltimore: Johns Hopkins University Press, 1939), 55.

5. David M. Rabban, *Free Speech in Its Forgotten Years* (New York: Cambridge University Press, 1997), 113.

6. Nicholas Karolides, Margaret Bald, and Dawn Sova, *100 Banned Books* (New York: Checkmark Books, 1999), 48–51; Jacqueline G. Sherman, *The Oklahomans in California During the Depression Decade, 1931–1941* (Ph.D. diss., University of California, Los Angeles, 1970), 131–34.

7. Adolf A. Berle, Jr., and Gardiner C. Means, *The Modern Corporation and Private Property* (New York: Macmillan, 1932), 2.

8. For a discussion of the impact of anti-Communism on U.S. journalism, see Edward S. Herman and Noam Chomsky, *Manufacturing Consent* (New York: Pantheon, 1988).

9. Edwin Emery and Michael Emery, *The Press and America* (Englewood Cliffs, NJ: Prentice-Hall, 1978), 382–84; Thomas C. Reeves, *The Life and Times of Joe McCarthy* (New York: Stein and Day, 1982), 220–21.

10. *Moose Lodge No. 107 v. Irvis*, 407 U.S. 163 (1972).

11. *Shelley v. Kraemer* 334 U.S. 1 (1948). Because of these contradictory opinions, an article in *Pennsylvania Law Review* concluded that the state action doctrine "encompasses contradictions and invites manipulation and mystification." See Paul Brest, "State Action and Liberal Theory: A Casenote on *Flagg Brothers v. Brooks*," *University of Pennsylvania Law Review*, 130 (1982): 1296.

12. George W. Pring and Penelope Canan, *SLAPPs: Getting Sued for Speaking Out* (Philadelphia: Temple University Press, 1996), 3.

Notes to Chapter 1

1. Henry Weinstein, "Tobacco Firms Threaten Assault on Cigarette Bill," *Los Angeles Times*, April 4, 1998.

2. For a discussion of the contest, see Bruce Horowitz, "Essay Contest Touches Off Ethics Contest," *Los Angeles Times*, December 23, 1986.

3. According to Philip Morris (see www.philipmorris.com/corporate/ir/investor/sec_filings.htm), the corporation's operating revenues for 1998 were $74.4 billion and its net earnings were $7.8 billion. By comparison, the gross domestic product of Iraq, the United States' *bête noire*, was $41.1 billion, according to *The World Almanac 1998* (Mahwah, NJ: World Almanac Books, 1997), 775.

4. Robert Laurence, "Sponsors' Ties to Content Could Bind TV," *San Diego Union-Tribune* August 17, 1999.

5. Louis Banks, "Memo to the Press: They Hate You Out There," *The Atlantic*, April 1978, 38.

6. Ben Bagdikian, *The Media Monopoly*, 5th ed. (Boston: Beacon Press, 1997), 156, 171.

7. K. E. Warner, L. M. Goldenhar, and C. G. McLaughlin, "Cigarette Advertising and Magazine Coverage of the Health Hazards of Smoking—A Statistical Analysis," *New England Journal of Medicine*, January 30, 1992, 305–11.

8. "Saatchi Plays Down RJR's Move," *Financial Times*, April 7, 1988, 26.

9. Quoted in Kenneth Warner, "Cigarette Advertising and Media Coverage of Smoking and Health," *New England Journal of Medicine*, February 7, 1985, 387.

10. Alex Kuczynski, "Big Tobacco's Newest Billboards Are on the Pages of Its Magazines," *New York Times*, December 12, 1999, 1.

11. Amanda Locy, "Tobacco Industry Secret Project Goes Up in Smoke," (Wauwatosa, WI) *Express News*, October 25, 1999.

12. Howard Kurtz, "'60 Minutes' Kills Piece on Tobacco Industry," *Washington Post*, November 10, 1995.

13. "Self-Censorship at CBS," *New York Times*, November 12, 1995.

14. Judith Michaelson, "Morning Report," *Los Angeles Times*, November 9, 1999.

15. For examples of the evidence, see discussions in Henry Weinstein, "Key Tobacco Witness Gets Immunity, Sources Say," *Los Angeles Times*, July 13, 1997; "Tobacco Firm Chief Lied in Testimony Before Congress, Ex-Employee Says," *Chicago Tribune*, January 28, 1996; "UC to Release Tobacco Firm's Papers in Wake of Ruling," *Los Angeles Times*, July 1, 1995.

16. Barry Meier, "Cigarette Makers' Strategy of '94 Is Echoed Today," *New York Times*, May 2, 1998; Philip J. Hilts, "A Law Opening Research Data Sets Off Debate," *New York Times*, July 31, 1999.

17. John Schwartz, "ABC Issues Apology for Tobacco Report," *Washington Post*, August 22, 1995.

18. Benjamin Weiser, "ABC and Tobacco: The Anatomy of a Network News Mistake," *Washington Post*, January 7, 1996; Steve Weinberg, "Smoking Guns," *Columbia Journalism Review*, November 1995, 29.

19. Doug Levy, "ABC Brief Backs Nicotine Claim," *USA Today*, January 16, 1996.

20. Robert P. Laurence, "ABC's Snuffing of Tobacco Film Leaves Foul Odor," *San Diego Union-Tribune*, April 22, 1996.

21. Quoted in Larry C. White, *Merchants of Death* (New York: Beech Tree Books, 1988).

22. Lawrence Soley, "The Power of the Press Has a Price," *Extra!*, July/August 1997, 11–13.

23. "University Won't Get Donation," *Milwaukee Journal Sentinel*, April 25, 2000.

24. Douglas Frantz, "Alaskans Choose Sides in Battle Over Cruise Ships," *New York Times*, November 29, 1999.

25. "Company Policy Bans Solicitation of Money at Malls," *Milwaukee Journal Sentinel*, November 14, 2000.

26. Quoted in Davan Maharaj, "Firestone Recall Puts Spotlight on Secret Liability Agreements," *New York Times*, September 10, 2000.

27. Ibid.

28. David Blumenthal, et. al., "Relationships Between Academic Institutions and Industry in the Life Science—An Industry Survey," *New England Journal of Medicine*, February 8, 1996, 371.

29. Steven A. Rothenberg, "Secrecy in Medical Research," *New England Journal of Medicine*, February 8, 1996, 392.

30. Ralph T. King, "How a Drug Firm Paid for University Study, Then Undermined It," *Wall Street Journal*, April 25, 1996.

31. "Campus Fight Leads Reebok to Modify Shoe Contract," *New York Times*, June 28, 1996.

32. "Federal Judge Clears Way for 'Million Youth March,'" *Chicago Tribune*, August 27, 1998 Patricia Hurtado, "Victory for Rally," *Newsday*, September 1, 1999.

33. Nancy Meersman, "Suspended, Stayed Sentences for Free Speech Activists," (Manchester, NH) *Union Leader*, May 18, 1999; "Activists Argue for Free Speech at Mall of N.H.," *Union Leader*, September 23, 1998.

34. Linda Greenhouse, "Justices, a Bit Amused, Ponder a Ban on Signs," *New York Times*, February 24, 1999; Linda Greenhouse, "In Broad Ruling, Court Prohibits Banning of Homeowners' Signs," *New York Times*, June 14, 1994.

35. 779 S.W. 2nd 603, 607–8 (1989); 24 P. 2nd 948 (1992).

36. Ibid., 951. The court reached the opposite conclusion in *Century 21 v. City of Jennings* (700 S.W. 2nd 809 [1985]) when a similar prohibition on signs was adopted by a city. However, the court based its decision on a Missouri statute prohibiting municipalities from banning "For Sale" signs on owners' properties, rather than on the First Amendment.

37. Craig Savoye, "KKK Comes to Town—On Highway Signs," *Christian Science Monitor*, December 9, 1999. In Texas, state officials claimed they would sue the Klan after it applied to Adopt-A-Highway because the Klan signs were designed to intimidate minorities. In that case, the Klan withdrew its application rather than go to court. See Will Sentell, "Missouri Is Reeling from Ruling," *Kansas City Star*, December 6, 1999.

38. David Savage, "High Court Voids Law Against Burning Flag," *Los Angeles Times*, June 12, 1990.

39. Court decisions distinguish between traditional public spaces such as sidewalks and parks that constitute "public forums" and other public property that is (a) "limited purpose" or semi-public and (b) traditionally not used for public communication. "Limited purpose" public space is exemplified by school board meetings, where limits can be placed on expression. Government space that not used for public expression include military bases, where expression can be banned. Laurence H. Tribe, *American Constitutional Law* (Mineola, NY: The Foundation Press, 1988), 986–97, argues that the distinctions among these categories are blurred, artificial, and irrelevant.

40. For a discussion of the persecution of the I.W.W., see "Criminal Syndicalism," in Zechariah Chafee, Jr., *Free Speech in the United States* (Cambridge: Harvard University Press, 1948), 326–42.

41. Eldridge Foter Dowell, *A History of Criminal Sydicalism Ledislation in the United States* (Baltimore: Johns Hopkins University Press, 1939), 55.

42. Floyd Norris, "How to Make a Scientific Breakthrough Seem Horrifying," *New York Times*, December 17, 1999.

43. "House Panel Defeats Bill for Protection From Suits," *Orlando Sentinel*, March 11, 1994; Frank Phillips, "Approved Bill Would Stifle Developers' SLAPP Suits," *Boston Globe*, November 30, 1994.

44. John Schwartz, "Drug Company Admits Fraud, Agrees to Pay $10 Million Fine," November 29, 1995; David Shook, "N.J. Firm Oks $3.75 Billion to End Diet Drug Suits," *Bergen Record*, October 8, 1999; Kara Sissell, "Rhode Island Sues Lead Pigment Makers," *Chemical Week*, October 20, 1999, 19.

45. "SEC Proposes Rule Barring Selective Disclosure of Information," *Milwaukee Journal Sentinel*, December 16, 1999; Floyd Norris, "Wall St. Snarls at S.E.C. Proposal on Disclosure," *New York Times*, December 16, 1999.

46. For a discussion of the U.S. Freedom of Information Act and state open records laws, see Robert F. Bouchard and Justin D. Franklin, eds., *Guidebook to the Freedom of Information and Privacy Acts* (New York: Clark Boardman Co., 1980).

47. Quoted in Glen O. Robinson and Ernest Gellhorn, *The Administrative Process* (St. Paul: West Publishing, 1974), 791.

48. H.R. Report 1497, 89th Cong., 2nd sess., 1986, 10.

49. *Chrysler v. Brown*, 441 U.S. 281 (1979). See also discussion op. cit. in Robert F. Bouchard and Justin D. Franklin, 248–64.

50. Gretchen Morgenson, "Fearing Investors' Wrath, More Companies Hiding Bad News," *Milwaukee Journal Sentinel,* December 26, 1999.
51. Statistics from E. J. Hobsbawm, *Industry and Empire* (New York: Penguin Books, 1977), 115. For a discussion of the importance of railways in corporate evolution, see Oliver E. Williamson, "The Modern Corporation: Origins, Evolution, Attributes," *Journal of Economic Literature,* December 1981, 1537–68.
52. *Santa Clara County v. Southern Pacific Railroad,* 118 U.S. 394 (1886).
53. Howard Zinn, *A People's History of the United States* (New York: Harcourt Brace Jovanovich, 1980), 255.
54. Quoted in Frank Tracy Carlton, *The History and Problems of Organized Labor* (New York: D. C. Heath & Co., 1911), 273.
55. Laurence H. Tribe, op. cit., 567–74.
56. *U.S. v. Hutcheson,* 312 U.S. 219 (1941).
57. Robert Sherrill, "Big Business Takes the First," *Harper's,* January 1988, 22.
58. Mark Curriden, "Exxon-Mobil Merger Assured, Lawyers Say," *Dallas Morning News,* November 27, 1999.
59. Associated Press, "Big Business Reroutes PAC Money," *Chicago Tribune,* September 16, 1999.
60. Juliet Eilperin, "House Whip Wields Fund-Raising Clout," *Washington Post,* October 18, 1999.
61. Robert R. Rankin and Josh Goldstein, "Ethics Flap Seen as Threat to McCain's Image," *Milwaukee Journal Sentinel,* January 8, 2000.
62. Herbert I. Schiller, *Culture, Inc.* (New York: Oxford University Press, 1989), 28–29.
63. For a discussion of this evolution, see Alfred D. Chandler, Jr., "The Structure of American Industry in the Twentieth Century: A Historical Overview," *Business History Review,* Autumn 1969, 473–503. Chandler's approach was criticized by Richard B. Du Boff and Edward S. Herman, "Alfred Chandler's New Business History: A Review," *Politics and Society* 10 (1), 87–110.
64. Susan Byrnes, "Ruling Favors Protestors of Auto Dealer," *Seattle Times,* November 16, 1994.

Notes to Part I

1. Craig Earnshaw, "Workers Vital to Fulfilling Dreams," *Salt Lake City Deseret News,* December 31, 2000.
2. Dan Grinfas, "On the Job," Column, *Eugene Register Guard,* December 11, 2000.

Notes to Chapter 2

1. Matewan was a civil rather than a company-owned town adjacent to the Red Jacket Coal Company in West Virginia, where miners struck in 1920. On May 19, 1920, a dozen Baldwin-Felts agents tried evicting striking workers from company-owned housing in Matewan and were stopped by the town's chief of police, Sid Hatfield. When the Baldwin-Felts agents attempted to arrest Hatfield, a gunfight broke out that killed seven Baldwin-Felts agents, Matewan's mayor, and three other Matewan residents. See West Virginia State Archives, *West Virginia's Mine Wars,* http://www.wvlc.wvnet.edu/history/ minewars.html.
2. "The Strange Death of Corporationville," *The Economist,* December 23, 1995, 74; Stanley Buder, *Pullman: An Experiment in Industrial Order and Community Planning 1880–1930* (New York: Oxford University Press, 1967).
3. John S. Garner, *The Model Company Town* (Amherst: University of Massachusetts Press, 1994), 1.
4. 329 U.S. 501 (1945).
5. Interview with former Newton resident, Robert L. Craig, March 28, 2000.

6. Scott Thomsen, "Realities of the 90s Strain Bean, Freeport Relationship," *Freeport Press Herald,* February 25, 1996.
7. William Glaberson, "Claiming a Right Not to Know," *New York Times,* September 22, 1997.
8. Kirsten Downey Grimsley, "More Jobs Offer Living Wage Plus Living Quarters," *Memphis Commercial Appeal,* December 6, 1998.
9. 323 NLRB No. 127.
10. The Slater-Tiffany records in Harvard University's Baker Library show that some small farms became indebted to company stores and eventually abandoned farming to work in the mill. For example, farmer William Davis began purchasing supplies from the Slater-Tiffany Cotton Mill store in February 1812. Three years later, Davis moved his family into a mill-owned tenement, after which he and three children worked full-time in the mill. They work regularly until June 1819, when the family account is closed. Some members of the family continued working in the mill until 1827. The Davis records are publicly accessible in Greg Kulak, Roger Parks, and Theodore Z. Penn eds., *The New England Mill Village, 1790–1860* (Cambridge: The MIT Press, 1982), 415–19.
11. Hiram Munger, *The Life and Religious Experience of Hiram Munger* (Chicopee Falls, MA: self-published, 1856), 11.
12. Hannah Josephson, *The Golden Threads* (New York: Duell, Sloan and Pearce, 1949), 3–10.
13. Caroline Ware, *The Early New England Cotton Manufacture* (New York: Houghton Mifflin Co., 1931), 255; Lucy Larcom, *A New England Girlhood* (Boston: Houghton Mifflin Co., 1889), 175, 181.
14. Ware, op. cit., 263.
15. Ibid., 261.
16. Josephson, op. cit., 201–2. Josephson's account of the *Lowell Offering* and early mill life paint an idyllic, but fictional, picture of Lowell.
17. Helen C. Camp, *Iron in Her Soul* (Pullman, WA: Washington State University Press, 1995), 27.
18. *ABC World News Tonight,* 4 August 1995, transcript in Lexis-Nexis; Jess Katz and Tony Perry, "Immigrant Smugglers Ply an Oft-Brutal Trade," *Denver Post,* April 13, 1996; Kim Murphy, "Smuggling of Chinese Ends in a Box of Death, Squalor," *Los Angeles Times,* January 12, 2000.
19. Jessica McBride, "With State's Work Dispute Decisions, Some Can't Believe Their Ears," *Milwaukee Journal Sentinel,* March 21, 2000.
20. AFL-CIO, "America@Work: Recognizing our Common Bonds," http://www.aflcio.org/articles/commonbonds/.
21. Peter Roberts, *Anthracite Coal Communities* (New York: Macmillan Co., 1904), 19.
22. Chapter 1 of David Alan Corbin, *Life, Work and Rebellion in the Coal Fields* (Urbana, IL: University of Illinois Press, 1990) contains and excellent description of how the steel and railway trusts had existing deeds to West Virginia lands invalidated, and then transferred to their control.
23. Brian M. Kelly, "Having It Their Way: Alabama Coal Operators and the Search for Docile Labor, 1908–1921," in Edwin Brown and Colin Davis, eds., *It Is Union and Liberty* (Tuscaloosa: University of Alabama Press, 1999), 54, 58.
24. An exception to this was Buxton, Iowa, where the Consolidation Coal Company created a paternalistic company town, in which workers were completely dependent upon the company for housing, recreation, religion, and social services. Dorothy Schweider, Joseph Hraba, and Elmer Schweider, *Buxton: Work and Racial Equality in a Coal Mining Community* (Ames, IA: Iowa State University Press, 1987) describes Buxton as an idyllic company town, ruled by an extremely benevolent company. However, the independent observers they cite, such as newspaper reports, draw a picture of a company that controlled all aspects of life, providing its workers with reasonable wages, access to religion, and recreation in return for unfettered loyalty. The book never mentions what happened

to critical workers, but an article in the *Buxton Eagle*, suggests that dissent was not tolerated by the company. See pages 110–11.

25. Peter Roberts, p. 122; Peter Alexander, "Rising from the Ashes," in Brown and Davis, eds., op. cit., 64; Robert Fagge, *Power, Culture, and Conflict in the Coalfields* (New York: Manchester University Press, 1996), 36.

26. Winthrop D. Lane, *Civil War in West Virginia* (New York: B. W. Huebsch, 1921), 29. Price V. Fishback, "Did Coal Miners 'Owe Their Souls to the Company Store?'" Theory and Evidence from the Early 1900s," *Journal of Economic History*, December 1986, 1011–1029, using traditional economic theories of competition and rational choice, argues that miners often shopped at independent stores. However, the study never empirically examined the proximity of independent stores and coal towns, leaving one doubtful that miners or their spouses would hike through several miles of hilly terrain to shop at independent stores, even if they were cheaper than company stores.

27. Crandall A. Shifflett, *Coal Towns* (Knoxville: The University of Tennessee Press, 1991), 179–185; Fishback, ibid.

28. Fishback, op. cit., 1024. In Pennsylvania, where few lived in company towns, miners received more than 60 percent of their wages in cash.

29. Corbin, op. cit., 148.

30. Fagge, op. cit., 46; Morris, op. cit., 93.

31. Morris, op. cit., 93.

32. See Roger Fagge, op. cit., 128–29; Lane, op. cit., 62–63.

33. Homer Lawrence Morris, op. cit., 123.

34. Brian M. Kelly, op. cit., 52.

35. Schweider, Hraba, and Schwieder, op. cit., 95.

36. Crandall A. Shifflett, op. cit., 123. Lane, op. cit., 48–50, contains a discussion of how the coal companies pursued this legal strategy that eventually resulted in mass evictions during strikes.

37. Corbin, op. cit., 123.

38. Sylvester Petro, *The Kohler Strike* (Chicago: Henry Regnery Company, 1961), 79.

39. Corbin, op. cit., 51; Kelly, op. cit., 51.

40. Quoted in Lane, op. cit, 65.

41. An investigation of arbitration practices by *San Francisco Chronicle* reporter Reynolds Holding (October 7 and 8, 2001) found that arbitration companies are not unbiased. Some have undisclosed contracts with firms for which they are engaged in arbitration, selling the firms other "administrative and consulting services." Arbitration companies may also own stocks or bonds in the companies for which they provide arbitration. Moreover, the employers usually choose, and may even pay, the arbitration company, making the arbitration company indebted to the employer. As a result of these conflicts of interest, arbitrators are far more likely to rule in favor of an employer than an employee. A 1997 study in Indiana, described by Holding, found that employees won only 16 percent of arbitration cases against firms who repeatedly use the same arbitration company, suggesting that arbitration is "stacked against" the employees. As a result of these problems with arbitration, some California legislators are seeking to outlaw forced arbitration to settle discrimination complaints against employers (see Reynolds Holding, "Labor Agencies Join Battle Against Forced Arbitration," *San Francisco Chronicle*, March 1, 2002).

42. Quote from James B. Allen, *The Company Town in the American West* (Norman: University of Oklahoma Press, 1966), 58.

43. Shifflett, op. cit., 41–42.

44. Stanley Buder, *Pullman: An Experiment in Industrial Order and Community Planning 1880–1930* (New York: Oxford University Press, 1967), 82.

45. Lane, op. cit., 82.

46. Buder, op. cit., 62–64.

47. Ibid., 107.

48. Ibid., 112–13, 140.

49. Allen, op. cit., 65–66, 85, 112–13.

50. Ross Glass Cleland, *A History of Phelps Dodge* (New York: Alfred A. Knopf, 1952), 181–92. This is an authorized, pro-company history of Dodge Phelps.

51. *Marsh v. Alabama,* 236 U.S. 501 (1945).

52. Ibid., 509.

53. "Scotia in the Redwood Country . . . Still a Company Town," *Sunset,* April 1990, 76; "The Strange Death of Corporationville," *The Economist,* December 23, 1995, 73.

54. 495 Pa. 158, 432 A. 2nd 1382 (1981).

55. 84 N.J. 535, 423 A. 2nd 615 (1980).

56. Although Bob Jones University publicly announced that it had rescinded this policy, it is apparently still in effect. See "Makin' Out at Bob Jones U.," *Salon,* http://www.salon.com/books/it/2000/03/22/bobjones/index2.html.

57. Art Thomason, "Humiliation Only Price ASU Paid," *Arizona Republic,* November 11, 1997.

58. Allen Turner, "Group Challenges UT Over Its Flier Policy," *Houston Post,* November 22, 1998; Cara Tanamachi, "Erwin Center Pamphlet Case Argued," *Austin American-Statesman,* November 20, 1998.

59. Patrick Healy, "U.S. Judge Upholds U. of Texas Ban on Leafleting by Outsiders," *Chronicle of Higher Education,* January 22, 1999.

60. Lynda V. Mapes, "Migrant Workers in Washington," *Seattle Times,* August 2, 1998.

61. Diana Marcum, "In Mecca, A Debate Over Housing," *Los Angeles Times,* January 23, 2000.

62. Mapes, op. cit.

63. Ed Vogel, "Bill Would Force Mobile Home Parks to OK Political Signs," *Las Vegas Review-Journal,* February 4, 1999, 4B.

64. Susan Salisbury, "A New Harvest of Union Members," *Miami Daily Business Review,* December 10, 1999, A8.

65. Alec Wilkinson, in *Big Sugar* (New York: Alfred A. Knopf, 1989), 226–27, described growers as favoring immigrant laborers because they "form a labor force that is docile; labor difficulties of any seriousness the growers resolve by shipping home the discontented cutters." Wilkinson provides examples of mass deportations occurring in 1982 and 1986 to quiet labor protests. The workers were kidnapped and held hostage at the Florida Fruit and Vegetable Association headquarters before being deported.

66. Ibid., 30–31.

67. *Petersen v. Talisman Sugar Corp.,* 428 F. 2d 73 (5th Cir. 1973).

68. Bruce Goldstein, "'Guestworker' Labor Programs: Fighting Attacks on Agricultural Workers' Rights," *Guild Practitioner,* Winter 2000, 19.

69. Ibid., 22.

70. AFL-CIO, "AFL-CIO Delgates Deliberate Immigrants' Rights," http://www.aflcio.org/convention99/conv_updates_immigrants.htm.

71. Ibid.

Notes to Chapter 3

1. Robert F. Hoxie, *Trade Unionism in the United States* (New York: D. Appleton and Co., 1931), 237.

2. Philip S. Foner, *History of the Labor Movement in the United States,* vol. 1 (New York: International Publishers, 1982), 101.

3. Clarence E. Bonnett, *History of Employers' Associations in the United States* (New York: Vantage Press, 1956), 57.

4. Foner, op. cit., 154–56.

5. Bonnet, op.cit., 42, 44, 52.

6. "Address of the Founders' and Machine Builders' Association of the Falls of Ohio," *Fincher's Trades' Review,* October 3, 1863; reprinted in Leon Littwack, *The American Labor Movement* (Englewood Cliffs, NJ: Prentice-Hall, 1962), 85; and discussed in Philip S. Foner, op. cit., 353.

7. Foner, op. cit., 211.

8. Gordon M. Haferbecker, *Wisconsin Labor Laws* (Madison: University of Wisconsin Press, 1959), 157.

9. Ibid.; Wisconsin Rev. St. 1898, c. 182, sec. 4466.

10. Grover G. Huebner, *Blacklisting* (Madison: Wisconsin Free Library Commission, 1906), 8–10, 21.

11. Ibid., 19.

12. Frank Tracy Carlton, *The History and Problems of Organized Labor* (New York: D. C. Heath & Company, 1911), 181.

13. Clinch Calkins, *Spy Overheard: The Story of Industrial Espionage* (New York: Harcourt, Brace and Company, 1937), 20–21. These court decisions occurred during an era when courts routinely struck down laws regulating businesses on "substantive due process" grounds. For a brief discussion of this, see Ronald Rotunda and John E. Nowak, *Treatise on Constitutional Law,* vol. 2 (St. Paul: West Group, 1999), 582–92.

14. U. S. Senate Committee on Education and Labor (Subcommittee on Senate Resolution 266), *Violations of Free Speech and Rights of Labor* (Washington, D. C.: U.S. Government Printing Office, 1936–40).

15. Calkins, op. cit., 235.

16. Philip S. Foner, in *History of the American Labor Movement,* vol. 2 (New York: International Publishers, 1980), 86, described the travails of Martin Irons, a railroad worker and district union leader, who was blacklisted and forced into poverty. Irons was "forced out of every job he tried . . . and during the last years was reduced to keeping a lunch counter in a small basement saloon in Missouri." Also see the reports in Stewart Bird et al., *Solidarity Forever* (Chicago: Lakeview Press, 1985).

17. Harry A. Millis and Emily Clark Brown, *From the Wagner Act to Taft-Hartley* (Chicago: University of Chicago Press, 1950), 24; U.S. Senate Committee on Education and Labor, op. cit., Part 15A, 1937, 5501–509.

18. "Loyalty and Private Employment: The Right of Employers to Discharge Suspected Subversives," *Yale Law Journal* 62 (1953), 958–59.

19. California Labor Code Sec. 1101-2 (1943). A version of the law is quoted in John Cogley, *Report on Blacklisting I: Movies* (New York: Fund for the Republic, Inc., 1956), 89. Another version of the law is quoted in footnote 29.

20. 318 NLRB No. 54.

21. 322 NLRB No. 115; 322 NLRB No. 116.

22. 116 F. 3rd 1039 (4th Cir.), 155 LRRM 2691.

23. 327 NLRB No. 065.

24. 324 NLRB No. 014.

25. 323 NLRB No. 149.

26. *It's Time to Shine a Light* (Washington, D. C.: AFL-CIO, undated), brochure; Milwaukee County Labor Council statistics, undated, c. 2000.

27. Interview with John Goldstein, February 26, 2000.

28. For an in-depth description on the formation of the trust, see Eileen Bowser, *The Transformation of American Cinema 1907–1915* (New York: Charles Scribner's Sons, 1990), 21–36.

29. Gerald Mast and Bruce Kawin, *A Short History of the Movies* (Boston: Allyn and Bacon, 2000), 48.

30. Robert Vaughn, *Only Victims* (G. P. Putnam's Sons, 1972), 171.

31. Mike Nielsen and Gene Mailes, *Hollywood's Other Blacklist* (London: British Film Institute, 1995), 21.

32. FBI Los Angeles, "Communist Infiltration of the Motion Picture Industry," February 18, 1943, file 100–15732, declassified FBI document.

33. FBI Los Angeles, "Communist Infiltration of the Motion Picture Industry," September 12, 1945, file 100–15732, declassified FBI document, 5–6; FBI-Los Angeles, "Communist Infiltration of the Motion Picture Industry," January 20, 1946, file 100–15732, declassified FBI document, 9; "IATSE Local Not to Pass Film Pickets," *Los Angeles Examiner*, October 10, 1946.

34. The only in-depth discussion of these blacklists is Neilsen and Mailes, op. cit.

35. *Guilty by Suspicion* dramatizes the career of David Merrill, a fictitious film director played by Robert DeNiro, who is encouraged to testify before HUAC by Twentieth Century Fox head Daryl Zanuck. In the film, Zanuck tells Merrill his opinion of blacklisting, saying, "I don't like what's happening one bit. These politicians think they're doing me a favor by letting me know who they're going to call and how I can get you off before hand. . . . I wouldn't let these guys run a tractor, much less a country."

36. Some of the MPA's allegations were based on documents the MPA had illegally obtained through the Office of Naval Intelligence. The documents had come from the FBI, which took the documents back. See D. M. Ladd, "Communist Influence in the Motion Picture Industry," July 9, 1945, FBI Office Memorandum, file 100–15732, declassified FBI document; Edward Dmytryk, *Odd Man Out* (Carbondale: Southern Illinois University Press, 1996). HUAC did not need much encouragement to investigate Hollywood. HUAC member and anti-Semite John Rankin had been attacking Hollywood for several years before the HUAC investigation was launched.

37. See "Confidential File," FBI-Los Angeles Office to FBI Director, August 9, 1943, file 100–15732. The FBI apparently also bugged the homes and offices of some Communist Party members. For example, see D. M. Ladd to FBI Director, "Office Memorandum," July 13, 1945, file 100–15732.

38. Volumes have been written on these hearings. See Gordon Kahn, *Hollywood on Trial* (New York: Arno Press, 1972); Kenneth Lloyd Billingsley, *Hollywood Party* (Rocklin, CA: Rorum, 1998); and Griffin Fariello, *Red Scare* (New York: Avon Books, 1995). Billingsley's book is a hard-right defense of the Hollywood purge.

39. The membership cards came from the FBI. See R. B. Hood to FBI Director, "RE: Communist Infiltration of the Motion Picture Industry," September 17,1947; Clyde Tolson to FBI Director, September 11, 1947; D. M. Ladd to FBI Director, "Subject— Communist Infiltration Motion Picture Industry," May 13, 1947, file 100–15732.

40. See Edward G. Robinson's posthumous autobiography, *All My Yesterdays* (New York: Hawthorne Press, 1973) for a description of how the graylist operated and when he learned of its existence.

41. Michael C. Burton, *The Making of a Liberated Mind* (Austin, TX: Eakin Press, 1995), 114; and John Cogley, *Report on Blacklisting II: Radio-Television* (New York: Fund for the Republic, Inc., 1956), 3; Merle Miller, *The Judges and the Judged* (New York: Doubleday & Co., 1953), 80.

42. *Counterattack*, Letter 230, October 19, 1951, 1.

43. See Harold W. Horowitz, "Legal Aspects of 'Political Blacklisting' in the Entertainment Industry," *Southern California Law Review*, April 1956, 278–91, for a discussion of the difficulties in winning a defamation suit against American Business Consultant, Inc.

44. The Civil Rights Congress and the National Wallace for President Committee were among the "subversive" organizations listed in *Red Channels*.

45. *Red Channels* (New York: American Business Consultants, 1950), 9.

46. For examples, see Jack Gould, "Network Rejects Protest by Legion," *New York Times*,

September 13, 1950, 9; and "Hazel Scott Denies Red Sympathies," *New York Times*, September 16, 1950, 5.

47. Vincent W, Hartnett, "Rascalry on the Air Waves," *Catholic World*, June 1950, 166–71.

48. Members of HUAC insulted these witnesses. See Robinson, *All My Yesterdays*, 264.

49. The FBI already had the names of these individuals because of its "black bag jobs." However the FBI apparently never made these available to the HUAC out of fear that its illegal methods would be publicized.

50. In form and content, *The Firing Line* was childlike plagiarism. Compare the biographies of Lee J. Cobb (August 15, 1952) and Ruth Gordon (June 1, 1952) with the biographies in *Red Channels*. *The Firing Line* biographies look like a fourth-grader's rewriting of an encyclopedia entry for a homework assignment

51. Interview with Norman Corwin, February 3, 2000. Brewer cleared people based on his own prejudices, not facts, and was vindictive toward individuals whom he thought had not "come clean." See his statements about John Garfield and Lee J. Cobb in Fariello, *Red Scare*, 116–117; 120.

52. "Who's Blacklisted?" *Time*, August 22, 1949, 81–82.

53. "Narrowing Channels," *Newsweek*, October 9, 1950, 60; "Purge of Performers," *Newsweek*, September 11, 1950, 51–52; "On the Air: Trial by Sponsor," *New Republic*, September 11, 1950, 22–23; Jack Gould, "General Foods Seeks Radio Unit to Set Policy on Pro-Red Charges," *New York Times*, September 12, 1950; Jack Gould, "TV 'Red Ban' Lifted by General Foods," *New York Times*, September 27, 1950.

54. "Committee to Get TV 'Red' Problem," *New York Times*, October 3, 1950.

55. Cogley, *Report on Blacklisting II*, 23.

56. Miller, *Judges and the Judged*, 85. Given the situation in broadcasting, some liberals like Norman Corwin, who had worked in broadcasting and was named in *Red Channels*, moved to Hollywood and successfully found employment in the motion picture industry, which primarily blacklisted proven Communists. Interview with Norman Corwin.

57. John Sibley, "$3,500,000 Award Is Made to Faulk in Libel Verdict," *New York Times*, June 22, 1962.

58. "The Official Smothers Brothers Website," http://www.smothersbrothers.com/press_room/ censorship_p2.html.

59. Susan King, "Reactivating 'Rockford," *Los Angeles Times*, November 27, 1994; Carole Cheatham, Dorothy Davis and Leo Cheatham, "Hollywood Profits: Gone with the Wind?" *The CPA Journal*, February 1996, 32.

60. John Engstrom, "After Battle with Studios, Garner Is Anxious to Get Back to Work," *Seattle Post-Intelligencer*, July 30, 1991; Glenn Whip, "James Garner Is Still Having Fun," Copley News Service, December 23, 1996; Susan King, op. cit.

61. Julie Miller, "Paying the Price for Blowing the Whistle," *New York Times*, February 12, 1995; Katherine Sopranos, "Taking a Stand: The Risks and Rewards of Whistle-Blowing," *Chicago Tribune*, July 19, 1998.

62. Todd Gitlin, *Inside Prime Time* (New York: Pantheon Books, 1983), 3–7.

63. Joe Rhodes, "Rosie's New Trial: Ed Asner," *Los Angeles Times*, September 8, 1991.

64. As a few examples, see *Counterattack*, August 17, 1951, 1–2, which accused Columbia professors Manfred Kridl and Ernest Simmons of Communist associations; August 31, 1951, 2–3, which accused Harvard professor Howard Mumford Jones and MIT professor Dirk Struik of Communist activities; and October 19, 1951, 1, which accused Yale law professors Thomas Emerson, Fowler Harper, and David Haber of being "supporters of [Communist] party fronts."

65. Eugene Lyons, "Our New Privileged Class," *American Legion Magazine*, September 1951, 39.

66. George Sokolsky, "Watch Out for These Commie Swindles: Culture," *American Legion Magazine*, May 1952, 15, 44.

67. "Communism in Education," *The Firing Line,* February 1, 1955, 1.
68. "Combating Communism in Education," *The Firing Line* March 15, 1952, 3.
69. Lionel S. Lewis, *Cold War on Campus* (New Brunswick, NJ: Transaction Books, 1988), 86–89.
70. The Mundel case is described in detail in Charles H. McCormick, *This Nest of Vipers* (Urbana: University of Illinois Press, 1989).
71. "Gag Rule in Ohio," *Time,* November 5, 1951, 85; "Ohioans Condemn Order," *New York Times,* October 10, 1951; "Ohio State to Weigh Plea on Speech Ban," *New York Times,* October 6, 1951.
72. Ellen W. Schrecker, *No Ivory Tower* (New York: Oxford University Press, 1986), 89–92.
73. Benjamin Fine, "Educators Insist on Ouster of Reds," *New York Times,* May 30, 1949; "Columbia Board Bars Communists," *New York Times,* March 29, 1952.
74. These cases are discussed in Schrecker, *No Ivory Tower,* and Lionel S. Lewis, *Cold War on Campus.*
75. Interview with Staughton Lynd, February 3, 2000.
76. Interview with Ira Standig, February 27, 2000.
77. Lionel S. Lewis, *Scaling the Ivory Tower* (Baltimore: Johns Hopkins University Press, 1975).
78. For a brief discussion of the harassment, firing, and graylisting of whistle-blowers in the academy, see Lawrence Soley, *Leasing the Ivory Tower* (Boston: South End Press, 1995), 47–51.
79. John Dingell, "The Elusive Truths of the Baltimore Case," *Washington Post,* July 18, 1996. Several scientists—associates of David Baltimore—reportedly snickered when O'Toole described her difficulties in finding a job after leaving Tufts during a congressional hearing about the alleged fraud, according to David Hamilton, "White Coats, Black Deeds," *Washington Monthly,* April 1990, 28. Eventually, an NIH appeals panel sided with Imanishi-Kari, concluding that there were errors but no intentional fraud on her part. See Philip Hilts, "'I Am Innocent,' Embattled Biologist Says," *New York Times,* June 4, 1991; "Cleared of Fraud, Scientist Is Rehired," *New York Times,* August 2, 1996; K. C. Cole, "Fraud Charge Shakes Faith in Ground Rules of Science," *Los Angeles Times,* July 15, 1996.
80. Patrick Sweeney, "Renowned 'U' Professor Found Guilty in Fraud Case," *St. Paul Pioneer Press,* August 6, 1993; Doug Grow, "Jury Gives to Garfinkel's Former Aide What 'U' Didn't—Vindication," *Star Tribune,* August 8, 1993; Jean Hopfensperger, 'U' Told to Release Data on Discipline Cases," *Star Tribune,* June 11, 1993.
81. Charles Nicodemus, "High-Profile Whistle-blower Sues ComEd," *Chicago Sun-Times,* November 25, 1999.
82. Julie Miller, "Paying the Price for Blowing the Whistle," *New York Times,* February 12, 1995.
83. Ibid.
84. Jeff Nash, "Wheat First Socked with $25M Suit by Ex-Broker: First Case to Test Whistle-blower Law," *Investment News,* August 16, 1999.
85. "California Whistle-blower Awarded $1.38 Million," *Liability Week,* August 8, 1994.
86. Alison Bass, "Therapists Say Gag Order Hurts Patients; Health Professionals Tell of Blacklist," *Boston Globe,* December 20, 1995.

Notes to Part II

1. Abby Goodnoug,,"Limit on Use of City Hall Steps Faces Assault," *New York Times,* December 7, 1998; Michael Blood, "AIDs Rally," *Bergen Record,* December 2, 1998.
2. "Judicial Protection of Civil Rights," *New York Times,* November 19, 1998.
3. Benjamin Weiser, "Deal Allows Partial Return of Preachers to Times Square," *New York Times,* December 18, 1998.
4. Fiona J. L. Donson, *Legal Intimidation* (London: Free Association Books, 2000), 41.
5. Lee Hawkins, Jr. and Lee Bergquist, "Universal Foods Tries to Block Story," *Milwaukee*

Journal Sentinel, September 24, 1999.

6. Tom Held, "Judge Dismisses Suit Against Ex-Employee of Universal Foods," *Milwaukee Journal Sentinel,* December 17, 1999.

Endnotes to Chapter 4

1. "Deals and Suits," *Legal Times,* July 6, 1998, 10.

2. Amy Argetsinger, "Lawsuit Puts Southern Md. Activists on Defensive," *Washington Post,* May 25, 1997.

3. Catherine Brennan, "House Bill Calls for Stop to SLAPP Lawsuits," (Baltimore) *Daily Record,* January 17, 1997.

4. Ibid.

5. Andrea Siegel and Dan Thanh Dang, "Jury Favors County Activists in Libel Action," *Baltimore Sun,* June 12, 1998.

6. Alexandra Dylan Lowe, "The Price of Speaking Out," *American Bar Association Journal,* September 1996, 48–49; "South County Journal Guardians of Free Speech," *Providence Journal,* November 27, 1996.

7. *Hometown Properties, Inc. v. Fleming,* 680 A.2d 56, 58 (1996).

8. Ibid., 58–59.

9. Lowe, op. cit., 50.

10. *Hometown Properties, Inc. v. Fleming,* op. cit., 59; Lowe, op. cit., 49.

11. *Hometown Properties, Inc. v. Fleming,* ibid., 58.

12. Quoted in Lowe, op. cit., 50.

13. Diane Sepanski, "Seal of Disapproval," *Seattle Weekly,* March 3, 2000.

14. Quoted in Lowe, op. cit., 47.

15. George Pring and Penelope Canan, *SLAPPs: Getting Sued for Speaking Out* (Philadelphia: Temple University Press, 1996), 8–9; Richard Zitrin and Carol M. Langford, "Striking Back at SLAPPs," *The Recorder,* April 28, 1999; "Getting SLAPPed," *Consumer Reports,* July 2000, 7.

16. Pring and Canan, SLAPPs, 10.

17. *Gordon v. Marrone,* 590 N.Y.S. 649 (1992).

18. David Kaplan and Debra Rosenberg, "They Want Their MTV Back," *Newsweek,* May 20, 1991, 68; Zan Dubin, "A Critical Look at Women of MTV," *Los Angeles Times,* March 10, 1994.

19. Art Golab, "Developers SLAPP Homeowners; Lawsuit Aim to Be a Pain in the Wallet," *Chicago Sun-Times,* April 5, 2000.

20. Art Golab, "SLAPP Suit Ends With Settlement," *Chicago Sun-Times,* July 8, 2000.

21. David Rubenstein, "Six Environmental Groups Slapped by Coal Association," *Corporate Legal Times,* July 2000, 69.

22. "WFA Ponders Next Step After Legal Setback with Environmentalists," *Coal Outlook,* April 9, 2001.

23. Marnie Stetson, "Reforming SLAPP Reform: New York's Anti-SLAPP Statute," *New York Univ. Law Review* 70 (1995): 1324.

24. See Charles Alan Wright and Arthur R. Miller, *Federal Practice and Procedure,* vol. 5A (St. Paul: West Publishing Co., 1990), 460–63.

25. *Webb v. Fury,* 167 W. Va. 434 (1981); Pring and Canan, SLAPPs, 90.

26. *Webb v. Fury,* op.cit.

27. Ibid., 437.

28. Ibid., 460.

29. Ibid., 467–468.

30. *Protect Our Mountain Environment, Inc. v. District Court,* 677 P.2d 1361, 1362-63 (1984).

31. Ibid., 1369.
32. Cal. Civ. Proc. Code sec. 425.16; Del. Code Ann. Tit. 10, secs. 8136–8138; Fla. Stat. sec. 768.29; Ga. Code Ann. 9-11-11.1; Mass. Gen. Laws Ann. Ch. 231, sec. 59H (effective Jan. 1, 1995); Me. Rev. Stat. Ann. Tit. 14, sec. 556; Minn. Stat. Ann. secs. 554.01–554.05; Neb. Rev. Stat. secs. 25–21,241 to 25–21, 246; Nev. Rev. Stat. Ann. secs. 41.635– 41.670; N.Y. Civ. Rights Law secs. 70-a, 76-a; N.Y. C.P.L.R. secs. 3211(g), 3212(h); Pa. Consol. Stat. Chs. 77, 83;
33. "Judge Rejects Hometown's Try to Sink Suit," *Providence Journal-Bulletin*, May 20, 1999.
34. "Ban on SLAPP Lawsuits Nearer," *St. Petersburg Times,* April 30, 2000; "SLAPP Measure: Takes Path of Least Resistance," *Tampa Tribune*, November 4, 1999; Logan D. Mabe, "Lake Group Disbands in Face of Lawsuit," *St. Petersburg Times*, January 20, 1999.
35. "Business Needs Muzzle, Not Just Government," *Palm Beach Post,* February 21, 1998.
36. For examples of SLAPPs filed by the private sector in Florida, see *Florida Fern Growers Ass'n, Inc. v. Concerned Citizens of Putnam County*, 616 So. 2d 562 (1993); *Londono v. Turkey Creek Inc.*, 609 So. 2d 14 (1992).
37. Available at California Anti-SLAPP Project website, http://www.casp.net/nairon.html; also described in *Nairon v. Land*, 242 Ga. App. 259 (2000).
38. Cathy Cleland-Pero, "SLAPP at Resident Dismissed," *Atlanta Constitution*, September 26, 1996.
39. Cathy Cleland-Pero,"Developer's SLAPP Suit Dismissed," *Atlanta Constitution*, September 19, 1996.
40. Cindy Pearson, "Network Sued by Matria Healthcare," *The Network News,* May 1997, 3.
41. June D. Bell, "Women's Group Asks Sanctions Under SLAPP Law," *Fulton County Daily Report,* December 11, 1997; "Daily Briefing," *Atlanta Constitution*, November 27, 1997; June D. Bell, "Firm Eludes Grasp of SLAPP Law by Ending Suit," *Fulton County Daily Report,* February 3, 1998.
42. Cal. Civ. Proc. Code sec. 425.16 (e).
43. Michael O. Allen, "Organizers for Clothing Workers Win Legal Round," (New York) *Daily News*, October 31, 2000: *Street Beat Sportswear v. National Mobilization Against Sweatshops,* 698 N.Y.S. 2d 820 (1999).
44. Barbara Arco, "When Rights Collide: Reconciling the First Amendment Rights of Opposing Parties in Civil Litigation," *Univ. of Miami Law Review* 52 (1998): 587.
45. New York C.P.L.R. sec. 3211(e).
46. Massachusetts General Laws Annual Ch. 231, sec. 59H.
47. California Civil Procedure Code sec. 425.16(b)-(c).
48. Just what those attorneys fees should be has been disputed. In California, attorney Mark Goldowitz, who operates the California Anti-SLAPP Project and specializes in defending against SLAPPs, often on a contingency basis, submitted a bill of $118,000 for his work getting a SLAPP against a client dismissed. Goldowitz's office claims to have spent 395 hours on the action, compared to $40,000 charged by another attorney on the case. Goldowitz was involved in two other, similar controversies. See Shannon Lafferty, "Attorneys Battle Over Size of SLAPP Bill Suit," *The Recorder,* January 17, 2001; Shannon Lafferty, "California Judge Slashed Legal Fee," *The Legal Intelligencer,* January 30, 2001.
49. N.Y. Civ. Rights Law sec. 70-a; Minn. Stat. Ann. sec. 554.045.
50. *United States v. Lockheed Missiles & Space Co.*, 171 F.3d 1208, 1217–18 (1999); Paul Elias, "Anti-SLAPP Debuts in Federal Court," *National Law Journal,* April 5, 1999.
51. Pring and Canan, SLAPPs, 168–79, 185.
52. *Baglini v. Lauletta*, 315 N.J. 225, 717 A.2d 449 (1998); Martin Haines, "Slapping Back," *New Jersey Law Journal*, September 21, 1998, 23. In their 29 page complaint, Lauletta and his company asserted eleven separate claims against Baglini and the others, demanding in excess of $1 million in damages on each claim.
53. Ibid.

54. Ibid.

55. The punitive damage award was reduced by the trial judge. See Haines, op.cit., 23.

56. Stetson, "Reforming SLAPP Reform."

57. Lowe, op. cit., 53.

58. Pring and Canan, SLAPPs, 172–79.

59. To prevail, a plaintiff must prove that the defendant brought a lawsuit against the plaintiff without probable cause and with malice, that the suit terminated favorably to plaintiff, and that the proceedings did not end before causing injury to the plaintiff. See, for example, *Franklin v. Grossinger Motor Sales, Inc.,* 259 N.E.2d 307, 309-10 (1970); *Penwag Property Co., Inc. v. Landau,* 372 A.2d 1162, 1165 (1977). See also Pring and Canan, SLAPPs, 179–80.

60. Compare *Lobiondo v. Schwartz,* 733 A.2d 516, 534 (1999) and *Levin v. King,* 648 N.E.2d 1108 (1995).

61. Stetson, "Reforming SLAPP Reform," 1324, 1352.

62. Chip Johnson, "Oakland Newspaper Wines Suit," *San Francisco Chronicle,* January 22, 2000.

63. Kenneth Ofgang, "C.A. Upholds Dismissal of GOP Consultant's Libel Suit Against Magazine," *Metropolitan News-Enterprise* (Los Angeles), April 8, 1999.

64. "C.A. Orders New Hearing in Suit Over 'Hard Copy' Exposé of Modeling Management," *Metropolitan News-Enterprise,* November 9, 1998; Stan Soocher, "Nonmutual Bonds," *Entertainment Law & Finance,* December 1997, 8.

65. Mark Truby, "Consumer Reports Under Attack," *Detroit News,* March 20, 2000.

66. Joel Brown, "Judge Clears WCVB in Metabolife Lawsuit," *Boston Herald,* November 18, 1999; *Metabolife International, Inc. v. Wornick,* 72 F. Supp. 2d 1160 (1999).

67. *Metabolife International, Inc. v. Wornick,* 1163–64.

68. Ibid.

69. Don Aucoin, "Ch. 5 Vindicated in Diet-Pill Suit," *Boston Globe,* November 18, 1999.

70. Dave Daley, "Briggs Libel Suit Against Catholic Paper Dismissed," *Milwaukee Journal Sentinel,* April 14, 1998; National Public Radio, Morning Edition, "'National Catholic Reporter' Target of Defamation Suit," June 27, 1996 (Lexis transcript).

71. "Paper Purges Mower Men's Strange Suit," *Media & the Law,* April 24, 1998; "$30 Million Can Make Media Shy of Truth," *National Catholic Reporter,* April 24, 1998.

72. Daley, op. cit.; "Man Loses Suit Against Paper That Calls Him Catholic," *Corporate Legal Times,* June 1998, 16.

73. *Food Lion, Inc. v. Capital Cities/ABC, Inc.,* 194 F.3d 505 (1999).

74. Ibid., 511.

75. Russ Baker, "Damning Undercover Tactics as 'Fraud,'" *Columbia Journalism Review,* March/April 1997, 28–34; Robert D. Richards and Clay Calvert, "Counterspeech 2000: A New Look at the Old Remedy for 'Bad' Speech," *Brigham Young Univ. Law Review* (2000): 553.

76. Quoted in Baker, op.cit., 29.

77. *Food Lion, Inc. v. Capital Cities/ABC, Inc.,* 511. In its appeal brief, Food Lion mentioned the difficulty of proving "malice" as the reason it did not file a defamation lawsuit against ABC.

78. Ibid. 522–24.

Notes to Chapter 5

1. See Richard Paddock and Douglas Jehl, "Preschoolers Face 'Intolerable Risk' from Pesticides, Group Says," *Los Angeles Times,* February 28, 19893; Michael Weisskopf, "Pesticides Pose Higher Risk to Children, Group Says," *Washington Post,* February 25, 1989; Sharon Begley et al., "Dangers in the Vegetable Patch," *Newsweek,* January 30, 1989, 74.

2. A transcript of the *60 Minutes* segment appears in the appendix of *Auvil v. CBS, Inc.* 800 F. Supp. 928, 20 Media L. Rep. 1361 (1992).

3. Ibid., 930–931.

4. Philip Shabecoff, "Apple Chemical Being Removed in U.S. Market," *New York Times*, June 3, 1989; "EPA to Phase Out Alar Use in Apples by June 1991," *Los Angeles Times*, September 2, 1989.

5. Charles Fulwood, "Alar Report Right From the Start, But You'd Never Know It," *Public Relations Quarterly*, June 1996, 9.

6. See "Conscious Consumers," *New York Times*, October 26, 1996; Donella Meadows, "The 'Great Alar Scare': Fact or Fiction?" *Charleston Gazette*, March 3, 1997.

7. *Auvil v. CBS, Inc.*, 928.

8. *Auvil v. CBS, Inc.*, 941.

9. *Auvil v. CBS, Inc.*, 67 F. 3rd 816; 23 Media L. Rep. 2454 (1995).

10. Thomas Goetz, "After the Oprah Crash," *Village Voice*, April 29, 1997 (and correction of May 20, 1997); Brian Ford, "Guarding the Environment; Feds Overreact, Coalition Claims," *Tulsa World*, April 25, 1996.

11. David Helvarg, "Poison Pens," *Sierra*, January 11, 1997.

12. David Helvarg, *The War Against the Greens* (San Francisco: Sierra Club Books), 1994, 365–66; John Stauber and Sheldon Rampton, *Toxic Sludge Is Good for You!* (Monroe, ME: Common Courage Press, 1995), 5–13.

13. David Bederman, "Food Libel: Litigating Unscientific Uncertainty in a Constitutional Twilight Zone," *DePaul Bus. L. J.* 10 (Spring/Summer 1998): 191.

14. Goetz, "After the Oprah Crash;" Rosalind Truitt, "Food for Thought," *Presstime*, November 1997, 59.

15. American Feed Industry Association, "Food Disparagement," http://www.afia.org/Government_Affairs/FDA_CVM_Issues/Food_Disparag_.html.

16. Bob Dart, "Case May Signal Fate of Other States' Laws on Talk About Veggies," *Dayton Daily News*, January 21, 1998; Anne Presley, "Testing a New Brand of Libel Law," *Washington Post*, January 17, 1998.

17. Quoted in Katherine Pfleger, "Coalition Takes Aim at 'Veggie-Libel' Laws," *St. Petersburg Times*, April 30, 1998, p. 5A.

18. A version of the AFIA model statute is in Appendix B of Ronald Collins, "Free Speech, Food Libel & the First Amendment . . . in Ohio," *Ohio Northern University Law Review* 26:1. This statute simply defines a "false statement" as one that "is not correct," but provides no standard for determining correctness. It nevertheless contains many frequently adopted provisions of state statutes, such as treble damages and the claim that adoption "enhanc[es] public welfare."

19. Quoted in Elizabeth Allen, "Bill Filed Opposing 'Veggie Libel' Law,'" *San Antonio Express-News*, December 19, 1998.

20. David Bederman, "Food Libel."

21. Idaho Code sec. 6-2002 (2000).

22. Idaho Code sec. 6-2003 (2000).

23. O.C.G.A (Official Code of Georgia). sec. 2-16-1 (2000).

24. O.C.G.A. sec. 2-16-2 (2000).

25. Rosalind Truitt, "Food for Thought," 60; *Action for a Clean Environment v. Georgia*, 457 S.E. 2nd 273 (1995).

26. N.D. Cent. Code sec. 32-44-01 (2000), subsection 5. Although broader than the Georgia statute, the wording may not contradict the Supreme Court's 1990 conclusion that opinions may be actionable if the opinion is "sufficiently factual to be susceptible of being proved true or false." See *Milkovich v. Lorain Journal Co.*, 110 S. Ct. 2695 (1990).

27. N.D. Cent. Code sec. 32-44-02 (2000). The North Dakota statute also states that farmers will be awarded attorneys' fees and other incurred costs.

28. Tim Pareti, "What's Eating Oprah Winfrey?" *Texas Lawyer*, January 5, 1998, 1.
29. Tex. Civ. Prac. & Rem. Code sec. 96.002 (2000).
30. Tex. Civ. Prac. & Rem. Code sec. 96.003 (2000).
31. Allen, op. cit.; Pareti, op. cit.
32. Eric Jan Hansum, "Where's the Beef?" *Rev. Litig.*19 (2000): 261.
33. Sheldon Rampton and John Stauber, "Mad Cow Disease: Industrial Farming Comes Home to Roost," *CAQ,* Fall 1997, 54–63.
34. Portions of the *Oprah Winfrey Show* transcript can be found in Bederman, op. cit.; and Margot S. Fell, "Agricultural Disparagement Statutes: Tainted Beef, Tainted Speech, and Tainted Law," *Fordham Intellectual Property, Media & Entertainment Law Journal* 9 (1999): 981.
35. Rampton and Stauber, "Mad Cow Disease," 60.
36. Pareti, op. cit.
37. Jim Henderson, "Cattle Country Is Mad About Oprah," *Milwaukee Journal Sentinel,* February 17, 1998.
38. Chip Chandler, "Jurors in Winfrey Case Won't Consider Texas's Food-Libel Law," *Amarillo Daily News,* Februaty 18, 1998; Tim Jones, "Winfrey Receives a Bit of Relief," *Chicago Tribune,* February 18, 1998.
39. Kay Ledbetter and Chip Chandler, "Texas Jury Rejects Cattlemen's Suit Against Television Talkshow Host," *Amarillo Daily News*, February 27, 1998; Stephen Braun, "Jury Rejects Cattlemen's Legal Beef with Winfrey," *Los Angeles Times,* February 27, 1998.
40. Tim Jones, "Oprah Verdict Could Tongue-Tie Her and Others," *Chicago Tribune*, February 16, 1998.
41. "Texas Rejects Repeal of 'Veggie Libel' Law," *Nation's Restaraunt News*, May 31, 1999, 22; "'Veggie Libel' Law Leaves Bad Taste," *Fort Worth Star Telegram*, May 8, 1999, 1; Allen, "Bill Filed Opposing 'Veggie Libel' Law."
42. Carol Marie Cropper, "Texas and Arkansas Emu Ranchers Sue Honda over a TV Spot They Say Disparages their Birds," *New York Times*, November 6, 1997.
43. "Ease Up on the Emus," *Austin-American Statesman* November 9, 1997; "Emu Farmers Take Offense," *Las Vegas Review-Journal*, March 9, 1998; Jones, op. cit.
44. Stephen Durchslag, "Limitations on Commercial Speech: Emu Ranchers v. American Honda Corporation," *DePaul Bus. Law. J.* 10 (Spring/Summer 1998): 179.
45. Anne Hawke, "Veggie Disparagement," *Quill,* September 1998, 14–15; "Veggie Libel Laws Tested in Courts, Considered by More Legislatures," *News Media and the Law,* Spring 1998, 27–29.
46. The eight states are Alabama, Arizona, Colorado, Florida, Lousiana, Mississippi, Ohio, and Oklahoma.
47. Julie Harders, "The Constitutionality of Iowa's Proposed Agricultural Food Products Act and Similar Veggie Libel Laws," *Drake J. Agric. Law* 3: 251; Truitt, op. cit. The states that considered but rejected the statutes are California, Delaware, Illinois, Iowa, Maryland, Michigan, Minnesota, Missouri, Nebraska, New Hampshire, New Jersey, Pennsylvania, South Carolina, Vermont, Washington, Wisconsin, and Wyoming. An Idaho bill (HB 389) would have strengthened that state's statute.
48. ORC Ann. 2307.81 (2000).
49. Marion Burros, "Can a Raspberry Really Hurt a Cow?" *New York Times,* June 3, 1998.
50. Brian Williams, "One AgriGeneral Lawsuit Dropped, But State Case Still to Be Heard," *Columbus Dispatch,* June 26, 1997.
51. Brian Williams, "AgriGeneral Lawsuit Claims Group Disparaged Its Product," *Columbus Dispatch,* May 1, 1997.
52. Jones, op. cit.
53. Brian Williams, "'Dateline' Forces Buckeye Egg to Scramble for Answers," *Columbus Dispatch*, April 12, 1998.

54. Vindu Goel, "Buckeye Egg Farm Drops Suit Against Ohio Consumer Group," *Cleveland Plain Dealer,* July 7, 1998.
55. Burros, op. cit.; Hawke, op. cit., 13–14.
56. Quoted in Melody Peterson, "Farmers' Right to Sue Grows, Raising Debate on Food Safety," *New York Times,* June 1, 1999.
57. J. Robert Hatherill, "Take the Gag Off Food Safety Issues," *Cleveland Plain Dealer,* April 19, 1999.
58. Quoted in "On Movies, Money, and Politics," *The Nation,* April 5, 1999, 20.
59. Marianne Lavelle, "Food Abuse: Basis for Suits," *National Law Journal,* May 5, 1997, A1.
60. Evan Halper, "Food Fight," *In These Times,* August 11, 1997, 24.
61. *Auvil v. CBS, Inc.,* (1992), 942.

Notes to Part III

1. 326 U.S. 501 (1946).
2. Rich Romell, "Judge Refuses to Halt Theater's First-Run Movies," *Milwaukee Journal Sentinel,* February 2, 2001.

Notes to Chapter 6

1. Marie Rhode, "Trespassing Charge Is Dropped," *Milwaukee Journal Sentinel,* January 20, 1996.
2. For example, see Jim Carpenter and Lawrence Soley, "Citizens Must Be Able to Exercise First Amendment Rights in Malls, *Milwaukee Journal Sentinel,* January 30, 1996.
3. Charles Nicodemus, "Pincham Says He'll Sue Mall Over Leaflets," *Chicago Sun-Times,* October 4, 1996.
4. The eight were convicted of trespassing on May 17, 1999, and fined $117 each and sentenced to 30 days in jail, with the jail terms suspended. See Nancy Meersman, "Suspended, Stayed Sentences for Free Speech Activists," *Manchester Union Leader,* May 18, 1999.
5. Clare Kittredge, "When Rights Collide at the Mall," *Boston Globe,* November 15, 1998; Tom Mooney, "Are Malls Public Spaces? 'Foot Locker 8' Trial Begins in N.H." *Montreal Gazette,* September 28, 1998.
6. *Marsh v. Alabama,* 326 U.S. 501, 66 S. Ct. 276 (1946).
7. Wisconsin Legislative Reference Bureau, *Wisconsin Blue Book 1999–2000* (Madison: Joint Committee on Legislative Organization, 1999), 688–89.
8. *World Almanac 2000* (Mahwah, NJ: World Almanac Books, 1999), 390.
9. Mark Alexander, "Attention, Shoppers: The First Amendment in the Modern Shopping Mall," *Arizona Law Review* 41 (Spring 1999): 1.
10. Ibid.; Deborah Jacobs, "Free Speech in Malls, the New Town Squares," *St. Louis Post-Dispatch,* November 13, 1998; "Valley Fair to Get a Face Lift as Key Retailer Plans a Move," *The Business Journal,* June 2, 2000, 4.
11. *New Jersey Coalition Against War in the Middle East v. J.M.B. Realty Corp.,* 138 N.J. 326 (1994).
12. Ibid.
13. Ron Marose, "Plan Boosts Skywalks for Downtown," *Milwaukee Sentinel,* February 13, 1979; "Tax Plan Pushed for Downtown," *Milwaukee Journal,* October 3, 1977; "Maryland Company Will Operate Downtown Mall," *Milwaukee Sentinel,* July 10, 1979.
14. Tom Daykin, "State Aid to Retail Sparks Debate," *Milwaukee Journal Sentinel,* March 28, 2001.
15. Steve Massey, "Public Cash Often Drives City Development," *Pittsburgh Post-Gazette,* July 30, 1995.
16. Ibid.; *State v. Wicklund,* 589 N.W. 2d, 795–96.
17. Alexander, "Attention Shoppers," 5.

18. Steve Raabe, "It's a Mall World, After All," *Denver Post*, August 18, 1996.

19. For additional reviews of these Supreme Court decisions, see Ian J. McPheron, "From the Ground to the Sky: The Continuing Conflict Between Private Property Rights and Free Speech Rights on the Shopping Center Front Seventeen Years After Pruneyard," 16 *Northern Illinois University Law Review* 16 (Summer 1996): 717; and Alexander, "Attention Shoppers."

20. *Amalgamated Food Employees Union Local 590 et al. v. Logan Valley Plaza, Inc., et al.* 391 U.S. 311 (1968).

21. Ibid., 312.

22. Ibid., 311–13.

23. Ibid., 319–20.

24. Ibid., 321–23.

25. Ibid., 330.

26. Ibid., 327–40.

27. *Diamond v. Bland*, 3 Cal. 3d 653 (1970) .

28. Burger was appointed to the Court in 1969, Blackmun in 1970, Powell in 1971, and Rehnquist in 1972.

29. Kermit Hall, ed., *The Oxford Guide to United States Supreme Court Decisions* (New York: Oxford University Press, 1999), 393.

30. *Lloyd Corp. v. Tanner*, 407 U.S. 554–55, 92 S. Ct. 2221 (1972).

31. Ibid., 556.

32. Ibid., 554–56.

33. Ibid., 557–63.

34. Ibid., 562–66.

35. Ibid., 572–76.

36. Ibid., 585–86.

37. *Diamond v. Bland II*, 11 Cal. 3d 331.

38. *Hudgens v. NLRB*, 424 U.S. 518 (1976).

39. Ibid., 518.

40. The Supreme Court remanded the case to the NLRB to reconsider under the National Labor Relations Act (NLRA). After reconsideration, the NLRB concluded that "Hudgens' property rights must yield to the pickets'. . . rights" under Section 7 of the National Labor Relations Act, and ordered Hudgens to grant the picketers permission to enter the mall. *Scott Hudgens and Local 315*, 230 N.L.R.B. 414 (1977).

Under the NLRB's interpretation of Section 7, employees have a statutory right to use their workplace as a forum for distributing literature, provided this is done in nonwork areas during nonwork times. However, nonemployee union organizers enjoy no right grounded in the Act to enter an employer's property except when there are no adequate, alternative means of communicating with the employees. *NLRB v. Babcock & Wilcox Co.*, 351 U.S. 105, 112 (1956); *Southern California Gas Co.*, 321 N.L.R.B. 551 (1996). Prior to 1992, this "no adequate, alternatives" exception was interpreted broadly, but the Supreme Court rejected the broad interpretation for a narrow one in 1992. See *Lechmere, Inc. v. NLRB*, 502 U.S. 527, 540 (1992).

Although declaring employers' property closed to nonemployee union organizers, the Court implied in *Babcock* that employers must allow nonemployee union organizers to distribute leaflets on their property if they "allow other distribution" on the property. The NLRB has interpreted this to mean that employers who open their property to charitable organizations must also provide nonemployee union organizers the same access. See *Be-Lo Stores*, 318 N.L.R.B. 1 (1995). This is why some malls have closed their doors to Salvation Army bell ringers.

41. Article I, sec. 5.
42. Article I, sec. 2.
43. Shirley Abrahamson, "Divided We Stand: State Constitutions in a More Perfect Union," *Hastings Const. Law Quarterly* 18 (1991): 723; "Private Abridgment of Speech and the State Constitutions," *Yale Law Journal* 90 (1980): 165, 180.
44. *Robins v. Pruneyard*, 23 Cal. 3d. 899; 592 P. 2d. 341 (1979).
45. Ibid., 344.
46. Ibid.
47. *Pruneyard v. Robins*, 447 U.S. 74 (1980).
48. California Code of Civil Procedures, Sec. 527.3.
49. *Sears, Roebuck & Co. v. San Diego County District Council of Carpenters*, 25 Cal. 3d 317; 599 P. 2d 676 (1979).
50. *Bock v. Westminster Mall Co.*, 819 P.2d 55, 56 (1991).
51. Ibid., 59–60.
52. For a discussion of the case, see Maurice Kirchofer III, "New Jersey State Constitution Requires Privately Owned Shopping Malls to Allow Access for Expressional Leafleting . . ." 27.
53. *New Jersey Coalition Against War in the Middle East v. J. M. B. B. Realty*, 138 N.J. 352 (1994).
54. Ibid., 361.
55. Ibid., 371.
56. Ibid., 374–77.
57. *Green Party of New Jersey v. Hartz Mountain Industries, Inc.*, 324 N.J. Super 197 (1999).
58. *Green Party of New Jersey v. Hartz Mountain Industries, Inc.*, 164 N.J. 127 (2000).
59. Ibid., 136–38.
60. Ibid., 146–58.
61. *Batchelder v. Allied Stores, Int.*, 445 N.E. 2d 590 (1983).
62. *Commonwealth v. Hood*, 452 N.E. 2nd 188 (1983).
63. *Lloyd Corp. v. Whiffen*, 773 P. 2d 1294 (1989); *State v. Cargill* 786 P. 2d 208 (1990).
64. *Alderwood Associates v. Washington Environmental Council*, 635 P.2d 108 (1981); *Southcenter Joint Venture v. National Democratic Policy Comm.*, 780 P.2d 1282 (1989); Bardy C. Williamson and James Friedman, "State Constitutions: The Shopping Mall Cases," *Wisconsin Law Review* 1998 (1998).
65. *Waremart, Inc. v. Progressive Campaigns, Inc.*, 989 P. 2d 524 (1999).
66. Contrast the college access case, *Commonwealth v. Tate*, 432 A. 2d 1382 (1981), with *Western Pennsylvania Socialist Workers 1982 Campaign v. Connecticut General Life Ins. Co.*, 512 Pa. 23, 515 A. 2d 1331 (1986). The court attempted to distinguish the private college from malls by stating that the "college had made itself into a public forum." This "flip-flop" is discussed in Williamson and Friedman, op. cit., 883.
67. *Fiesta Mall Venture v. Mecham Recall Committee*, 767 P. 2d 719 (1988); *Cologne v. Westfarms Associates*, 469 A. 2d 1201 (1984); *Citizens for Ethical Government v. Gwinnett Place Associates*, 392 S.E. 2d 8 (1990); *Estes v. Kapiolani Women's and Children's Med. Center* 787 P. 2d 216 (1990); *Woodland v. Michigan Citizen's Lobby*, 378 N.W. 2d 337 (1985); *State v. Lacey*, 465 N.W. 2d 537 (1991); *State v. Wicklund*, 589 N.W. 2d 793 (1999); *SHAD Alliance v. Smith Haven Mall*, 488 N.E. 2d 1211 (1985); *State v. Felmet*, 273 S.E. 2d 708 (1981); *Eastwood Mall Inc. v. Slanco*, 626 N.E. 2d 59 (1994); *Charleston Joint Venture v. McPherson*, 417 S.E. 2d 544 (1992); *Republican Party v. Dietz*, 940 S.W. 2d 86 (1997); *Jacobs v. Major*, 407 N.W. 2d 832 (1987).
68. *State v. Felmet*, 708. The state constitution reads: "Freedom of speech and the press are two of the great bulwarks of liberty and therefore shall never be restrained, but every person should be responsible for their abuse." The court emphasized the latter phrase, sug-

gesting that it applied to speech in malls rather than tortious speech! The Georgia high court was also slovenly in its decision. Rather than pondering the origins or meaning of the state constitution, or even citing canards like the "state action" doctrine, the court merely declared that signature gathering in malls was not protected. See *Citizens for Ethical Government*, op. cit.

69. *Cologne v. Westfarms Associates*, 192 Conn. 48, 469 A. 2d 1201 (1984).

70. Ibid., 51–56.

71. Ibid., 59–63.

72. Ibid., 64.

73. These states include Arizona,Connecticut, Indiana, Massachusetts, Michigan, New Jersey, New York, Oregon, and Wisconsin. Elizabeth Belkin, ed., *Key Shopping Center Legal Issues* (New York: International Council of Shopping Centers, 1995), 98, 113.

74. *State v. Wicklund*, 589 N.W. 2d 793 (1999).

75. *Mall of America Fun Facts,* brochure (Bloomington: Mall of America, n.d., ca. 1999).

76. "Mall Protests Legal? Justices Listen," *Minneapolis Star Tribune*, November 3, 1998.

77. *State of Minnesota v. Wicklund*, Hennepin County District Court, File no. 9642987 (1998).

78. Ibid., 23.

79. "Megamall Decision: A Lasting Victory for Free Speech," *Minneapolis Star Tribune*, July 27, 1997.

80. *State v. Wicklund*, 589 N.W. 2d, 798–803.

81. Michael Gardos Reid, "Letter to the Editor," *Minneapolis Star Tribune,* March 20, 1999.

82. "Public Square: Megamall Is One in Fact, If Not in Law," *Minneapolis Star Tribune,* March 20, 1999; "Giant Mall of America Aims for Success With Excess," *Chicago Sun-Times*, November 28, 1992; "Make Your Shopping Excursion to the Mall of America Enjoyable," *Des Moines Register,* September 18, 1992; "Indiana Economy," *Indiana Star*, September 15, 1992.

83. "Judge Lambasts State Supreme Court Over Ruling," *Minneapolis Star Tribune,* January 13, 2000.

84. Ibid.

85. "'Footlocker Eight' Say They're Mulling a Return to the Mall," *Boston Globe*, August 15, 1999; Nancy Meersman, "Supreme Court Won't Hear 'Footlocker Eight' Appeal," *Manchester Union Leader,* November 20, 1999.

Notes to Chapter 7

1. I am indebted to Laura J. Snoke of Wilner, Klein & Siegel for her thoughtful comments about this chapter, even though she disagreed with some of my interpretations and conclusion. She litigated several of the cases described in this chapter.

2. Community Associations Institute, "Facts About Community Associations," http://www.caionline.org/about/facts.cfm.

3. Stephen C. Fehr, "Homeowners Associations Feels Backyard Backlash," *Washington Post,* October 11, 1992; David Montgomery, "Md. Debates Giving Condos a Window on Democracy," *Washington Post*, February 20, 1997; Patricia Jacobus, "Living by the Rules," *San Francisco Chronicle*, October 1, 1998.

4. Community Associations Institute, "Facts About Community Associations," http://www.caionline.org/about/facts.cfm.

5. Marcia Mogelonsky, "Take My Property Rights, Please," *American Demographics,* December 1993, 22; Edward J. Blakely, "The Time Has Come to End Gated Communities," *San Francisco Examiner,* August 1, 1999.

6. Susan B. Davis, "Back to the Future," *San Diego Union-Tribune* (Books), September 26, 1999.

7. David Guterson, "No Place Like Home," *Harper's*, November 1992, 61, 62.
8. Seth Weissman, "Beware Overreaching Developers in Covenants," *Atlanta Business Chronicle*, March 29–April 4, 1996, 26B.
9. Some states, including California, have passed laws prohibiting developers from doing this.
10. Marilyn Kennedy Melia, "Altogether Now: Associations Become the Glue that Makes a Development a Community," *Chicago Tribune* (Home Guide), October 21, 1995.
11. "Dictator on the Doorstep," *Tucson Weekly*, March 23–29, 1995, available at http://www.tucsonweekly.com/tw/03-23-95/cover.htm.
12. Sharon Hormell, "For Homeowners, a Rude Awakening in New Tracts," *Riverside Press-Enterprise*, July 19, 1998.
13. Ibid.
14. Bill Teeter, "Council Candidate in Crowley Fights Removal of Signs," *Fort Worth Star-Telegram*, July 21, 1999.
15. Bill Teeter, "Crowley Homeowners Sue Developer Over Signs," *Fort Worth Star-Telegram*, June 24, 1999.
16. Bill Teeter, "Suit Over Candidate's Yard Sign in Crowley Neighborhood Settled," *Fort Worth Star-Telegram*, August 6, 1999.
17. Bill Teeter, "In Crowley, Richard Crowder Edged Kevin Carey for a New City Council Seat," *Fort Worth Star-Telegram*, August 15, 1999.
18. Michael Pollan, "Town-Building Is No Mickey Mouse Operation," *New York Times Magazine*, December 14, 1997, 56–60.
19. Randolph Smith, "Homeowner Pays Fine," *Richmond Times Dispatch*, August 3, 1996.
20. Frank Askin, "Free Speech, Private Space and the Constitution," *Rutgers Law Journal* 29: 947 (Summer 1998). These restrictions usually fall under the category of "equitable servitudes."
21. Marc Pearlstein, "Jackboot Diplomacy," *Chicago Tribune*, August 15, 1999.
22. Evan McKenzie, *Privatopia* (New Haven: Yale University Press, 1994), 163–66.
23. *Davis-Sterling Common Interest Development Act*, Ca Civil Code, sec. 1365.7(a).
24. Jean Pasco, "Associations Cleared to Fight El Toro," *Los Angeles Times* (Orange County Edition), June 2, 2000; Robert Bruss, "Can Association Fund Campaign?" *Orlando Sentinel*, September 3, 2000.
25. Randolph Smith, "Homeowner Pays Fines," *Richmond Times Dispatch*, August 3, 1996.
26. Katherine Snow Smith, "Dastardly Deeds?" *St. Petersburg Times*, March 6, 1998.
27. Marcia Mogelonsky, "Take My Property Rights"; Michelle Lerner, "PUD Buyers Get a Community, Not Just a Home," *Washington Times*, May 19, 1995; Ford Risley, "From Grass to Garages, a Litany of 'Don'ts,'" *New York Times*, May 12, 1991.
28. Taylor Lincoln, "Condo Owners Want 'Bill of Rights,'" (Baltimore) *Daily Record*, January 29, 1998; Timothy Egan, "The Serene Fortress," *New York Times*, September 3, 1995; Risley, op. cit.; Kathy Finberg, "HOA Sign Restrictions Can Damage Democracy," *Arizona Republic*, March 4, 2000.
29. Diane Jean Schemo, "Escape from Suburbia," *New York Times*, May 3, 1994.
30. Patricia Jacobus, "Living By the Rules," *San Francisco Chronicle*, October 1, 1998; Smith, op. cit.
31. Jerry Mesa, "Fear of the 'Association,'" letter to the Editor, *Arizona Republic*, November 27, 1999.
32. Laura Vozzella, "Columbia Elects to Prohibit Politics in Private Places," *Baltimore Sun*, August 20, 2000.
33. Lincoln, op. cit.
34. Quoted in Egan, op. cit.
35. Pollan, op. cit.
36. Wedgewood, "Facts," http//:www.wedgewood.com/faq/faq.html.

37. http://pantheridge.net/frequently.asp.

38. http://communitylink.koz.com/lvrj/gv/neighborhoodhoa.

39. Quoted in Pollan, op. cit.

40. Quoted in Risley, op. cit.

41. Roger Cannaday, "Condominium Covenants: Cats, Yes; Dogs, No," *Journal of Urban Economics* 35 (1994): 71–82.

42. William Hughes, Jr., and Geoffrey Turnball, "Uncertain Neighborhood Effects and Restrictive Covenants," *Journal of Urban Economics* 39 (1996), 160–72.

43. Timothy Egan, op. cit., was the first to make this observation.

44. Patricia Jacobus, op. cit. California statutes now allow CID residents to fly "Old Glory."

45. "Bill Would Let Neighbors Fly Old Glory at Their Homes," *Norfolk Virginian-Pilot*, November 18, 1999; Gary Poliakoff, "Condo Associations Unflagging in Pursuit of Bylaw Violations," *Palm Beach Post*, June 20, 1999.

46. Laurie Roberts, "Terravita's Price for Free Speech," *Arizona Republic* (Northeast edition), February 18, 1998.

47. David Matthews, "Legislative Bills Focus on Homeowners Associations," *Business Journal of Phoenix*, August 27, 1999, http://www.bizjournals.com/phoenix/stories/1999/08/30/focus2.html.

48. "Bill Would Let Neighbors Fly Old Glory in Their Homes," op. cit.

49. Florida Statutes, sec. 718.113 (4); Phillip Stern, "Letter About Women's Flag-Flying Was Insulting," *St. Petersburg Times*, February 1, 1991.

50. Sharon Weber, "Owners Can Use Clubhouse for Gathering," *Palm Beach Post*, March 27, 1994.

51. Thao Hua, "O.C. Homeowner's Cross Brought to Bear," *Los Angeles Times* (Orange County edition), January 28, 1998; Thao Hua, "Women Agrees to Remove Cross from Patio in $10,000 Settlement," *Los Angeles Times* (Orange County edition), April 9, 1998.

52. Art Thomason, "HOA: Sign Here, Trust Us, Obey Us," *Arizona Republic*, July 1, 2000.

53. Donya Currie, "Condo Owners Grill Legislator on Bill," *St. Petersburg Times*, May 22, 1991.

54. Joseph Adams, "Community Associations: 1998 Survey of Florida Law," *Nova Law Review* 23 (Fall 1998), 67.

55. Carol Sowers, "Homeowners Challenge Abusive Associations," *Arizona Republic*, January 23, 2000.

56. Maggie Galehouse, "Political Signs Point to Friction," *Sarasota Herald-Tribune*, October 9, 2000.

57. Kathy Finberg, "HOA Sign Restriction Can Damage Democratic Values," *Arizona Republic*, March 4, 2000; Christopher Combs, "Rules Can Stifle Campaign Signs," *Arizona Republic/Phoenix Gazette*, February 3, 1996.

58. 512 U.S. 43, 114 S. Ct. 2038 (1994); "Court Prohibits Ban on Homeowners' Signs," *New York Times*, June 14, 1994.

59. Stewart Sterk, in "Minority Protection in Residential Private Governments," *Boston University Law Review* 77 (1997): 273, reports that "courts typically have enforced use restrictions included in the Declaration, even against challenges that the restrictions inhibited free speech or undermined personal autonomy."

60. 779 S.W. 2nd 603 (1989). The court reached the opposite conclusion in *Century 21 v. City of Jennings* (700 SW 2nd 809 [1985]) when a similar prohibition on signs was adopted by a city. The court based its decision on the Missouri statute prohibiting municipalities from banning "For Sale" signs on owners' properties, not the First Amendment.

61. 824 P. 2nd at 951 (1992).

62. 673 A. 2nd 340 (1995); appeal denied, 679 A. 2nd 230 (1996).

63. See *Riss v. Angel*, 934 P.2nd 669 (1997), discussed in Casey Little, "*Riss v. Angel*: Washington Remodels the Framework for Interpreting Restrictive Covenants," *Washington Law Review* 73 (1998): 433.

64. *Nuzzo v. Board of Managers of Jefferson Village Condominiums No. 1*, 644 N.Y.S. 2nd 546 (1996).

65. *Killearn Acres Homeowners Association v. Keever,* 595 So. 2nd 1019, 1022 (1992); *Nahrstedt v. Lakeside Village Condominium Ass'n, Inc.,* 33 Cal. Rptr. 2nd 63 (1994). The latter is discussed in Paula Murray, "Restrictive Covenants in Homeowners Associations: Are They Going to the Dogs?" Real Estate Law Journal 23 (1995): 356.

66. *Stone Hill Community Association v. Norpel,* 492 N.W. 2nd 409 (1992).

67. *Clem et al. v. Christole, Inc.,* 582 N.E. 2nd 780 (1991).

68. Gary Moore, Gerald Smolen, and Lawrence Conway, "Disclosure of Rights and Obligations in Homeowners Associations," *Real Estate Review* 22 (Summer 1992): 78–81.

69. Matthews, "Legislative Bills Focus on Homeowners Associations."

70. Maryland H.B. 36 (1998); David Montgomery, "Md. Debates Giving Condos a Window on Democracy," *Washington Post*, February 20, 1997.

71. 765 ILCS 605/18.4, 18.4 (h) (West).

72. Mark Pearlstein, "Getting Ready to Dish It Up," *Chicago Tribune,* July 7, 1996; Federal Communications Commission, "Commission Adopts Rule on Use of Satellite Dishes," Federal Documents Clearing House, November 20, 1998 (FCC 98-273).

73. Doug Abrams, "FCC Overrules Covenants Restricting TV Antennas," *Washington Times,* October 15, 1997; Joe Estrella, "DBS Battles Pesk Homeowners' Associations," *Multichannel News,* December 2, 1996, 150.

74. 334 U.S. 1 (1948).

75. 824 P. 2nd 948 (1992); *Midlake on Big Boulder, Condominium Association v. Cappuccio,* 673 A. 2nd 340 (1996).

76. *Gerber v. Longboat Harbour North Condominium* 724 F. Supp. 884 (1989). The court's decision in Gerber was subsequently codified by the Florida legislature.

77. Askin, "Free Speech," 948.

78. 326 U.S. 501 (1946).

79. 182 Cal. Reptr. 813 (1982).

80. Ibid., 825.

81. Ibid., 829.

82. *Guttenberg Taxpayers and Rentpayers Association v. Galaxy Towers Condominium Association,* 688 A. 2nd at 158-159 (1996).

83. 182 Cal. Reptr. 342 (1982).

84. 502 So. 2nd 1380 (1987).

85. Jeffrey Lee Baker, "Federal Preemption of Radio-Restrictive Covenants: Homeowners Association and the Public Function," *Communication and the Law* 18 (September 1996): 21.

86. Stuart Leavenworth, "Fenced Towns: Security, Exclusivity and Now Taxing Power," *Raleigh News and Observer,* May 30, 1999.

87. Ray Tessler and David Reyes, "2 O.C. Gated Communities Are Latest to Seek Cityhood," *Los Angeles Times,* January 25, 1999; Ray Tessler and Jeff Gottlieb, "New O.C. City Puts a Gleam on Governing," *Los Angeles Times* (Orange County edition), March 4, 1999.

88. 405 U.S. at 341 (1972).

89. Rachelle Garbarine, "Municipal Services for Condos and Co-ops," *New York Times,* January 31, 1993; Karen Klein, "Owners Complain of Double Tax," *Los Angeles Times,* March 5, 1995; "Condos and Co-ops Ask Equity," *New York Times,* December 6, 1992.

Notes to Part IV

1. Fred Siebert, Theodore Peterson, and Wilbur Schramm, *Four Theories of the Press* (Urbana: University of Illinois Press, 1956), 93.

2. Ibid., 74.

3. Sydney Head, *World Broadcasting Systems* (Belmont, CA: Wadsworth, 1985), 70–73.

4. Ken Silverstein, "His Biggest Takeover—How Murdoch Bought Washington," *The Nation,* June 8, 1998, 18–32.

5. For a discussion of this MBA control, see Doug Underwood, *When MBAs Rule the News Room* (New York: Columbia University Press, 1993).

6. "Restrictions on Cable TV Firms Scrapped," *Milwaukee Journal Sentinel,* March 3, 2001.

Notes for Chapter 8

1. George Seldes, *Freedom of the Press* (New York: Bobbs-Merrill, 1935), 42, 43.

2. Jim Willis, *Surviving in the Newspaper Business* (New York: Praeger, 1988), 25; Vincent Norris, "Consumer Magazine Prices and the Mythical Advertising Subsidy," *Journalism Quarterly,* Summer 1982, 205–11, 239.

3. Doug Grow, "Column Was Too Smart for Duluth Newspaper," *Minneapolis Star Tribune,* January 28, 1992.

4. Seldes, op. cit., 43.

5. Gloria Cooper, "Darts and Laurels," *Columbia Journalism Review,* May 1993, 23.

6. Blake Fleetwood, "The Broken Wall, *Washington Monthly,* September 1, 1999, 41.

7. Robert Laurence, "Sponsors' Ties to Content Could Bind TV," *San Diego Union-Tribune,* August 17, 1999; Louis Banks, "Memo to the Press: They Hate You Out There," *The Atlantic,* April 1978, 38.

8. Ben H. Bagdikian, *The Media Mononoly* (Boston: Beacon Press, 1997), 156–57.

9. Ibid.

10. Banks, op. cit., 38.

11. Kim Nauer and Steve Rhodes, "Pottsville's 'Better' Paper," *Columbia Journalism Review,* March/April 1992, 12–13.

12. Lauren Donovan, "Businesses Pull Out of Velva Newspaper," *Bismarck Tribune,* March 15, 1999.

13. Josephine Marcotty, "Airline Ads Fly Away," *Minneapolis Star Tribune,* March 28, 1992. *The Reader* is no longer published.

14. Fleetwood, op. cit., 44.

15. Howard Kurtz, ""'Primetime' Exposé Hits Close to Home," *Washington Post,* December 16, 1996; Erik Mink, "'Primetime' Looks at How Big Auto Dealers Steer Local Coverage," *New York Daily News,* December 18, 1996; KCBS, "Primetime," December 18, 1996.

16. Dean Krugman et al. *Advertising, Its Role in Modern Marketing* (New York; The Dryden Press, 1994), 93.

17. Nan Robertson, *The Girls in the Balcony* (New York: Random House, 1992), 82–83.

18. Cooper, "Darts and Laurels," 15.

19. Ibid., 22.

20. Fleetwood, op. cit., 44.

21. When co-owned or co-published under the Newspaper Preservation Act, newspapers often force advertisers to buy space in both newspapers or pay a hefty premium to advertise in just one. For example, the *Detroit News* and *Detroit Free Press* charge advertisers $537 per column inch when both papers are purchased. If an advertiser wants to buy just one newspaper, the rate is $483 per column inch, according to Standard Rate and Data Service, *Newspaper Rates and Data,* April 1999, 308. Clearly, the rates strongly encourage advertisers to buy advertising in both.

22. Donna Lawrence, "Group Questions Dealer Ad Clout," *Automotive News,* July 17, 1995, 8.

23. Steve Singer, "Auto Dealers Muscle the Newsroom," *Washington Journalism Review,* September 1992, 25–28.

24. Kurtz, "'Primetime' Expose Hits Close to Home."

25. Yvonne Chiuy, "FTC Settles Ad Boycott Case," *Washington Post,* August 2, 1995; Shelby

Gilje, "Ad Boycott Catches FTC Eye," *Seattle Times,* August 2, 1995; Anthony Ramirez, "FTC Slams Car Dealers on Axed Ads," *Houston Chronicle,* August 6, 1995.

26. Quoted in Singer, op. cit., 26.

27. See *Milwaukee Journal Sentinel* "Transportation" sections of September 12 and 19, 1999.

28. Wendy Swallow Williams, "Two Surveys Show the Industry's Reach," *Washington Journalism Review,* November 1991, 24.

29. Sally McInerney, " Tide Turns Fortunes of Edisto Beach, Newspaper," *Atlanta Journal and Constitution,* June 25, 1994.

30. Elizabeth Lesly, "Realtors and Builders Demand Happy News and Often Get It," *Washington Journalism Review,* November 1991, 22.

31. Marcotty, "Airline Ads Fly Away."

32. Cooper, "Darts and Laurels," 21.

33. "Ad Pressures Up, Business Journalists Say," *Atlanta Journal and Constitution,* May 1, 1992.

34. "Some ABC Affiliates Feel Brunt of '20/20' Piece," *Broadcasting,* December 18, 1989, 50.

35. Kurtz, op. cit., C1.

36. The decision to spike *Primetime Live* in Buffalo was made by General Manager Paul Cassidy, whom the *Buffalo News* described as having made "very occasional attempts to interfere with the way that news stories are presented [out of sensitivity to advertisers]." See Alan Pergament, "Dropping of Car Leasing Story Backfires on Ch. 7's Cassidy," *Buffalo News,* February 21, 1996.

37. Dan Trigoboff, "Dealer Ads Motor from WXYZ-TV," *Broadcasting & Cable,* June 7, 1999, 27.

38. Ronald K. L. Collins, *Dictating Content* (Washington, D.C.: Center for the Study of Commercialism, 1992), 22–23.

39. Andee Beck, "A Bigger Chill—The Terrifying Trend to Clamp Down on Advertiser-Sensitive Reporting in Television," *IRE Journal,* Fall 1990, 17; Herb Weisbaum, "Advertisers Fight Back," *IRE Journal,* Fall 1990, 18.

40. Frederic Biddle, "WHDH Defends Axing Story," *Boston Globe,* December 1, 1995.

41. For a more detailed summary of the findings, see Lawrence Soley, "The Power of the Press Has a Price," *Extra!,* July/August 1997, 11–13.

42. Robert Hays and Ann Reisner, "Feeling the Heat from Advertisers: Farm Magazine Writers and Ethical Pressures," *Journalism Quarterly,* Winter 1990, 941.

43. Jennifer Howland, "Ad vs. Edit: The Pressure Mounts," *Folio,* December 1989, 952.

44. Standard Rate & Data Service, *Consumer Magazine Rates and Data,* April 1999, 587.

45. David Shaw, "Magazines Feel Increased Pressure from Advertisers," *Los Angeles Times,* March 31, 1998.

46. David Phillips, "Chrysler Drops Censorship Policy," *Detroit News,* October 14, 1997.

47. Quoted in G. Bruce Knecht, "Big Retail Chains Get Special Advance Look at Magazine Content," *Wall Street Journal,* October 22, 1997.

48. Ibid.

49. "Discounting Lyrics to Maximize Sales," *San Francisco Chronicle,* November 18, 1996.

50. Steve Mores, "Up Against the Wal-Mart," *Boston Globe,* December 6, 1996.

51. Karen Schoemer, "To Her Own Self Be True," *Newsweek,* September 16, 1996; D. R. Stewart, "Wal-Mart Says Customers Understand Ban on Crow CD," *Arkansas Democrat-Gazette,* September 12, 1996.

52. Thomas Palmer, "Procter Lays Down the Law on Anti-Folgers Ads," *Boston Globe,* May 17, 1990.

53. Mark Stencel, "Boycotts a Touchy Business for Targeted Firms," *Los Angeles Times,* September 11, 1990.

54. "Anti-Insurance Ads Banned in Boston," *United Press International,* May 25, 1993.

55. See Spencer Rich, "Hospital Administration Costs Put at 25%," *Washington Post,* August

6, 1993. The *New England Journal of Medicine* article, written by Drs. Steffie Woolhandler, David Himmelstein, and James Lewontin of Harvard Medical School, concluded that 25 percent of U.S. hospital expenses could be saved by converting to a Canada-style, single-payer health plan.

56. Mark Shone, "Advocacy Ads Rejected," *Inside Media,* August 25, 1993, 20.

57. Howard Kurtz, "Local Stations Bar Ad Attacking Pizza Hut," *Washington Post*, July 21, 1994.

58. Doug Grow, "Ads Attacking NSP Nuclear Fuel Rods Storage Plan Didn't Meet Standards," *Minneapolis Star Tribune,* November 29, 1991.

59. "Radio Stations Shy Away from Anti-Hudson Ads," *Minneapolis Star Tribune,* November 30, 1991.

60. Cooper, "Darts & Laurels," 23–24.

61. "Leading National Advertisers," *Advertising Age,* September 27, 1999, 1.

62. Neil Rosenberg, "Billboard Firms Take a Pass on Sexy Ads," *Milwaukee Journal Sentinel,* August 3, 1999.

63. "'Bad Taste' Pitches Polygamy Porter Off Billboards," *Milwaukee Journal Sentinel,* November 7, 2001.

64. Debbie Seaman, "Hot Potatoes: It's a Safe Bet that Any TV Station Will Air Your Fab New Detregent Spot—But What if Your Client Is Planned Parenthood or a Gay Action Group?" *Creativity,* December 1, 1997, 32.

65. Carol Bodensteiner, "Special Interest Group Coalitions," *Public Relations Review,* March 22, 1997, 34; Geoffrey Foisie, "Harry and Louise: The Sequel," *Broadcasting and Cable,* July 4, 1994, 39.

66. Brad Hayward, "Hiding in the Grass Roots," *San Francisco Examiner,* July 23, 1995.

67. Max Barker, "Corporations Sow Seeds of Many Grass-Roots Efforts," *Fort Worth Star-Telegram,* April 25, 1999.

68. Another example of a substantiated grassroots commercial was Neighbor to Neighbor's ad asserting that buying coffee prolonged the Salvadoran civil war. WHDH-TV hired former *Washington Post* reporter Scott Armstrong to investigate claims in the anti-Folgers commercial after Procter & Gamble initiated its boycott. When the investigation was complete, WHDH-TV refused to publicly release the report, but leaked portions stated that Salvadorean coffee producers "have been tied, historically and up to the present, to human rights violations against coffee workers, union leaders and other peasants." The report concluded that Salvadoran death squads have received "continuous financing from the coffee industry since the late 1970s." See Richard Higgins, "Ch. 7 Is Urged to Release Study on Anti-Folgers Ad," *Boston Globe,* April 16, 1991.

Notes to Chapter 9

1. Carl Jensen and Project Censored, *Censored— The News That Didn't Make the News* (New York: Seven Stories Press, 1996), 50–52, 283–86.

2. Ibid., 31.

3. Robert McChesney, "Exposing Flaws in Telecom Law," *Journal of Commerce*, February 16, 1996, 6A.

4. Kathryn Harris, "Tisch Makes Most of His Piece of the Action at CBS," *Los Angeles Times*, April 27, 1986; "Tisch: From an Investor to an Insider," *New York Times,* September 11, 1986.

5. Michael Hiltzik, "Creating a Media Giant," *Los Angeles Times,* September 8, 1999.

6. Joe Flint, "In a CBS Shakeup, Mel Karmazin, the Exec Behind Howard Stern's Racy Radio Show and Its Upcoming TV Offshoot, Emerges as the Latest Hope for Jolting the Sleepy Eye," *Entertainment Weekly,* April 24, 1998, 20.

7. Steve Massey, "Who Killed Westinghouse?" *Pittsburgh Post-Gazette Online,* http://www.post-gazette.com/westinghouse/cbsempire.asp.

8. Geraldine Fabrikant, "Two Radio Giants to Merge, Forming Biggest U.S. Chain," *New York Times,* June 21, 1996.

9. Viacom owns half of the UPN network.

10. Steve McClellan, Joe Schlosser, and John Higgins, "Merger Gains and Pains," *Broadcasting and Cable,* May 8, 2000, 6.

11. Cumulus Media website, http://www.cumulusb.com/

12. Melanie Wells, "Hicks Muse Tunes in American Music as Next Target," *USA Today,* August 26, 1997.

13. "History of the A.H. Belo Corporation," http://www.wvec.com/about_belo.htm.

14. Pamela Shoemaker and Steven Reese, *Mediating the Message,* 2nd ed. (New York: Longman, 1996); Edward Herman and Noam Chomsky, *Manufacturing Consent* (New York: Pantheon Books, 1988).

15. Erik Barnouw, *The Golden Web* (New York: Oxford University Press, 1968), 42, 129–30, 283–84.

16. Lawrence Laurent, "Pay Television or A Cash Box in Every TV Set," in Newton Minow, *Equal Time* (New York: Atheneum, 1964), 229.

17. *Weaver v. Jordan,* 49 Cal. Rptr. 537.

18. August Gribbin, "When Press Protects Its Turf," *Newspaper Research Journal,* Spring 1995, 138–47.

19. Reynolds Holding, "Hearst Insisted Examiner Hold Story on Chronicle," *San Francisco Chronicle,* June 9, 2000.

20. Ibid.; "Paper's Policies to be Reviewed," *Milwaukee Journal Sentinel,* May 11, 2000.

21. Gloria Cooper, "Darts & Laurels," *Columbia Journalism Review,* May/June 1997, 23.

22. James Ledbetter, "Aborting the Issue," *Village Voice,* August 20, 1996.

23. Richard Pollak, "The Trial of Donald and Si Newhouse," *The Nation,* March 13, 1989, 340, 342–45.

24. A Reagan-appointed judge sided with the family, ruling that common and preferred stock had equal value, even though the preferred stock paid nominal dividends and had no voting rights. There was coverage of the Newhouse-IRS case in a few non-Newhouse publications, such as the *New York Times* (October 12, 1983) and *Time* (October 23, 1983, 72), before the court decision in 1990. After the Newhouse victory, there was significant coverage. For example, see Pat Guy, "Newhouse Empire Wins IRS Battle," *USA Today,* March 1, 1990. Ironically, *USA Today* is published by the Gannett Co., whose vice-chair Douglas McCorkindale testified on behalf of the Newhouses, according to Geraldine Fabrikant, "Newhouses Win Fight with I.R.S.," *New York Times,* March 2, 1990.

25. See *Cleveland Plain Dealer,* July 17, 1993; *New Orleans Times-Picayune,* March 12, 1993; Newhouse News Service article in *Chicago Sun-Times,* October 11, 1992; and *St. Louis Post-Dispatch,* October 3, 1993.

26. William Henry III, "The House of Newhouse Pursues a Winning Formula with Toughness— and a Revolving Door," *Time,* June 4, 1990, 76; David Streitfeld, "Pantheon and the War of Words," *Washington Post,* March 18, 1990.

27. Thomas Maier, "Fear and Favor," *Columbia Journalism Review,* May/June 1997, 77.

28. Henry III, op. cit.; Paul Richter, "Quirky Si Newhouse Becomes a Media Power," *Los Angeles Times,* November 28, 1989.

29. Judy Quinn, "Colorado Press Takes on Si Newhouse," *Publishers Weekly,* February 10, 1997, 21.

30. Paul D. Colford, "Is Shelved Newhouse Bio a Harbinger?" *Los Angeles Times,* April 9, 1998; Dan Kennedy, "Don't Quote Me," *Boston Phoenix,* June 3–10, 1999, http://www.boston-phoenix.com/archive/features/99/06/03/ DON_T_QUOTE_ME.html; Jefferson Decker, "Too Hot to Handle," *In These Times,* May 31, 1998, 17.

31. Colford, op. cit.; Decker, op. cit.

32. Jon Wiener, "Murdered Ink," *The Nation,* May 31, 1995, 743–44.

33. Jane Mayer, "Bad News, *The New Yorker,* August 14, 2000, 33.

34. Weiner, op. cit., 744–45.

35. United Press International, "Nebraska Radio Station Boycotts k.d. lang Over Meat Campaign," June 26, 1990; Richard Harrington, "Cattle Country's Beef with k.d. lang," *Washington Post,* July 2, 1990; "Big Stink in the Beef Belt," *Time,* July 16, 1990, 51.

36. Jim Goget, "Talk Radio Catches Static for Cynicism in U.S.," *San Diego Union,* January 3, 1994.

37. Jim Naureckas, "Corporate Ownership Matters: The Case of NBC," *Extra!,* November/December 1995.

38. Ken Auletta, *Three Blind Mice* (New York: Random House, 1991), 11, 21–23

39. James Ledbetter, "When Big Media Gets Too Big, What Happens to Open Debate?" *Village Voice,* January 16, 1996, 30.

40. Based on a search of the online Vanderbilt Television News archives for 1987–1992. The search terms were "nuclear and power and safety not Chernobyl." Only stories devoted to nuclear plants in the United States were counted.

41. Tom Feran, "Pekar Is Still with Letterman," *Cleveland Plain Dealer,* April 20, 1993; Harvey Pekar, "Letterman Is a True Lightweight," *Boston Herald,* May 22, 1994.

42. Diane Mermigas, "'Today' Airs Follow-up After GE Controversy," *Electronic Media,* December 11, 1989, 2; Tom Shales, "At NBC, A Question of Censorship," *Washington Post,* December 2, 1989.

43. Todd Putnam, "The GE Boycott: A Story NBC Wouldn't Buy," *Extra!,* January/February 1991, at http://www.fair.org/extra/best-of-extra/ge-boycott.html.

44. Sharon Bernstein, "'Today' Cancels Appearance of Author Who Criticizes GE," *Los Angeles Times,* April 6, 1992.

45. David Shaw, "Media Credibility Shrinking," *Dallas Morning News,* June 20, 1993; David Shaw, "Trust in Media on Decline," *Los Angeles Times,* March 31, 1993.

46. Jane Mayer, "Bad News," *The New Yorker,* August 14, 2000, 32.

47. Ibid.; Mike Drew, "All Kinds of Experts Rail at the Slide of TV News," *Milwaukee Journal Sentinel,* August 24, 2000.

48. James Squires, *Read All About It!* (New York: Times Books, 1993), 28.

49. Edwin Emery and Michael Emery, *The Press and America,* 4th ed. ((Englewood Cliffs, NJ: Prentice-Hall, 1978), 490.

50. John Carver Edwards, *Berlin Calling* (New York: Praeger, 1991), 149–85.

51. Quoted in Edwards, ibid., 150.

52. Frank Brady, *Citizen Welles* (New York: Charles Scribner's Sons, 1989), 278–81, 310–11; Barbara Leaming, *Orson Welles* (New York: Viking, 1985), 204–17.

53. Hearst initially supported Roosevelt, but when Roosevelt's actions strengthened unions and others groups that Hearst could not control, Hearst's support quickly turned to opposition. Quoted in Emery and Emery, op. cit., 487; *San Francisco Examiner,* May 6, 1933.

54. Evelyn Seeley, "Journalistic Strikebreakers," *New Republic,* August 1, 1934, 310; "The Press as Strikebreakers," *New Republic,* August 8, 1934, 333; "Hitlerism by the Golden Gate," *New Republic,* August 29, 1934, 61; also quoted in George Seldes, *Freedom of the Press* (New York: Bobbs-Merrill, 1935), 288.

55. Leon Harris, *Upton Sinclair: American Rebel* (New York: Thomas Y. Crowell Co., 1975), 306; Greg Mitchell, *The Campaign of the Century* (New York: Random House, 1992), 422–24.

56. Harris, op. cit.

57. Mitchell, op. cit., 499–501.

58. Described in Jerry Rollings, "Mass Communications and the American Worker," in Vincent Mosco and Janet Wasko, eds., *The Critical Communications Review,* vol. 1 (Norwood, NJ: Ablex Publishing, 1983), 131–45; Sara U. Douglas, *Labor's New Voice* (Norwood, NJ: Ablex Publishing, 1986), 83–88.

59. D. Charles Whitney et al., "Geographic and Source Biases in Network Television News, 1982–1984," *Journal of Broadcasting and Electronic Media,* 1989, 159–74.

60. Sara Douglas, Norma Pecora, and Thomas Guback, "Work, Workers and the Workplace: Is Local Newspaper Coverage Adequate?" *Journalism Quarterly,* Winter 1985, 855–60.

61. Isabel H. Boyles, "The Washington Post Pressman's Strike: How the Press Covered the Press," *Mass Comm Review,* Winter 1976/77, 7–12.

62. Cooper, "Darts & Laurels," 27.

63. Nat Hentoff, "Censorship at Pacifica," *Washington Times,* February 21, 2000.

64. Debra Levi Holtz, "Nearly $500,000 Spent During KPFA Lockout," *San Francisco Chronicle,* September 8, 1999.

65. In addition to WTMJ-AM, only one other Milwaukee radio station, public broadcasting affiliate WUWM-FM, is classified as an "all news" station, according to the *Gale Directory of Publications and Broadcast Media,* 127th ed., vol. 3 (New York: Gale Research, 1995), 3351. Other television newscasts are carried by the Hearst-Argyle owned WISN (channel 12), but these newscasts focus heavily on "soft news" rather than breaking news.

66. At the end of one story on the stadium financing controversy, "Brewers Set Lobbying Legislators on Stadium Proposal," *Milwaukee Journal Sentinel,* September 19, 1995, reporter Daniel Bice revealed that Journal Communications, Inc., was a registered lobbyist for stadium financing. After the stadium financing plan was approved by the legislature, Brice disclosed the real extent of Journal Communications, Inc., lobbying: The corporation spent 420 hours in the last six months of 1995 and $57,311 lobbying for the bill. Journal Communications, Inc. chairman and CEO Robert Kahlor also personally lobbied for the bill and served on the Governor's Milwaukee Stadium Commission, which urged that tax dollars be used to build a new stadium. See Daniel Bice, "Money Abundant Near Stadium Vote," *Journal Sentinel,* February 5, 1996, p. 1.

67. Interview with former *Milwaukee Journal* columnist Joel McNally, July 18, 2000;

68. "Time Warner Loses Ruling in ABC Blackout," *Milwaukee Journal Sentinel,* May 4, 2000; Keith Alexander, "Time Warner Agrees to Air ABC For Now," *USA Today,* May 3, 2000.

69. Bill Carter with Stephen Labaton, "Heavily Pressured Time Warner Puts ABC Back on Cable, For Now," *New York Times,* May 3, 2000.

70. Paul Farhi and Peter S. Goodman, "Blackout of ABC Ends, For Now; Media War Raises Fears of AOL Deal," *Washington Post,* May 3, 2000.

71. Lawrence K. Grossman, "Bullies on the Block," *Columbia Journalism Review,* January/February 1997, 19. According to Grossman, the Murdoch-Time Warner dispute was partly the result of personal animosities between Murdoch and Ted Turner, who called Murdoch a "disgrace to journalism." In retaliation, Murdoch ordered his newspaper, the *New York Post,* to delete CNN listings from its television section and Murdoch's Fox network would not show CNN during its telecasting of Atlanta Braves games. After much public bickering and time in court, which involved New York Mayor Rudolph Giuliani, the Murdoch-Time Warner dispute was resolved through horse trading by Time Warner head Gerald Levin, according to Lawrie Mifflin, "In the Murdoch-Levin Dispute, Money Talked," *New York Times,* July 28, 1997.

72. Erik Ness, "Big Brother @ Cyberspace," *Progressive,* December 1994, 6.

73. Shannon Duffy, "Attorneys Seek Dismissal of AOL Junk E-Mail Lawsuit," *Legal Intelligencer,* October 11, 1996, 3.

74. Ralph Jacobs and Richard Bernstein, "AOL's E-Mail 'Censorship': Another View," *Legal Intelligencer,* October 17, 1996, 9.

75. *Cyber Promotions, Inc. v. America Online, Inc.,* 948 F. Supp. 436.

76. "AOL Rejects E-mail from Harvard to Anxious Applicants as Spam," *Milwaukee Journal Sentinel,* January 2, 2002.

77. Randall Broberg, Eric Hagen, and Cory Krell, "Internet Providers fight Back Against

Spammers," *New York Law Journal*, April 13, 1987; "Memorandum Opinion and Order," *CompuServe Incorporated v. Cyber Promotions, Inc.*, Case No. C2-96-1070 (February 3, 1997), U.S. District court for the Southern District of Ohio, Eastern Decision, available at http://www.loundy.com/CASES/CompuServe_v_Cyber_Promo.html

78. Ariana Eunjung Cha, "America Online Officials Pledge to Cooperate with TV Networks, But Many Worry About Venture," *Milwaukee Journal Sentinel*, July 31, 2000.

79. Simson Garfinkel, "Computer Network Users Attempt a Mutiny," *Christian Science Monitor*, December 5, 1990.

80. Joseph Menn, "Software Giants Flexing Muscle for Tough Laws," *Milwaukee Journal Sentinel*, February 4, 2000.

81. John Schwartz, "Microsoft, Slashdot Exchange Volleys," *Washington Post*, May 12, 2000.

82. Richard Higgins, "Dialect Web Site Now a Free E-Speech Issue," *Memphis Commercial Appeal*, June 23, 2000.

83. Menn, op. cit.

84. *Ascertainment of Community Problems by Broadcast Applicants*, 53 FCC 2nd 3 (1975), in Douglas H. Ginsburg, *Regulation of Broadcasting* (St. Paul: West Publishing Co., 1979), 176.

85. *Revision of Programming and Commercialization Policies, Ascertainment Requirements and Program Log Requirements for Commercial Television Stations*, 98 FCC 2nd 1076 (1984).

86. *In the Matter of Editorializing by Broadcasting Licensee*, 13 FCC 1246 (June 1, 1949), in Frank Kahn, ed., *Documents of American Broadcasting* (Englewood Cliffs, NJ: Prentice-Hall, 1973), 392.

87. *Banzhaf v. FCC*, 405 F. 2nd 1082.

88. R. D. Hersey, Jr., "F.C.C. Voted Down Fairness Doctrine in a 4–0 Decision," *New York Times*, August 5, 1987.

89. Cited in Ben H. Bagdikian, *The Media Monopoly*, 5th ed. (Boston: Beacon Press, 1997), xx.

90. Ibid., xii–xx.

91. Sean Scully, "FCC Opens Up Expanded AM Band," *Broadcasting & Cablecasting*, April 19, 1993, 7.

92. Dale Hatfield, Chief of Engineering and Technology, and Roy Stewart, Chief, Mass Media Bureau, "Statement Concerning Low Power FM Engineering Issues," http://www.fcc.gov/Bureaus/Engineering_ Technology/New_Releases/2000/nret0005.txt. The statement reported that "members of Congress have received misleading engineering information about alleged interference from low power FM radio stations" from the NAB.

Notes to Chapter 10

1. Frank Askin, "This Is the Place for a Turf Lawyer!" *New Jersey Lawyer*, April 7, 1997, 7.

2. In Milwaukee County, all of these privatizations have occurred. Milwaukee County's Doyne Hospital was sold to the private Froedtert Memorial Hospital in 1995; the county museum is now operated by Milwaukee Public Museum, Inc.; and students in the city of Milwaukee can attend private schools, paid for with tax-funded "vouchers." Students in these schools clearly lack the constitutional protections afforded students in public schools. The sale of the county hospital is discussed in John Fauber, "End of an Era: County Prepares to Close Doyne," *Milwaukee Journal Sentinel*, December 21, 1995.

3. J. R. S. Owczarski, "Development Plan Irks Residents," *Milwaukee Journal Sentinel*, January 16, 1997.

4. See Joanna Cagan and Neil deMause, *Field of Schemes* (Monroe, ME: Common Courage Press, 1998), 82.

5. Telephone interview with Mike Duckett, August 17, 2001.

6. Telephone interview with Scott Jenkins, August 21, 2001.

7. Ibid.

8. See Tom Haudricourt, "Second Largest Crowd of '96," *Milwaukee Journal Sentinel,* June 17, 1996; Tom Haudricourt, "Rally Brings Cheers for Selig, Petak, Jeers for Norquist," *Milwaukee Journal Sentinel,* June 23, 1996.

9. Bylaws of Wisconsin Center District.

10. Telephone interview with Richard A. Geyer, July 12, 2001. Geyer is mistaken about the policy at other convention centers. In Ohio, even a privately owned center was required to open its facilities to the soliciting of political signatures. See *Ferner et al. v. Toldeo-Lucas Convention and Vistitors Bureau. Inc.,* 80 Ohio App. 3rd 842 (1992).

11. The questionnaire was sent in late July 2001 by mail to 200 residents of Eau Claire, a city frequently used as test market by producers of package goods. The sample was selected from the Eau Claire telephone directory using a systematic sampling method, and each questionnaire was sent with a brief cover letter and a self-addressed stamped envelope. The response rate was 51.6 percent, with eight of the questionnaires returned as undeliverable. One hundred and one questionnaires were returned, but two were unusable.

12. The percentage is based on respondents answering "yes" or "no." Four of the respondents did not answer the question, and an additional two were unable to answer for sure. The other responses had similar "missing values" or nonresponses.

13. AT&T website, August 1, 2001, http://www.att.com/att/.

14. Brendan I. Koerner, "AT&T's First Amendment Problem, and Ours," *New Republic,* May 14, 2001, 19.

15. *Comsat Cablevision of Broward County, Inc. v. Broward County, Florida,* 124 F. 2nd 685 (2000).

16. *U.S. West, Inc. v. Federal Communications Commission,* 182 F. 3rd 1224 (1999). Trans Union Corp. and several database firms unsuccessfully sued the Federal Trade Commission on First Amendment grounds for a proposed regulation that limited their ability to sell social security numbers and other information about consumers. See Edmund Sanders, "Corporate Free Speech Battle Is Escalating," *Los Angeles Times,* May 27, 2001.

17. *Time Warner Entertainment Co. v. Federal Communications Commission,* 240 F. 2nd 1126 (2001).

18. *U.S. West, Inc. v. Federal Communications Commission,* 182 F. 3rd 1224 (1999)

19. 425 U.S. 728 (1976).

20. *Central Hudson Gas & Electric Corp. v. Public Service Commission,* 447 U.S. 557 (1980).

21. Quoted in Sanders, op. cit.

22. *First National Bank of Boston v. Bellotti,* 435 U.S. 765 (1978).

23. California Code of Civil Procedures, Part II, Sec. 527.3 (b) (1).

24. California Education Code 66301 (2001), sec. 66301.

25. For example, Marquette University in Milwaukee has such a rule.

26. California Code of Civil Procedures, Part II, sec. 425.16.

27. "3 of 4 Firms Monitor Workers," *Milwaukee Journal Sentinel,* June 17, 2000.

28. Susan Miller, "Cable Ready," *Miami Daily Business Review,* July 26, 2001, A12.

29. About the closest that the American Bar Association's "Rules for Professional Conduct" say about the public interest is in the preamble, which states that lawyers are "public citizen[s] bearing a special responsibility for the quality of justice." August 17, 2001. See http://abanet.org/cpr/mrcp/mrcp_home.html.

30. Keith Bradsher, "Lawyers Knew about Firestone Defects in 1996, Partner Says," *Milwaukee Journal Sentinel,* June 24, 2001.

31. Ibid.

Index